West Aegean

The Attic Coast,
Eastern Peloponnese and
Western Cyclades

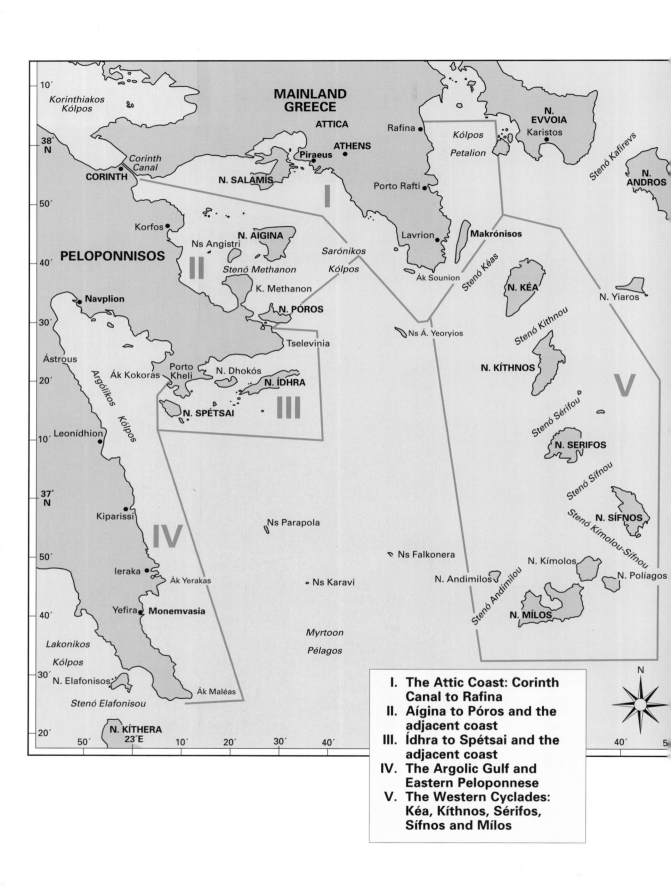

MAINLAND GREECE

ATTICA

Korinthiakos Kólpos

38° N

Corinth Canal

CORINTH

50′

Korfos

Ns Angistri

N. SALAMIS

Piraeus

ATHENS

Rafina

Kólpos Petalion

Porto Rafti

N. EVVOIA

Karistos

Stenó Kafirevs

N. ANDROS

PELOPONNISOS

N. AIGINA

Stenó Methanon

40′

K. Methanon

Sarónikos Kólpos

Lavrion

Makrónisos

Ák Sounion

Stenó Kéas

N. KÉA

N. Yiaros

I

II

Navplion

N. PÓROS

30′

Tselevinia

Ns Á. Yeoryios

Stenó Kithnou

N. KÍTHNOS

V

Ástrous

Ák Kokoras

Porto Kheli

N. Dhokós

N. ÍDHRA

20′

Argólikos Kólpos

N. SPÉTSAI

III

Stenó Sérifou

Leonídhion

10′

N. SERIFOS

37° N

Kiparissi

IV

Stenó Sífnou

N. SÍFNOS

Stenó Kímolou-Sífnou

Ns Parapola

50′

Ieraka

Ák Yerakas

Ns Falkonera

N. Kímolos

N. Políagos

N. MÍLOS

Yefira

Monemvasia

Ns Karavi

N. Andimilos

Stenó Andímilou

40′

Myrtoon Pélagos

Lakonikos Kólpos

30′

N. Elafonisos

Ák Maléas

Stenó Elafonisou

N. KÍTHERA

20′

23° E

50′   10′   20′   30′   40′

40′   5

N

I. **The Attic Coast: Corinth Canal to Rafina**
II. **Aígina to Póros and the adjacent coast**
III. **Ídhra to Spétsai and the adjacent coast**
IV. **The Argolic Gulf and Eastern Peloponnese**
V. **The Western Cyclades: Kéa, Kíthnos, Sérifos, Sífnos and Mílos**

West Aegean

The Attic Coast, Eastern Peloponnese and Western Cyclades

Rod Heikell

Imray Laurie Norie & Wilson Ltd

Published by
Imray Laurie Norie & Wilson Ltd
Wych House The Broadway St Ives
Cambridgeshire PE27 5BT England
☎ +44(0)1480 462114 *Fax* +44(0)1480 496109
Email ilnw@imray.com
www.imray. com
2002

A catalogue record for this book is available from the British
Library.

ISBN 0 85288 447 8

CAUTION

Every effort has been made to ensure the accuracy of this
book. It contains selected information and thus is not
definitive and does not include all known information on the
subject in hand; this is particularly relevant to the plans,
which should not be used for navigation. The author believes
that his selection is a useful aid to prudent navigation, but
the safety of a vessel depends ultimately on the judgement of
the navigator, who should assess all information, published
or unpublished.

PLANS

The plans in this guide are not to be used for navigation.
They are designed to support the text and should at all times
be used with navigational charts.

This work has been corrected to May 2002.

Printed in Great Britain at
The Bath Press

Author's note
Photocopies and downloaded information from my
books circulate around the Mediterranean. For those
of you sitting and reading a photocopy or
information downloaded off internet sites, I suggest
you reflect on the fact that you forfeit your own
moral basis for objecting to any theft from yourself
or your boat. You have after all stolen something
from me and my publishers, both in a moral and
legal sense, so when you have something stolen,
think about how it feels.

RJH

Contents

Preface

Preface to *Saronic*

In the spring of 1978 I set off on my first flotilla from Spetsai with the brochure produced by the company and a couple of charts. I hadn't been to half of the places and my apparent knowledge for the skippers' briefings was derived from deciphering every mark and squiggle on the chart and adding a large dollop of bull. I soon decided that I'd keep my job and the charterers would be better served if they had plans of the places they were going to and some pilotage notes. The hostess decided the notes should also indicate what facilities there were and what there was of interest to see and do ashore. That first rough guide for the Saronic flotilla in 1978 set in motion a whole series of yachtsmen's guides for countries in the Mediterranean and it is ironic that it has now turned full circle and here I am producing a guide to the Saronic again.

There were a number of reasons the area was chosen for flotilla sailing. It has a good mix of sophisticated towns and tourist resorts and small villages and anchorages off the tourist track. The wind and weather are benign and consistent, with good sailing winds throughout the season and few gales. It has ancient sites close by for history buffs to ponder over. And an almost perpetually blue sky and translucent water. This all remains true of the area and it is as good a sailing area as it ever was, particularly when the *meltemi* is howling down through the Cyclades to the east.

Inevitably it is popular in the summer and its proximity to Athens means it is within easy reach for weekend excursions. Fortunately most boats from Athens have a magnetic attraction towards the main ports of Aígina, Ídhra and Spétsai and these are good places to stay away from on busy summer weekends. Little is lost because there are numerous harbours or anchorages nearby and you can nip around to the busy harbours in the morning when everyone has left. I hope this book enables you to navigate your way around the area and persuades you to look at some of the lesser known spots off the better known 'milk run'.

If things have changed in the time between writing and going to print, then write to me care of the publishers. To those who helped me put this book together, my thanks. I would especially like to thank Willie Wilson of Imray, Laurie, Norie & Wilson for his encouragement and for the production of the plans from my originals; Roy and Barbara Stacey dreaming of boats in landlocked Tooting; Rob and Nell Stuart for digital knowledge; Chris and Luvvy in Póros - thanks for fixing the masthead light on the green teashop; to Sotiros Kouvaras of Greek Sails for dinners and good company; to Julian Blatchley and Nicole for the mini-cruise while waiting (in vain) for the *meltemi* to subside; to Graham and Katrina Sewell of SY *Songline*, proofer of the Aegean award; to Joe and Robin Charlton for shelter and company; to the large motorboat in Ídhra who dropped its anchor across mine – I told you I'd be able to haul it up in the morning; and to Odile who edited this book and struggled with the layout on screen, my thanks for the perseverance and long hours you put into it all.

Rod Heikell
London and Homps 1993

Preface to *West Aegean*

This second edition of what is effectively the old *Saronic*, albeit in colour and much updated, covers a wider remit than the first edition. In a way the title *West Aegean* is a bit misleading, as it doesn't cover all of the west Aegean, but it could hardly be called the *Saronic Gulf, eastern Peloponnese, Gulf of Evia to Rafina and western Cyclades including Kéa, Kíthnos, Sérifos, Sifnos and Mílos Pilot*, so I decided that *West Aegean* best described the cruising area in this book.

Things are still pretty much as I described it in the preface to *Saronic*. At weekends the boats pour out of Athens and head to Aígina, Ídhra and Spétsai, and at these times and on national holidays it is best to steer clear of these places. Outside of the 'big three' above, there are a lot of harbours and anchorages which are not crowded, surprisingly so given their proximity to Athens. It always confounds me that there seem to be yachting 'motorways' all around the Mediterranean, but if you simply nip off on a sideroad you can find all sorts of little-visited places without too much trouble.

I hope this new edition will help to get you around this area and also tell you a little about things on the shore. There are lots of additional plans covering small places not shown in my other books and a lot more detail on archaeological and other sites of note. And I couldn't help but include some favourite tavernas.

To all who helped me put this book together, my thanks. I would especially like to thank Lu Michell, who still loves the sound of water hissing by the bows of *seven tenths* and helped with editing. She also took many of the photos in this edition. Willie Wilson at Imrays put the book together and kept everything going smoothly until it went off to the printers. The girls in the drawing office at Imrays translated my plans into the digital ones you see here, and Julia put the text in order. Richard Kouvaras helped in Póros, and Sotiros Kouvaras was true to form and had an excellent taverna picked out for a meal. Anthony in Póros pointed out a few things in the islands for me to look at and Julian in Aígina filled in a few queries. Robyn and Joe Charlton provided shelter and a table to read the proofs on in Levkas. Thanks also to Nigel Patten for photos. From all of us who sat in Vathí on Sífnos with a Force 8 heaving over the hills and wondered if it would ever end, my admiration for the patience of those who had to re-anchor more than a few times. The mistakes in here are mine, though I hope there are not too many and you always have a bit of water under the keel.

Rod Heikell
London 2002

KEY TO SYMBOLS USED ON PLANS

 depths in METRES

 shallow water with a depth of 1m or less

 rocks with less than 2 metres depth over them

 rock just below or on the surface

 a shoal or reef with the least depth shown

⌐ wreck partially above water

◎ ◎ eddies

⊕ wreck

 dangerous wreck with depth over it

 rock ballasting on a mole or breakwater

 above-water rocks

cliffs

⚓ anchorage

prohibited anchorage

church

mosque

windmill

chimney

castle

airport

ruins

houses

port police

fish farm

customs

travel-hoist

yacht club

water

electricity

fuel

post office

O.T.E telecommunications

tourist information

pine

trees other than pine

▲ port of entry

Ⓥ visitors' berths

⊕ waypoint

yacht berth

local boats (usually shallow or reserved)

⊙ beacon

port hand buoy

starboard hand buoy

mooring buoy

Characteristics

light

lighthouse

F fixed

Fl. flash

Fl(2) group flash

Oc. occulting

R red

G green

W white

M miles

s sand

m mud

w weed

r rock

KEY TO QUICK REFERENCE GUIDES

Shelter
A Excellent
B Good with prevailing winds
C Reasonable shelter but uncomfortable and sometimes dangerous
O In calm weather only

Mooring
A Stern-to or bows-to
B Alongside
C Anchored off

Fuel
A On the quay
B In the town
O None or limited

Water
A On the quay
B In the town
O None or limited

Provisioning
A Excellent
B Most supplies can be obtained
C Meagre supplies
O None

Eating out
A Excellent
B Average
C Poor
O None
(*Note* These ratings are nothing to do with the quality of food served in restaurants, but relate only to the number of restaurants.)

Plan
• Harbour plan illustrates text

Introduction

About Greece

History

One of the problems I constantly encounter in Greece is putting historical events into perspective. When did the Venetians colonise the Greek islands? And which islands? When was the Classical period in Greek antiquity? Who were the Myceneans? I am not going to elaborate on any of these, but I have assembled the following historical order of things in Greece (with a slight bias to the western Aegean) to give some perspective to historical events. For detail, wrangling over dates and places, and for explanations of what went on, the reader will have to consult other sources.

Neolithic Period
Little is known of early Neolithic life in Greece. Around 6500BC early Stone Age settlers crossed the Bosphorus to mainland Europe and probably used primitive boats and rafts to get to islands close to the Asian shore. In the Franchthi Cave in the cliffs near Koilas in the Argolic Gulf numerous prehistoric remains have been found, including a skeleton from the Mesolithic period that may provide important clues to early Neolithic life in Europe. Around 4000BC the Cycladic civilisation was well established, and from the wide distribution of their distinctive geometric designs we know that there was communication between the islands on a regular basis.

Minoan Period
(2000 to 1450?BC) Around 2500BC new colonists moved down into Greece from the Balkans and Turkey, bringing bronze weapons and tools with them. The Minoan civilisation was concentrated on Crete and Thira, where the pottery and metalwork was brought to a high art, as was the art of comfortable and civilised living. The Minoans colonised few places, appearing happy to police the seas with their vessels and so procure order and peace while permitting other peoples to go about their business. The civilisation ended abruptly around 1450BC, probably from one of the biggest eruptions known, when Thira exploded and tidal waves estimated to be 70ft high together with earthquakes and ash, destroyed the civilisation overnight.

Mycenean Period
(1500 to 1100BC) With the demise of the Minoans the Myceneans, a Greek-speaking race based at Mycenae in the Argolid, stepped into the power vacuum. These are the Acheaens of Homer, and the Trojan War, fought around 1200BC, is thought to be a battle brought about by the Myceneans seeking trade outlets in the Black Sea. The centre of power appears to have been at Mycenae on the Plain of Argos, and excavations have revealed extensive fortifications, a palace, and the characteristic beehive tombs in one of which Schliemann found what he believed to be the death mask of Agamemnon. The Myceneans were displaced by the Dorians, who invaded from the north bringing with them Iron Age technology.

Greek Civilisation
(1100 to 200BC) This title covers a multitude of sins. From around 1100 to 900BC the Greek 'Dark Age' wiped out not only culture, but also written language. While the Greek-speaking Dorians existed in this dark twilight, the Phoenicians from the Levant (possibly Syria or Lebanon) took control of the sea routes. By 800BC a new written language was emerging and Homer, possibly a native of Khios, penned the *Iliad* and the *Odyssey*. From 750 to 500BC (the Archaic or Classical period) city-states (*Pólis*) sprang up all over Greece, some more powerful than others, some in alliance with others, but all

trading with one another and bound together in a loose defence pact. Colonies were established all around the Mediterranean.

The Persian Wars

(500 to 478BC) The Persian invasion pulled the city-states together round Athens and cemented the Delian league, based around the tiny island of Delos in the Cyclades. The Hellenic period arrived with the final defeat of the Persians and the establishment of Athens as the power base. The Battle of Salamis (see separate box) was instrumental in rebuffing the Persians and establishing Athens as the centre of things Greek. The Peloponnesian War (431 to 404BC) between Athens and Sparta divided the islands and the city-states, causing much hardship for inhabitants whose government opted for the wrong side at the wrong time as the war raged back and forth. The war weakened both Athens and Sparta, leaving the way open for Phillip II of Macedonia and later his son Alexander the Great to take control of Greece, though little changed under the Greek-educated Alexander.

The Romans

(200BC to AD295) A weak Greece was easy prey for the Romans and they declared war on Phillip V of Macedonia in 202BC. Octavius defeated Antony and Cleopatra at Actium near Preveza and after a decade of infighting cemented the Roman Empire into a whole. Roman rule had little cultural influence on Greece, whereas everything Greek, from architecture to cuisine, had a profound effect on the Roman way of life. Greek cities were largely autonomous, owing allegiance to Rome, and Greek remained the official language. In AD295, weakened by attacks from tribes on the edges of the empire and beset by difficulties within, Diocletian split the empire into two.

Byzantium

(AD330 to 1204) The foundation of Constantinople and the rise of Byzantium marks the rise of the first Christian Empire. Byzantine rule of its empire was constantly beset by invasions from the north and south. The Slavs, Avars, Goths, Huns, Vandals, and Bulgars came down from the north, while the Saracens sailed across from the south. The islands were depopulated and towns and villages contracted in size and moved away from a precarious shoreline. At times the Byzantines drove the invaders out, but as Ottoman power grew, the empire shrank away from its island territory in Greece.

The Venetians

(1204 to 1550) In 1204 the Fourth Crusade sacked Constantinople (ostensibly allies!) and parts of the Byzantine Empire were parcelled out to adventurers from the European nobility. The Venetians, who had transported the crusaders, emerged with a large chunk of Byzantine territory as their prize. The sea route down through the Ionian islands and around the Peloponnese into the Aegean was established, but although the Venetians secured some parts of the western Aegean, the area was not critical for their trade routes to the E and was often ignored.

The Turks

(1460 to 1830) In 1453 the Ottoman Turks took Constantinople and ended the rule of Byzantium. By the end of the 16th century most of Greece was under Turkish control. Around the Peloponnese and the Aegean islands the Venetians continued to battle for territory, though it was a losing battle against the omnipotent Turk.

The War of Independence

(1822 to 1830) In 1821 the Greek flag was raised at Kalavrita in the Peloponnese. In 1822 the Turks massacred 25,000 people on the island of Khios and so aroused Greek passions that many took up arms against them. Spétsai and Ídhra were among the first islands to commit their hitherto commercial fleets to the war effort and harried the Turks in the Saronic and Argolic gulfs, scoring some notable successes with their use of fire-ships. The war was effectively won when a combined English, French and Russian fleet destroyed the larger Turkish and Egyptian fleet at Navarino. The provisional capital of newly liberated Greece was at Aígina until it was moved to Navplion in 1828. Athens was made the capital in 1834.

Modern Greece

The newly born republic got off to a shaky start, and after a series of assassinations the western powers put a Bavarian prince on the throne. He proved an insensitive and unpopular ruler and was deposed by a popular revolt in 1862. In 1863 a new ruler, George I from Denmark, was chosen, and the British relinquished control of the Ionian islands to encourage support. The boundaries of Greece expanded with the acquisition of Thessaly

The Battle of Salamís

The survival of Greece as Greece and of Athens as the centre of Greek civilisation hinged on this sea battle in the narrow channel at the eastern end of Salamís. Today as you survey the topography of the place it is difficult to reconcile what you see with the events. Industrial and naval installations cover the land to make it one of the least evocative sights around. Yet the geography of the place remains the same, despite some scholarly wrangling over what was where and the fact that the land has sunk some two metres since the Greeks and Persians fought it out here.

By 480BC Xerxes had conquered a large part of Greece. From Persia he easily subdued the Greek colonies on the coast of Asia Minor and marched his army up the coast and across the Dardanelles on a floating bridge made up of his naval fleet. The vast army and the fleet crossed northern Greece and then headed south to take Athens. At this stage all that opposed his total conquest of Greece was the Greek fleet at Salamís and the Spartans on the Peloponnese.

Before the Persians had arrived at Athens most of the population had been evacuated, many of them to nearby Troezen (near present-day Galatas opposite Póros), as the discovery of the Troezen stone detailing Themistokles' evacuation plans now makes apparent. The remainder of the population was assembled at Salamís and when the Persians arrived at Athens there

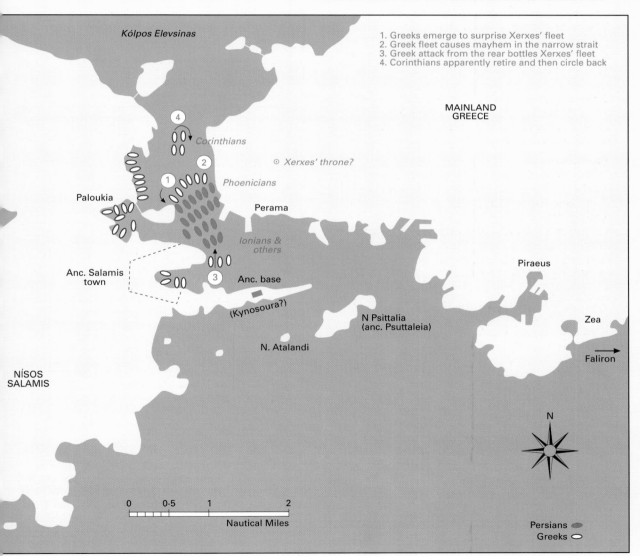

Kólpos Elevsinas

1. Greeks emerge to surprise Xerxes' fleet
2. Greek fleet causes mayhem in the narrow strait
3. Greek attack from the rear bottles Xerxes' fleet
4. Corinthians apparently retire and then circle back

MAINLAND GREECE

4

Corinthians

⊙ Xerxes' throne?

2

1

Phoenicians

Paloukia

Perama

Ionians & others

Piraeus

Anc. Salamis town

3

Anc. base

(Kynosoura?)

N Psittalia (anc. Psuttaleia)

Zea

N. Atalandi

Faliron

NÍSOS SALAMIS

N

0   0·5   1   2
Nautical Miles

Persians
Greeks

TLE OF SALAMIS

was some panic to get them away. After evacuating the last of the population, Themistokles persuaded the assorted admirals to stay with their boats in the narrows under Salamís and engage the Persian fleet there. This was not easy for him to do. The Spartans wanted to retire to the isthmus at Corinth where most of their army was assembled. Others wanted to retire to the Peloponnese and take on the Persians there. Themistokles pointed out that if they did not engage the Persian fleet at Salamís, then the islands of Aígina and Póros and the city states on the eastern Peloponnese would be easy prey for the Persians. Agreement was somehow reached and Themistokles put his cunning plan into action.

At this point, sometime in September 480BC, the Persian fleet was assembled in Faliron and the Greek fleet in the narrows at Salamís. The Persian fleet far outnumbered the Greeks, though the Persians did not have anything like the thousand ships the Greeks later credited them with. On the open water the Persians would certainly have defeated the Greeks. Xerxes' army could then have mopped up the remnants of the combined Greek army and Greece would be in Persian hands. The Persian generals and admirals advised on different strategies, with some wanting to sail to the Peloponnese and others wanting to starve the Greeks out of Salamís. Then Themistokles sent his false message.

Xerxes had numerous spies in the Greek camp and via one of them Themistokles leaked a message that the Greeks were squabbling amongst themselves (which in fact they were) and that if the Persian fleet attacked then certain of the Greek factions would come over to the Persian side. Ignoring the advice of his admirals Xerxes ordered the fleet to sea to attack the Greeks at Salamís. The Egyptian squadron of around 200 ships was dispatched to guard the western entrance and stop the Greeks escaping that way. The remainder of the fleet rowed into the narrows on the east side of Salamís.

The number of Greek ships is variously numbered at 310 (Aeschylus) or 380 (Herodotus). Most of these were smaller and more manoeuvrable than the ships of the Persian fleet. The best of Xerxes' fleet, the Phoenicians, squeezed through the narrows and then attempted to fan out into battle formation. At this point the Greek fleet emerged from behind the small island in the narrows and caught the Phoenicians in disarray. Aeschylus tells us that the first ship rammed was hit on the stern and must therefore have been turning. The crippled ships in front were prevented from retiring by the ships coming up behind and the Persian fleet was soon jammed in a hopeless muddle in the narrows. The Greeks picked off those ships penetrating through the crippled ships in the front. Such was the confusion that the Persians rammed their own ships – Herodotus tells us that Artemisia, queen of Halicarnassos and the Carians, rammed and sank one of her own ships in the chaos.

There are some elements of the accounts which are difficult to piece together. The Corinthian fleet apparently headed north away from the battle, only to turn abruptly and row back into the melée. Herodotus tells us that the Corinthian fleet was distinguished in battle, so it has been assumed that the retreat by the Corinthian ships was a feint designed to entice the Persian fleet into the narrows when they saw Greek ships apparently fleeing. Aeschylus in his dramatic rendering of the battle gives much prominence to the capture of the island of Psittalaia by the Greek army after the sea battle. Commentators suggest this was because Aeschylus had been with the Greek land force and wanted them to have a little bit of glory after the brilliant triumph of the navy.

Xerxes had a silver throne set upon the heights over the narrows to watch what he thought was going to be his great victory over the Greeks. Instead he saw his best ships destroyed and within a few days he returned to Persia. The remainder of his fleet returned to Asia Minor and was destroyed the next year. This marked the end of Persian designs on Greece and indeed the decline of the Persian empire.

The battle ranks as one of those decisive battles that turned world history around. Without the strategy of Themistokles there might have been no continuation of the Greek civilisation – and all it bestowed upon us for better or worse – that evolved in the centuries after the battle. Salamís did not acquire the legendary status of Marathon, but it was in every way a more significant event.

An exact copy of a trireme designed in England and constructed in Greece. Speeds of up to 8 knots could be achieved for brief periods and the Epirus in 1881 and Macedonia and the northern Aegean islands in the Balkan wars (1912–13).

The Greeks fought on the Allied side in the First World War and, with the defeat of the Axis Turks, embarked on a disastrous campaign to acquire territory in Asia Minor. When the Greeks were finally driven out, the remaining Turkish population in Greece was exchanged for Greeks in Turkey. Greece fought in the Second World War on the side of the Allies and obtained the last of her territory, the Dodecanese, from the Italians at the end of the war. Civil war split the country until 1947 when a Conservative government was elected. In 1967 the army took power with the notorious junta of the Colonels, which ushered in seven years of autocratic and harsh rule. Democracy returned in 1974 with Karamanlis. The first Socialist government, PASOK, under Papandreou, was elected in 1981. In 1986 Greece joined the European Community.

Language

It should be remembered that the Greek spoken today (Demotic Greek) is not ancient Greek, though it is largely derived from it. Anyone with a knowledge of ancient Greek will be able to pick up a little over 50 per cent of the Greek spoken today, though the pronunciation may not be what you expect. Rendering Greek into the Roman alphabet also presents some difficulties.

Although at first it seems impossible to master, the Greek alphabet can be conquered with a little persistence, and common words and phrases to get you by in the tavernas and bars and on the street can be picked up by ear. One of the obstacles to learning Greek is that you so often come across someone speaking English that the need to learn Greek evaporates. However, if you can only learn a few phrases such as 'hello' and 'goodbye' and 'how are you?', the effort will be repaid, especially in out-of-the-way places. A few useful phrases will be found in the Appendix.

The Greek Orthodox church

For someone from the west, from the world of Roman Catholicism and Protestantism, the churches and the black-robed priests of the Greek Orthodox church seem to constitute another religious world; and so indeed it is. Until the last meeting of the Council of Nicaea in 787, the western and eastern branches of the church had stumbled along together, growing apart but outwardly united. Post-Nicaea the churches grew apart, partly on doctrinal issues but mostly, one suspects, because of the geographical and cultural isolation between Rome and Constantinople. In Rome they spoke mostly Latin, in Constantinople Greek. In the west priests were celibate, in the east they married. In Rome the Pope was infallible, in Constantinople articles of faith were decided by a council of bishops. In the west the spirit of God came from the Father and the Son, in the east from the Father.

The overthrow of Constantinople by the Turks in 1453 had a far-reaching effect on Orthodoxy, and the Russian branch finally severed its connections with the Greek parent church. In Greece under the Turks the church was allowed to continue, and it later became a focus of rebellion against the occupiers.

Today the church, although much weakened in this secular age, still permeates Greek life. For the Greeks the big event of the year is not Christmas, but Easter, *Paskha*. The date of Easter is reckoned in a different way to that in the west, and the celebration is focused on the Resurrection rather than the Crucifixion. On Good Friday a service marks the descent from the Cross and the *Epitafion* containing the body of Christ is paraded through the streets. In some places an effigy of Judas Iscariot is burnt or blown up. This latter can be a spectacular event, as Greek men love playing with dynamite and the effigy is inevitably stuffed with it. All Greek homes brew up a soup from the offal of the lamb which is to be eaten on the Resurrection, but depending on your inclination the soup may be tasty or you may have problems sampling even a spoonful of assorted organs.

Late on Saturday night there is the *Anestisi* mass to celebrate Christ's return. In the church all the lights are turned out, and then from behind the altar screen the priest appears with a lighted candle and proceeds to light the candles of those in the church. Everyone responds with *Kristos Anesti* (Christ is risen) and there is a procession

Left Orthodox Church and cemetery near Kastro on Sifnos
Lu Michell

Opposite
Mikhali, Leonidhion

with the lighted candles through the streets to the sound of firecrackers and skyrockets, or any other explosive devices that are to hand. This is not a good time to be in trouble at sea as a lot of out-of-date flares are used up – though don't be tempted yourself as it is against the law to do so and there have been prosecutions. The traditional greeting at this time is *Kronia Polla* ('Many years' or 'Long life'). In the home boiled eggs, traditionally dyed red, are dished out and the normal sport is to bet your egg against the others, in the manner of conkers, or to surprise your friends with a solid rap on the head with the egg to crack the shell.

There are many local saints' days in the villages and towns, and the whole place will often close down for them even if they are not on the list of state holidays. Greeks normally celebrate not their birthday but the day of the saint they are named after – their name-day. In some churches there are icons to a saint reckoned to provide an above average service, and these will have numerous votive offerings. Many of these are simple affairs, a pressed metal disc showing what blessing is required, whether for an afflicted limb, safety at sea, a newborn baby or a family house. Some of the older votive offerings are more ornate and elaborate, sometimes a painting or a model of a ship where thanks are given for survival at sea, or a valuable brooch or piece of jewellery for some

other blessing. Greek churches are wonderful places, the *iconostasis* always elaborate and adorned, and the interior a dark and mystical place. It constantly amazes me that even in the most out-of-the-way places, on a rocky islet or a remote headland, every church and chapel and shrine will be newly whitewashed and cleaned, with an oil lamp burning or ready to burn in it.

Food

Greek food is not for the gourmet, but rather is plain wholesome cooking that goes with the climate and the Greek idea that a meal is as much a social occasion as a culinary experience. This is not, I emphasise, to say that Greek food is not enjoyable. I love the unadulterated flavours of charcoal-grilled fish with a squeeze of lemon over it, or a *salata horiatiki*, the ubiquitous mixed salad swimming in olive oil and peppered with *feta* and black olives – the simplicity of the combination of ingredients brings out the best in them. In some restaurants and in Greek family cooking you will come across dishes that have been lost in the tourist areas, where either the lethargy of taverna owners or the demands of visitors for a bland 'international' cuisine revolving around steak and chips has removed them from the menu. Some of the island tavernas still have a dish or two specific to the island or region, such as fish *à la Spetsiota*,

Wherever the Venetians went they stamped their standard, the Lion of Saint Mark, on their castles and forts

but for the majority the dishes on the menu are those which are simply prepared and cooked including a few favourites such as *moussaka* and *stifadho*.

The principal meal in Greece is the midday meal and most oven-cooked dishes are prepared in the morning for this meal. In the evening these dishes will simply be partially reheated and served up overcooked and lukewarm. Restaurants in Greece are categorised as either an *estiatorio* (a restaurant), a taverna (a simple tavern), or a *psistaria* (a restaurant specialising in fresh prepared food, mostly grilled meat), but the distinctions between these have now become so blurred that most restaurants call themselves a taverna.

The menu in a taverna will have two sets of prices, one with service and one without, and since all food comes with service you pay the higher price. In fact, waiters are paid on results and the difference between the two prices goes to them, which explains why some waiters are so attentive and others, often family who are not paid on results, loaf about ignoring your frantic pleas for a drink. In most Greek tavernas you will be invited into the kitchen or to a counter displaying the food to make your choice, a handy convention that gets over the problem of knowing what it is you are ordering from the menu. Only in the smarter restaurants will you be requested to order from the menu, and there will normally be an English translation on the menu, or on a board on the wall to help you out.

A typical Greek meal will be a starter and main course, with other side dishes ordered at random. Dessert is not normally served in a taverna although you may get fresh fruit or yogurt. When ordering, don't order everything at the same time as it will all arrive at once, or sometimes you will get the main course first and the starter second. Often the food will be just warm, it having been set aside to cool as Greeks believe hot food is bad for you, a belief that has some backing from the medical community. If you get everything in order and hot, and things have improved in recent years, you are on a winner. If you don't, just order another bottle of wine and settle yourself in for the evening like the Greeks around you – after all, what have you got to do that's so important after dinner?

On page 8 is a list of the common dishes you will come across, though obviously they vary in finesse and taste from taverna to taverna according to the skills of the cook.

Wine

Greek wine is a source of mystery to most western oenophiles. There are grape varieties in Greece few have ever encountered before. The production is so inconsistent that wines vary radically from year to year and most of the wines are oxidised or maderised. Storing wine properly is virtually unknown and most wine is new wine, and until 1969 there was no real government control over wines of a specific origin. To compound all of this, wine will often be sitting in a shop window where it gets a dose of sunlight every day. Given all these problems it is amazing

THE GREEK MENU

Soups, salads and starters

Avgolemono	Egg and lemon soup, often with a chicken and rice broth
Fakes	Lentil soup
Fasolada	Bean soup
Hortosoupa	Vegetable soup
Psarossoupa	Fish soup
Tzatziki	Yogurt and chopped cucumber dip
Taramasalata	Fish roe dip
Melitzanasalata	Aubergine dip
Patatasalata	Potato salad
Skordhalia	Potato and garlic dip, sometimes accompanies other dishes as a piquant sauce
Salata horiatiki	Mixed salad, usually tomatoes, cucumber, onion, green pepper, black olives, and *feta*
Domatasalata	Tomato salad
Salata marouli	Green salad, usually lettuce
Horta	Spring greens, often including rocket and spinach
Rizospanaki	Rice mixed with spinach
Piperies psites	Baked peppers
Melitzanes tiganites	Fried aubergines, delicious if freshly fried
Kolokithakia tiganites	Fried courgettes
Fasolia yigandes plaki	Giant or butter beans in a tomato sauce
Tiropita	Cheese wrapped in *filo* pastry, mini-versions of the large snack *tiropitas*

Some of the above can accompany the main course.

Main courses

Brizola khirino	Pork chop, normally charcoal-grilled
Brizola mouskhari	Beef chop, normally charcoal-grilled
Paidhakia	Lamb chop, normally charcoal-grilled
Souvlakia	Kebab, usually lamb or beef
Keftedhes	Meatballs in a sauce, usually tomato but may be an egg and lemon sauce
Bifteki	A burger, but usually homemade
Kotopoulo	Chicken, may be oven-roasted or spit-roasted
Kokoretsi	An offal (liver, kidneys, heart, tripe) kebab charcoal-grilled. Can be excellent
Moussaka	Aubergine and mince with a béchamel sauce, not unlike a Greek version of shepherds pie
Stifadho	A meat (usually lamb) and onion stew
Pastitsio	Pasta with a mince and cheese sauce, baked in the oven
Makaronia	Spaghetti, may be with a meat or tomato sauce
Domates yemistes	Stuffed tomatoes
Piperies yemistes	Stuffed peppers
Kolokithakia yemistes	Stuffed courgettes
Melitzanes imam bayaldi	Aubergines baked with tomatoes – a dish from the Turkish occupation that literally means: `the imam fainted'

Fish and seafood

Ohtapodhi	Octopus, may be charcoal-grilled or cooked in a wine or ink sauce
Kalamaria	Squid, normally coated in a light batter and deep fried
Soupia	Cuttlefish, normally deep fried
Psaria	Fish, normally fried or grilled
Barbouni	Red mullet
Fangri	Bream
Sfiritha	Grouper
Tonnos	Tuna
Xsifia	Swordfish
Marithes	Whitebait, normally deep fried (you eat them head and all)
Garidhes	Prawns, normally fried or grilled
Astakos	Crayfish

Desserts

Desserts and sticky sweets are usually found in a *Zakhoroplasteia* (patisserie) and in some of the up-market cafés.

Baklava	Honey and nut mixture in *filo* pastry
Kataifi	Honey and nut mixture in a sort of shredded wheat
Rizogalo	Rice pudding
Galaktobouriko	Custard pie
Loukoumadhes	Small doughnuts in honey
Pagota	Ice-cream

There will also be assorted sticky cakes, though I personally find most of them too sugary.

Above It may not all be gourmet cooking, but some of the locations are the best in the world. Often you will be berthed right outside the taverna you eat in

Right Over coffee. Ermioni

that some Greek wine is as good as it is. On the plus side, Greek oenology is on the mend and given the climatic conditions, the interesting grape varieties, and the excellent results of a few wine producers who have imported new wine-making technology and nurtured their product, the prospect for the future is good. Already some excellent wines are being produced in the Peloponnese, northern Greece and on some of the islands. Have a look at the *Real Greek* wine list at the end of this section.

Vines for wine-making were growing in Greece before anyone in France or Spain had ever seen or heard of the plant or its product. Estimates vary, but probably sometime around the 13th to the 12th centuries BC Greek viticulture was well established. The mythic origins of the introduction of the vine are associated with Dionysus and trace the route of the vine from India and/or Asia to Greece. Dionysus was said to be the son of Zeus and Semele (daughter of Cadmus, King of Thebes) who was brought up in India by the nymphs and taught the lore of the vine and wine-making by Silenus and the satyrs – sounds a wonderful childhood to me. He journeyed from India across Asia Minor to Greece bringing the vine and accompanied by a band of followers.

One can imagine a religious cult growing up around wine. The visions and hallucinations from imbibing it could only have been supernatural, and the introduction of it to Greece would have been unstoppable, hence its incorporation into the mythic universe of the ancients. The Homeric *Hymn to Dionysus* tells of his journey around the islands distributing the vine and describes vine leaves sprouting from the masthead of his ship. Nor is it surprising that the cult of Dionysus was associated with the release of mass emotion, was a fertility cult, and that the Dionysian Festival included wild uninhibited dancing and at times violence and sacrifice – all things associated in one way or another with alcohol today.

There is no way we can know what ancient wine was like. It was referred to by its place of origin, thus Pramnian, Maronean, Khian, Thasian, and Koan wine were mentioned by name much as we mention a Bordeaux or Côtes du Rhône today. Whether or not it was all resinated, as in the ubiquitous *retsina* surviving today, is unknown. Most likely amphoras of wine were sealed with a resin mixture to prevent oxidation and this imparted a flavour to the wine. Over time it was assumed that the resin itself, and not the exclusion of oxygen, prevented wine going sour and oxidising and so resin was added directly to the wine to produce *retsina*. It is unfortunate that many people only get to drink bottled *retsina* today as the stuff from the barrel is superior and should be drunk as a new wine. Much of the bottled *retsina* and some of the barrel *retsina* is simply bad wine that can only be made to taste palatable by resinating it.

At *The Real Greek* restaurant in London the owner has put together a fine list of bottled wines that are reproduced here and would be hard to better. The cooking is good too, with the normally robust Greek cuisine refined and fused

'Grub's up!', Cyclades

THE REAL GREEK WINE LIST

All-rounders
Whites Cambas White, Kretikos White, Asprolithi, Ilioni, Semeli White, Viognier.
Reds Cambas Red, Kretikos Red, Nemea, Porfyros.

Crustacea and fish
Whites Spiropoulos Mantinea, Roditis Alepo, Tselepos Mantinea, Adoli Ghis, Robola of Kefallonia, Thalassitis White, Athiri-Assyrtiko, Tselopos Barrique, Traminer (Averoff), Sauvignon Blanc (Hazimichalis).

Poultry and pork
Whites Strofilia White, Notios White, Megas Oenos, Chateau Julia Chardonnay (Lazardis).
Reds Athanassiadi, Notios Red, Ampellochora, Katogi Averoff, Domaine Mercouri, Satirikon (Oenotekhniki).

Red meat and game
Whites Amethystos (Lazaridis), Minoiko, Antonopoulos Chardonnay.
Reds Naoussa, Strofilia Red, Ramnista, Naousa Grand Reserve, Amethystos, Kava Red, Megas Oenos, Cabernet New Oak (Antonopoulos).

into one of the best Greek menus in London (book ahead for a table).

There are also a number of Muscats that are considered to be good quality, though they are not to my taste. The *Samos Muscat* from the island is considered the best, although *Muscat of Cephalonia* and *Muscat of Patras* produced by Achaia Clauss also get a mention. Sweet red liqueur wine vaguely resembling port is produced from the Mavrodaphne grape and *Mavrodaphne of Patras* (produced by Achaia Clauss) and *Mavrodaphne of Cephalonia* are passable port-type wines. Many of the local wine shops have a local Mavrodaphne in stock and this is often acceptable.

Retsina

Much of the ubiquitous *retsina* found in Greece is made from the savatiano grape grown in Attica and brewed and bottled there for the mass market. As I have indicated, the bottled variety is best avoided and *retsina* should be drunk fresh from the barrel. *Retsina* should really be drunk with *mezes* and not with a full meal, but in practice you drink it with whatever you want.

Although *retsina* is traditionally identified with Attica and the savatiano grape, in fact it is made all over Greece from a variety of grapes. In Póros, George of the *Drougas* is something of an authority on *retsina* and when he produces his own is rumoured to take his bed down into the cellar so he can be closer to his 'baby'.

Normally the grapes are gathered in September and after mashing go straight into the barrels with the must and the pine resin. Around two kilograms of resin goes into a 1000 litre barrel and George collects his own resin locally. The wine ferments for around forty days before fermentation is stopped. Most of the barrels are old, around forty to fifty years old in George's case, and if a barrel should give bad wine it is immediately burnt. The *retsina* should always be drunk as a new wine within a year. Occasionally red *retsina* is made and George reckons he has produced acceptable resinated reds, but it is not common.

Background basics

Getting there

Anyone coming to the Saronic and Cyclades will almost inevitably arrive by air at Spata, the new airport for Athens. Properly the airport is called the Eleftherios Venizelos airport, but almost everyone refers to it by the easier name, Spata Airport. The new Athens International Airport is located at Spata 27 km NE of Athens, and is connected by a new motorway to the Athens ring road. You can get to and from the airport in a number of ways.

Taxi The taxi rank is inside the airport perimeter and for two or more people this is arguably the easiest way to get anywhere. A taxi into Athens cost around 20–23 Euros (early 2002); it takes around 30–40 minutes depending on your final destination and the time of day. At rush hour it is likely to take somewhat longer to get to downtown Athens or Piraeus.

Bus A number of buses connect to various destinations as follows:

E94 connects the Ethniki Amina metro station with the airport. Passengers can transfer from the metro line to the Airport bus at this departure point.

E95 Syntagma Square – Airport Express has its departure point at the centre of Athens (Syntagma Square) and goes via Vas. Sofias Avenue, Mesogion Avenue and Attiki Odos before it terminates at the airport.

E96 Piraeus – Airport Express starts from the centre of Piraeus (Karaiskaki Square) and via Posidonos Avenue, Varis-Varkizas, and Varis-Koropiou Roads and then terminates at the airport.

KTEL Express to Rafina A daily service operates between the airport and Rafina approximately every 40 minutes from 0600 to 2100.

In early 2002 a ticket was 3 Euros and valid for 24 hours' travel on all public transport.

For more detailed information on buses you can look at AUTO (Athens Urban Transport Organisation) www.oasa.gr/e96d.htm

Rail The rail connection from the airport to join up with the Athens metro is under construction and should be ready for the Athens Olympics in 2004.

Getting around

Ferries

Passenger and car ferries all leave from Piraeus with a few exceptions. Passenger ferries operate on a regular basis to Aígina, Anghistri, Methana, Póros, Ermioni, Ídhra, Spetsai, and Porto Kheli. Obviously there are more frequent services to the more popular island destinations like Aígina, Methana, Póros, and Spétsai than to lesser known spots like Anghistri or Epidhavros.

Ferries to Kéa and Kíthnos leave from Lavrion and also connect down to the other western Cyclades. Ferries to Kíthnos, Sérifos, Sífnos and Mílos also leave from Piraeus.

Most of these ferries operate at least a daily service and to the Saronic islands there will be more than one daily service.

Some of these ferries will be regular car and people transporters and some will be faster semi-planing ferries taking just passengers or a few cars and passengers.

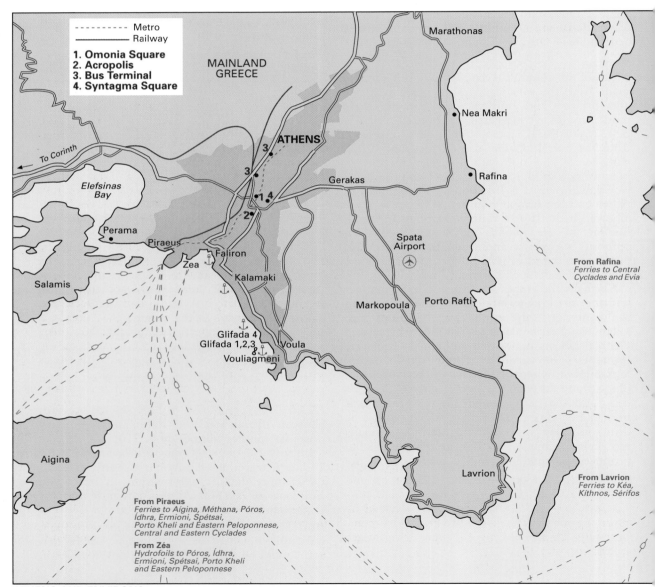

Key
- ----- Metro
- ——— Railway
- **1. Omonia Square**
- **2. Acropolis**
- **3. Bus Terminal**
- **4. Syntagma Square**

MAINLAND GREECE

Marathonas

Nea Makri

To Corinth

ATHENS

Gerakas

Rafina

Elefsinas Bay

Perama

Piraeus

Faliron

Zea

Kalamaki

Spata Airport

Salamis

Markopoula

Porto Rafti

Glifada 4
Glifada 1,2,3

Voula

Vouliagmeni

Aigina

Lavrion

From Rafina
Ferries to Central Cyclades and Evia

From Lavrion
Ferries to Kéa, Kíthnos, Sérifos

From Piraeus
Ferries to Aígina, Méthana, Póros, Ídhra, Ermioni, Spétsai, Porto Kheli and Eastern Peloponnese, Central and Eastern Cyclades

From Zéa
Hydrofoils to Póros, Ídhra, Ermioni, Spétsai, Porto Kheli and Eastern Peloponnese

ATHENS AND ENVIRONS

Hydrofoils

An extensive hydrofoil system connects most of the islands and main ports on the Peloponnese in this area and this is one of the best ways to get around. Most of the hydrofoils on the Flying Dolphin service leave from Zéa Marina except for Aígina where they run from Piraeus.

The hydrofoils are fast (32 or 36 knots), punctual, clean, and often fully booked in the height of summer and on national holidays. They may vibrate a lot and are noisy, but they run up until Force 6–7 depending on sea conditions. Most of the time you can book a seat half an hour before departure at the office near the hydrofoil berth at Zéa. Otherwise there is an office beside Platia Freatidis on the main road near Zéa.

Regular services run throughout the day to Aígina, Methana, Póros, Ídhra, Ermioni, Porto Kheli, and Spétsai. There are a number of express services which do not stop at every port. Less regular services run to Leonídhion, Tiros, Kiparíssi, Ieraka, Monemvasía and into the Argolic Gulf to Toló, Ástrous and Navplion.

Fast catamarans

In recent years a number of fast catamaran services have been introduced, running from Piraeus to Aígina, Póros, Ídhra and Porto Kheli. Services also run to the western Cyclades from Kíthnos to Mílos. Like the hydrofoils the service is punctual and the ferry modern and well equipped and just as fast or even faster than the hydrofoils.

Water-taxis and tripper boats

In the more touristy areas like Ídhra and Spétsai water-taxis run trips to nearby beaches or villages. Tripper boats also run from anywhere where there is a sizeable concentration of tourists, and it is possible to get a one-way trip on one of these.

Buses

Local bus services vary widely on the islands and Peloponnese, but even the best of the services are infrequent. To get about by bus you will need to check departure times the day before and to exercise a little, (and sometimes a lot of) patience. Between the larger towns and resorts on the Peloponnese there are more frequent services, but the best of these can still only be described as intermittent and you will have to budget to spend fairly large chunks of time if you are going to get around this way.

Taxis

Most of the islands and the mainland towns and larger villages have taxis or can phone for one. Fares are reasonable as long as there is a meter and it works, or the price is roughly agreed upon first. In some of the more touristy spots visitors are fleeced by drivers, but on the whole little of this goes on now.

Hire cars and bikes

In many of the tourist resorts you can hire a car or jeep, or a motor-bike-cum-scooter of some description. Hire cars and jeeps are expensive in Greece and unless there are three or four people it is not really worth it unless you are feeling frivolous.

Hire motor-bikes come in all shapes and sizes from battered Honda 50s to 500cc brutes. It is rare to be asked for a licence, but the operator will normally hold your passport. It is also rare to be offered a helmet. The reliability of hire bikes varies considerably, with some bikes only a year or so old and others still struggling along after years of battering by would-be TT riders. On the whole I have found even the older Honda/Suzuki/Yamaha step-through 50s or 80s to be the most reliable, and the larger tyres compared with scooters make them safer on gravel roads.

All of the operators charge you for insurance, but read the small print as it doesn't seem to cover you for very much. You are expected to return the bike if it breaks down and to pay for any damage to the bike if you have an accident. Bear in mind that Greece has the highest accident rate in Europe after Portugal and that on a bike you are vulnerable to injury. Even coming off on a gravel road at relatively low speed can cause serious gravel burns, so despite the heat it is best to wear long trousers and solid footwear. Roads on the islands are usually tarmac for the major routes and gravel for the others. Despite all these warnings a hire bike is the best way to get inland and with care you can see all sorts of places it would be difficult to get to by car.

Walking

There are some fine walks around the islands and on the Peloponnese coast. The main problem is finding a good map as most locally produced maps should be treated with a healthy scepticism. Tracks which have long since disappeared will be shown and new tracks omitted. The best policy is to set out with the spirit of exploration uppermost and plan not necessarily to arrive somewhere, but rather to dawdle along the way. This mode of walking is encouraged by the energy-sapping heat of the summer. Take stout footwear, a good sun-hat, sunglasses, sunblock cream and, most importantly, a bottle of water.

Shopping and other facilities

Provisioning

In all but the smallest village you will find you can obtain basic provisions and in the larger villages and tourist areas there will be a variety of shops catering for your needs. Greece now has a lot more imported goods from the other EU countries and you will be able to find familiar items – peanut butter, bacon, breakfast cereals, even baked beans – in the larger supermarkets and specialist shops. Imported items are of course more expensive than locally produced goods. Shopping hours are roughly 0800 to 1300 and 1630 to 2000, though shops will often remain open for longer hours in the summer if there are customers around, especially in tourist spots.

Meat Is usually not hung for long and is butchered in a peculiarly eastern Mediterranean way – if you ask for a chicken to be quartered the butcher picks up his cleaver and neatly chops it into four lumps. Salami and bacon are widely available in mini-markets.

Fish Is generally expensive except for smaller varieties. Some fish, like red snapper and grouper, are very expensive and prawns and crayfish have a hefty price tag except off the beaten track.

Fruit and vegetables Fresh produce used to be seasonal, but now EU imports mean more is available longer. It is prudent to wash fruit and vegetables before eating them raw.

Bread Greek bread straight out of the oven is delicious, but it doesn't keep well. Bakers are a growth industry in Greece and even small villages often have a good bakers with all sorts of bread, from white through all shades of brown. They will also often have mini-pizzas, cheese or spinach pies, bacon and egg pies, stuffed croissants, in fact whatever the baker thinks he can sell.

Staples Many items are often sold loose. Some staples, loose or packaged, may have weevils.

Cheese Imported cheeses such as *edam* or *gruyère* are now widely available courtesy of the EU. Local hard cheeses can also be found and *feta* is available everywhere.

Yogurt I think Greek yogurt is the best in the world. Use it instead of salad dressing or cream.

Canned goods Local canned goods (particularly canned fruit) are good and cheap. Canned meat is usually imported and expensive.

Coffee and tea Instant coffee is comparatively expensive. Local coffee is ground very fine for 'Greek coffee' and tends to clog filters. Imported ground coffee is available. Good tea bags can be hard to find.

Wines, beer and spirits Bottled wine varies from good to terrible and is not consistent, usually because it is not stored properly. Wine can be bought direct from the barrel in some larger villages and towns and at least you get to taste before you buy. *Retsina* is also available bottled or from the barrel. Beer is brewed under licence (*Amstel* and *Heineken* are the most common), is a light lager type and eminently palatable. Local spirits, *ouzo* (not dissimilar to *pastis*) and Greek brandy, often referred to by the most common brand name as just *Metaxa*, are good value and can be bought bottled or from the barrel.

Banks

Traveller's cheques, the major credit cards (*Access* and *Visa*) and charge cards (*American Express* and *Diners Club*) are accepted in the larger towns and tourist resorts. You will need your passport for identification. Many of the larger towns and tourist resorts now have an ATM, (automatic teller machine or 'hole-in-the-wall machine'), which will give you cash from the major credit cards such as *Visa* or *MasterCard* with a pin number.

For smaller places carry cash. Banks are open from 0800–1300 Monday to Friday. Most post offices and some travel agents will change traveller's cheques or foreign notes.

The ubiquitous *periptero*, a covered stall selling cigarettes, sweets, ice-cream and cold drinks, aspirin and sun-tan oil, useless beach toys, newspapers, indeed anything which can be squeezed into or around a couple of square metres. And it will probably have a metered telephone as well

Telephones

You can direct-dial from almost anywhere in Greece. The telephone system is not too bad although it is not unusual to get a crackly line and sometimes to be cut off or find someone else talking on your line. Telephone calls can be made from a kiosk with an orange top to it; a blue-top kiosk is for domestic calls only. In the towns there will be an OTE (Overseas Telephone Exchange) where you can make a metered call and pay the clerk on completion. Telephone calls can also be made from metered telephones in a *periptero* although the charge will be higher than at the OTE.

Telephone cards are now widely available and can be purchased from grocery and other shops, even from the *periptero* that have metered telephones. This is probably the most convenient and cheapest way to make phone calls.

Mobile digital phones using the GSM system can be used in Greece as long as your service provider has an agreement with one of the Greek mobile phone companies. You may be required to leave a deposit with your service provider before you leave. In most places the phones automatically lock into the system and coverage in Greece is good with this exception: if you are in a bay with high land blocking out the signal then you may not be able to use the phone. Paradoxically, the system often works better when you are out sailing around.

The IDD code for Greece is +30 and for the UK it is +44.

Email

There are a number of ways of sending and receiving email while afloat. The following is a brief roundup of ways and means of doing so.

1. Using a GSM phone and dedicated connection cord and appropriate modem you can connect at 9600 baud wherever you can get a signal. This is the system I most commonly use as it allows you to connect in the comfort of your boat. 9600 baud is not a very fast speed these days but it is sufficient for email. Transmission charges vary, not only with your local provider in Greece, but also with your provider in the UK or wherever your phone is registered. It is worthwhile doing a comparison of costs on providers to see who is giving the best deal.

   The new second generation phones (G2) only offer 14400 baud, which hardly makes it worthwhile investing in a new (very expensive) phone and invariably a new cable and perhaps a PC card modem for it. But in 2003 the third generation phones (G3) using the Unified Mobile Telephone Service (UMTS) will come into being and that should offer a whacking 2Mbps, faster than anything you can get on a landline at present. In the interim the so-called 2·5G transmission technologies (GPRS) are underway which offer up to 57·6kbps to 115kbps utilising the present GSM networks, and one of these technologies may be the way to go. Many European countries do not yet have transmitters (or many transmitters) for GPRS and G3 transmission so you may find you have an expensive new phone and subscription charges and nowhere to go with them. Invariably the different providers are using different transmission technologies and so compatibility with an overseas provider will be a problem. Why do they not just agree on one technology and roll it out across the board? For information on 2·5G (utilising HSCSD, GPRS, or EDGE) contact your service provider or change to another.

2. Cyber-Cafés. Many quite small places have a cyber-café these days and if you have an internet email provider such as *Hotmail* or *Yahoo!*, then it takes little time to download and send mail using a floppy disk. If you do not have a laptop to compile mail on and download it from the desktop in the café then most cyber-cafés will let you print out the mail for a small fee. Costs are low and of course connection rates are high at typically 56K

baud. I use this method of connecting when I cannot get a connection via GSM or when I feel like a coffee with my mail.

3. Plugging in to a conventional socket. If you can find somewhere to plug into a conventional socket ashore with (usually) a meter on the time used, then this is a quick and easy way to send and receive email using your own laptop. There are certain things to be borne in mind. If you connect to an ISP in the country you are in, then the cost is that of a local or at most a national call. Large companies like CompuServe and AOL will probably have a server in the country you are in, but unless your home ISP has a reciprocal agreement in other countries (and some do), you will have to dial up to the country your home ISP is in and this obviously will be an overseas call. Many marinas, service companies and a whole host of other places, will let you plug in to a metered telephone line. Remember you will need an adapter for the Greek telephone jack, although sometimes you will be able to connect simply through a normal US jack plug commonly found on many fax machines.

Public Holidays

Jan 1	New Year's Day
Jan 6	Epiphany
Mar 25	Independence Day
May 1	May Day
Aug 15	Assumption
Oct 28	Okhi ('No') Day
Dec 25	Christmas Day
Dec 26	St Stephen's Day

Movable
First Day of Lent
Good Friday
Easter Monday
Ascension

In addition many of the islands or regions have local saints' days when a holiday may be declared and some shops and offices will close.

Sailing information

Navigation

Navigation around the islands and along the coast is predominantly of the eyeball variety. The ancients navigated quite happily from island to island and prominent features on the coast and this is basically what yachtsmen still do in Greece. Eyeball navigation is a much maligned art, especially now that electronic position finding equipment has arrived on the scene, but for the reasons outlined below, it is still essential to hone your pilotage skills.

For good eyeball navigation you need the facility to translate the two-dimensional world of the chart into the three-dimensional world around you. Pick out conspicuous features like a cape, an isolated house, a knoll, an islet, and visualise what these will look like in reality. Any dangers to navigation such as a reef or shoal water may need clearing bearings to ensure you stay well clear of them. Any eyeball navigation must always be backed up by dead reckoning and a few position fixes along the way.

Anyone with electronic position finding should exercise caution using it close to land or dangers to navigation. The paradox of the new equipment is that while you may know your position, often to an accuracy of 20 metres or less, the chart you are plotting your position on is not accurate in terms of its latitude and longitude. Most of the charts were surveyed in the 19th century using astronomical sights, and the position of a cape or a danger to navigation, while proportionally correct in relation to the land mass, may be incorrect in terms of its latitude and longitude. Some of the charts carry a warning, and corrections for latitude and longitude (usually the latter). Consequently you are in the anomalous position of knowing your position to perhaps within 20 metres, but in possession of a chart which may have inaccuracies much greater than this. Blind acceptance of the position from electronic position finding equipment can lead and has led to disaster.

Navigation and piloting hazards

The comparatively tideless waters of the Mediterranean, a magnetic variation of just over 002°E, and the relatively settled summer patterns remove many of the problems associated with sailing in other areas of the world. Just having no tidal streams of any consequence to worry about enhances your sailing a hundredfold. Despite this, there are hazards to navigation which, while not specific to the Mediterranean, should be mentioned here.

Haze

In the summer a heat haze can reduce visibility to a mile or two, which makes identification of a distant island or feature difficult until you are closer to it. Sailing from Athens down to Aígina or Póros you may not be able to positively identify features until you are three miles or so off. Approaching Athens the dreaded *nefos* caused by air pollution, at times worse than Los Angeles, can make identification of features difficult until you are two or three miles off. Heavy rain in the spring and autumn cleanses the air and dramatically improves visibility.

Fog

In general fog is rare. In parts of the Aegean there may be a light radiation fog in the morning which can sometimes reduce visibility to a mile or less. The mist will gradually be burned off by the sun and by afternoon will invariably have disappeared.

Reefs and rocks

The Saronic has only a few isolated dangerous rocks and reefs and with care these are normally easily spotted. However, this absence of large areas of shoal water or extensive reefs can make the navigator lazy in his craft. The clarity of the water in the Mediterranean means you can easily spot rocks and shallows from the colour of the water. Basically, deep blue is good, deep green means it is getting shallow, lighter green means 'watch out', and brown lets you identify species of molluscs at first hand. However, with a bit of wind of any sort the whitecaps on the water can make identification of shallow water and reefs difficult and you should give any potential dangers a wide berth.

Fishing nets

Care is needed around local fishing boats or in isolated bays where there may be surface nets laid. Vigilance is needed not to run over a net and incur not just the wrath of a fisherman, but also most likely the net wrapped tightly around the propeller.

Lights

Although the islands and coast are quite well lit, the sheer extent of coastline means that it is impossible to light any but the most common routes used by ships and commercial fishermen. Navigation at night out of the common routes should be avoided unless you are familiar with the area.

Winds

The winds in this area are remarkably consistent in the summer. Details of the winds specific to the area are given at the beginning of each chapter, but in general the area can be divided into three.

Along most of the Attic coast around Athens and down over the sea area E of Póros and Ídhra the *meltemi* blows from the NE. The *meltemi* begins fitfully in July and builds up to full strength through August and early September, dying down in October. It will often blow up to Force 5–6 in this area and occasionally more. The *meltemi* tends to die off around Póros and Kólpos Idhras where it is funnelled in from the E. The *meltemi* will at times blow right down to Monemvasía and Cape Malea.

In Argolikos Kólpos and across to Ídhra the prevailing wind in the summer is a sea breeze from the SE which normally fills in around lunch time and dies down at night. It typically blows at around Force 4, sometimes a little less and sometimes a little more. The wind is reasonably reliable from June through to the end of September.

Over the western Cyclades the prevailing wind is the *meltemi* blowing from the N to NE. It can blow up to Force 7 or even 8 at times, though normally it is around Force 5–6. As in the Saronic Gulf, it generally gets up in July and blows through until the end of September.

In the evening there may a katabatic wind off the high mountains of the Peloponnese, though there are only a few places (Ástrous and Monemvasía are two) where you are likely to be affected by such a wind. On occasion the wind can get up to 30–35 knots though it is usually less and it generally lasts only a few hours before dying down. In the summer there may be isolated thunderstorms with an associated squall, but these seldom last for more than a few hours and are normally over in less than an hour.

In the spring and autumn depressions passing N over the mainland or S around Cape Malea can

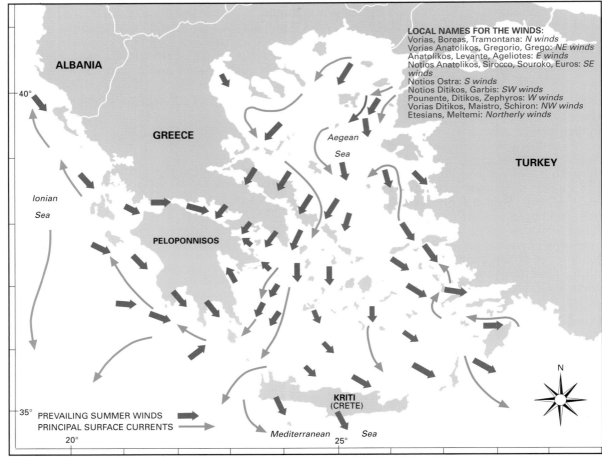

LOCAL NAMES FOR THE WINDS:
Vorias, Boreas, Tramontana: *N winds*
Vorias Anatolikos, Gregorio, Grego: *NE winds*
Anatolikos, Levante, Ageliotes: *E winds*
Notios Anatolikos, Sirocco, Souroko, Euros: *SE winds*
Notios Ostra: *S winds*
Notios Ditikos, Garbis: *SW winds*
Pounente, Ditikos, Zephyros: *W winds*
Vorias Ditikos, Maistro, Schiron: *NW winds*
Etesians, Meltemi: *Northerly winds*

PREVAILING SUMMER WINDS
PRINCIPAL SURFACE CURRENTS

WINDS AND CURRENTS

give rise to strong southerlies or northerlies.

For more detail on the prevailing winds see the section at the beginning of each chapter.

Berthing

Berthing Mediterranean-style with the stern or bows-to the quay can give rise to problems for those doing it for the first time, or even the second or third time. Describing the technique is easy: the boat is berthed with the stern or bows-to the quay with an anchor out from the bows or stern respectively to hold the boat off the quay. It is carrying out the manoeuvre which causes problems and here a few words of advice may be useful, but will not replace actually doing it.

Everything should be ready before you actually start the manoeuvre. Have all the fenders tied on, have two warps coiled and ready to throw ashore with one end cleated off, and have the anchor

ready to run; in the case of a stern anchor have the warp flaked out so it does not tie itself into knots as you are berthing. The manoeuvre should be carried out slowly, using the anchor to brake the way of the boat about half a boat length off the quay. The anchor should be dropped about three or four boat lengths from the quay and ensure you have sufficient chain or warp beforehand to actually get there.

Many boats have a permanent setup for going bows-to so there is not too much scrabbling around in lockers to extract an anchor, chain and warp. This can be quite simple: a bucket tied to the pushpit to hold the chain and warp and an arrangement for stowing the anchor on the pushpit. Boats going stern-to must have someone who knows what they are doing letting the anchor chain go. It should run freely until the boat is half a boat length off the quay. When leaving a berth haul yourself out with the chain or warp, using

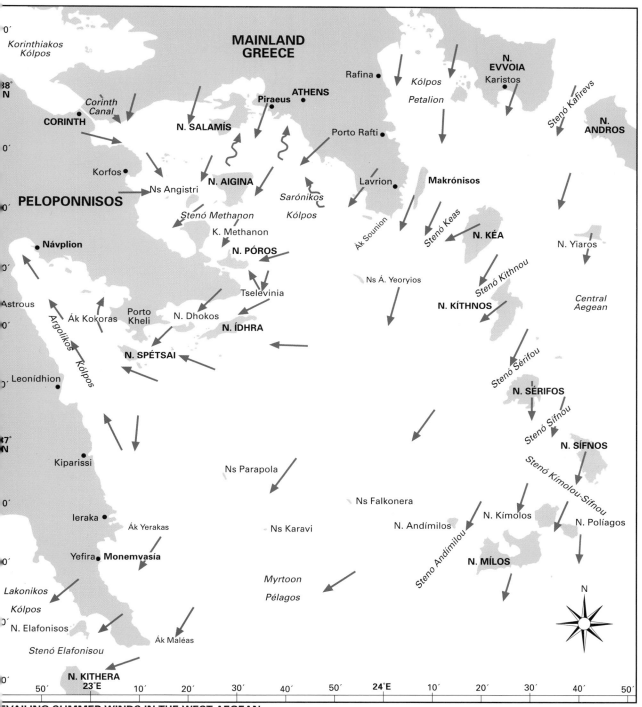

PREVAILING SUMMER WINDS IN THE WEST AEGEAN

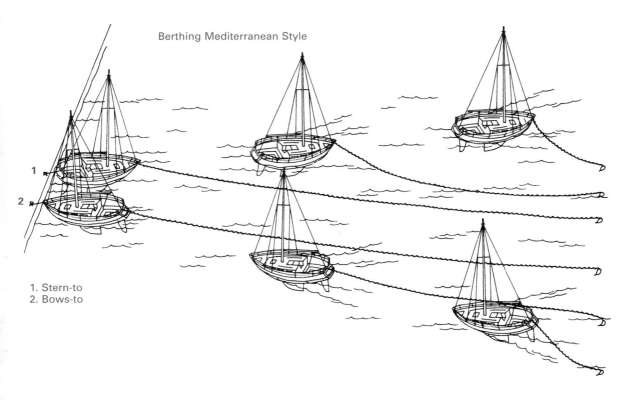

Berthing Mediterranean Style

1. Stern-to
2. Bows-to

the engine only sparingly until the anchor is up – it is all too easy to get the anchor warp caught around the propeller otherwise.

The good tourist

However much we hate being tagged with the label, we all are tourists, some longer term than others. If you like you can be the good holidaymaker, visitor, yachtsman, or whatever name is not offensive to your sensibilities. What is required of those of us who travel on the water around the Aegean or anywhere else in the world is that we do not stain the waters we travel on or the land we come to. Regrettably some tourists seem not to have any understanding of the delicate relationship between tourist and locals, and there are a number of substantial local complaints about us.

Rubbish

Many of the smaller islands are just not geared up to disposing of the rubbish brought in by tourists, and on the water you will be visiting some small

Right In the high season you will often have to berth two or even three out from the quay if you want to squeeze into popular places like Ídhra

Below In some places you need to go bows-to if you want to avoid underwater ballasting and rubble off the quay

villages or deserted bays where there are literally no facilities at all. You should take your rubbish with you to a larger island and dispose of it there. Even the larger islands have questionable methods of disposing of rubbish, and there is nothing wrong with trying to keep the number of convenience wrapped goods you buy to a minimum. My particular *bête noire* is bottled drinking water, as the discarded plastic containers can be found everywhere and when burnt (the normal method of disposal on the islands) produce noxious gases and dangerous compounds.

It hardly needs to be said that non-biodegradable rubbish should not be thrown into the sea. Even biodegradable rubbish such as vegetable peelings or melon rind should not be thrown into the water, except when you are three or more miles from land, as it ends up blowing back onto the shore before it has decayed or been eaten by scavengers. Toilets should not be used in harbour if there is one ashore, or they should be used with a holding tank. Holding tanks should not be emptied until you are well offshore.

Consciousness of pollution and individual responsibility for it is spreading through the villages and towns, and as tourists we also have a responsibility to keep the wilder parts of Europe free from pollution. Moreover, many of the sources of pollution are there to service the tourist trade and if there were no tourists then there would be less pollution.

Noise pollution

This comes in various forms, from the simple banality of making your presence known in an anchorage with the tape or CD player turned up full blast to inconsiderate motorboat owners with loud exhausts. Those who play loud music in deserted bays should reflect whether they would not be more comfortable in a noisy urban disco, preferably in their own country. Another annoying noise in an anchorage is the puttering of generators, and those who need to run their generator all day and night might consider whether they may not be more comfortable in a marina along the French or Italian Riviera where they can hook up to shore-power. Motorboaters with noisy outboards and inboards, and water-bikes which have the most irritating whine in their exhaust note, as well as the most irritating people driving them, should keep well clear of boats at anchor and keep noise levels to a minimum in any anchorage or harbour.

Safety and seamanship

In some places small powerboats and inflatables roar around an anchorage without regard for those swimming in the water. This is not just irritating but potentially lethal. If you have ever seen the injuries sustained by someone who has been hit by a propeller, you will immediately understand my concern. Accidents such as these frequently result in death, or for the lucky, horrible mutilation. Those on large craft should also keep a good lookout when entering an anchorage where people are in the water or when their own crew are swimming off the back of the boat.

Remember when picking up someone who has fallen overboard to engage neutral, or you may replace death by drowning with death by propeller injuries. Although water-bikes do not have a propeller they are just as lethal if they hit someone at speed and injure them – it doesn't take long to drown.

In many bays swimming areas are now cordoned off with a line of small yellow usually conical, buoys. Although this restricts the area you can anchor in, the swimming areas should be avoided and in fact you can be fined for anchoring in one of these areas. Certainly the locals will let you know in no uncertain terms that you should not be there.

Conservation

Under the aegis of organisations like the World Wildlife Fund, Greenpeace, and Friends of the Earth, conservation is coming of age in Greece.

A number of campaigns have been waged, amongst them a campaign to step up measures against oil pollution and one to reduce the amount of fertiliser and pesticides used in Greek agriculture. One of the problems in Greece is ensuring that action promised by the government is actually carried out, and so far there has been little success. There is an awful short-sightedness in all this, because failure to remedy environmental damage will have a catastrophic effect on the tourist industry in Greece and that would severely reduce already falling receipts from tourism. Those sailing around Greece should themselves avoid polluting the country in any way.

Weather forecasts

Because of the high and large land masses in Greece it is extremely difficult to predict what local winds and wind strengths will be. The Greek meteorological service does its best but nonetheless it faces an almost impossible task. Fortunately the wind direction and strength in the Aegean is remarkably consistent in the summer. For those who really want to listen to a weather forecast try the following sources, but remember to interpret them leniently.

VHF frequencies

A forecast for all Greek waters in Greek and English is given at 0600, 1000, 1600, 2200 UTC. For local time add 2 hours in the winter and 3 hours in the summer. The forecast covers all Greek waters for Z+12 hours. Gale warnings are given at the beginning of the broadcast.

A *sécurité* warning on Ch 16 gives all the VHF channels for the different shore stations and you will need to choose whichever shore station is closest to you. In fact the advice notice on shore stations is often mumbled and at such a speed that it can be difficult to hear, but is worth listening to in case VHF frequencies for the different shore stations are changed as occurred recently.

Western Aegean shore station list

Perama (Piraeus)	Ch 86
Saronic	Ch 25
Salamís	Ch 23
Síros	Ch 04

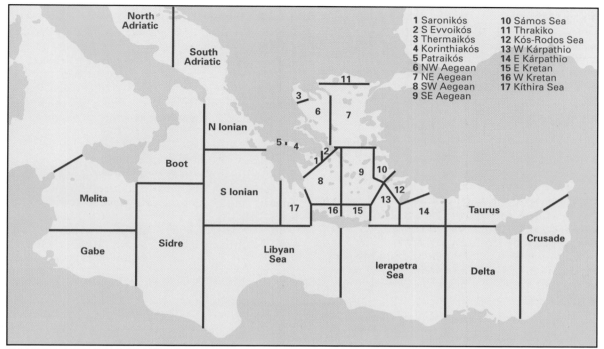

GREEK WEATHER FORECAST AREAS

1 Saronikós	10 Sámos Sea
2 S Evvoikós	11 Thrakiko
3 Thermaikós	12 Kós-Rodos Sea
4 Korinthiakós	13 W Kárpathio
5 Patraikós	14 E Kárpathio
6 NW Aegean	15 E Kretan
7 NE Aegean	16 W Kretan
8 SW Aegean	17 Kíthira Sea
9 SE Aegean	

HF Radio

A forecast in Greek and English is forecast on the following frequencies for SSB radios. (Receivers only will need a BFO switch).

Athens 2590kHz 0703, 0933, 1503, 2103 UT
Limnos 2730kHz 0703, 0903, 1533, 2133 UT
Iraklion 2799kHz 0703, 0903, 1533, 2133 UT
Rhodes 2830kHz 0703, 0903, 1533, 2133 UT

Broadcast Radio

Around Athens ERA radio 91·6FM is reported to have a forecast in English at 0630–0700 local time.

For the eastern Mediterranean a marine weather forecast is given by the Austrian short wave service (in German only) on 6150MHz/49m at 0945 and 1400 local time (from 1 May to 1 October only).

Television

On several of the television channels a weather forecast in Greek with satellite photos and wind forces and directions shown on the map is given after the news around 2100 local time. Many cafés and bars will have a television somewhere and you should ask for *o kairós parakaló*.

Port police and marinas

The port police get a weather forecast faxed to them several times a day. Depending on the inclination of the port police it is worthwhile asking them for a forecast.

Most of the few marinas in Greece post a forecast, often one taken off the internet.

Rescue services

Many of the larger harbours and some smaller harbours now have lifeboats. These range from all weather lifeboats to large RIBs. In addition many harbours have fast coastguard patrol boats ranging from large offshore craft to what are effectively fast speedboats.

Hellenic Radio monitors Ch 16 and 2182 MHz. Some coastguard stations are equipped with VHF and MF DSC facilities. In a number of recent situations the coastguard has responded reasonably quickly to distress calls and dispatched a craft to the scene.

Piraeus JRCC MMSI 237670000
VHF DSC
MF 2187·5kHz
HF DSC
☎ 01 411 2500 *Fax* 01 411 5798

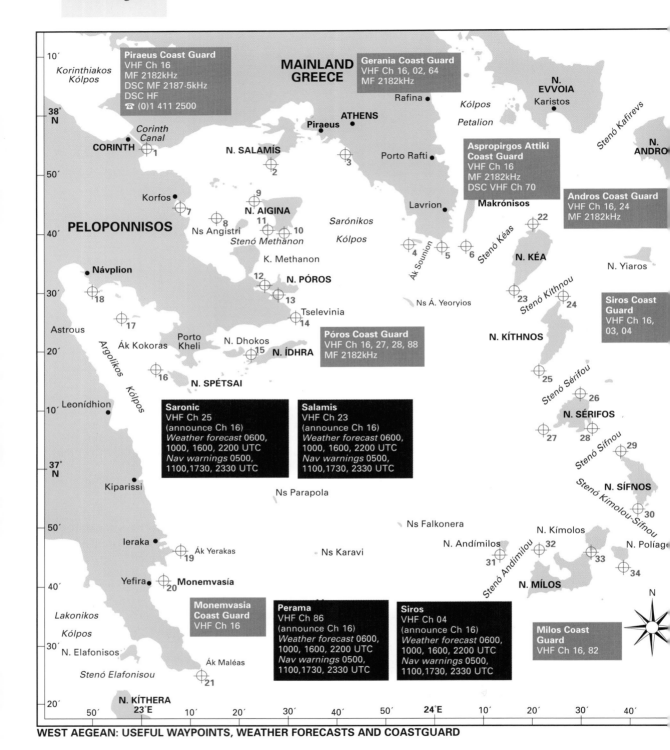

WEST AEGEAN: USEFUL WAYPOINTS, WEATHER FORECASTS AND COASTGUARD

USEFUL WAYPOINTS

⊕**1** Eastern entrance to Corinth
Canal
37°54'.9N 23°00'.5E
⊕**2** 0·5M S of Ák Kónkhi
(Salamina SW end)
37°52'.0N 23°27'.2E
⊕**3** Marina Alimos
(Kalamáki/Athens)
37°54'.8N 23°42'.1E
⊕**4** 0·5M S of W end of
Gaïdhouronisís
37°38'.45N 23°56'.04E WGS84
⊕**5** 0·25M S of temple on
Sounion
37°38'.63N 24°01'.31E WGS84
⊕**6** 0·15M S of S end of
Makrónisos
37°38'.56N 24°06'.25E WGS84
⊕**7** 1M S of Ák Trelli (Órmos
Sofikoú)
37°44'.49N 23°08'.93E WGS84
⊕**8** 0·25M N of N Kirá
37°42'.82N 23°16'.38E WGS84
⊕**9** 0·5M W of Ák Plakákia
(Aígina)
37°45'.8N 23°24'.6E
⊕**10** 0·10M S of Ák Pirgos (Aígina)
37°40'.29N 23°28'.82E WGS84

⊕**11** S end Stenón Monis (Aígina)
37°41'.26N 23°26'.82E WGS84
⊕**12** N Channel into Póros
37°31'.62N 23°25'.31E WGS84
⊕**13** SE Channel into Póros
37°29'.61N 23°27'.74E WGS84
⊕**14** S end of Tselevínia Channel
37°26'.05N 23°32'.15E WGS84
⊕**15** 0·5M S of Dhokós SE light
37°19'.30N 23°21'.48E WGS84
⊕**16** 0·1M W of Petrokáravo light
37°17'.08N 23°04'.67E WGS84
⊕**17** 1M W of Nisís Ípsili light
37°25'.9N 22°57'.1E
⊕**18** 1M W of Ák Megalí (Toló)
37°30'.6N 22°50'.3E
⊕**19** 0·25M E of Ák Yérakas
36°46'.17N 23°06'.90E WGS84
⊕**20** 0·25M E of Monemvasía
headland
36°41'.52N 23°03'.89E WGS84
⊕**21** 0·75M S of Ák Maleas
36°25'.48N 23°11'.62E WGS84
⊕**22** 1M N of Ák Perlevos (Kéa)
37°42'.3N 24°21'.0E
⊕**23** 0·2M S of Ák Tamélos (Kéa)
37°31'.14N 24°16'.50E WGS84
⊕**24** 0·25M N of Ák Kéfalos
(Kíthnos)
37°29'.21N 24°26'.01E WGS84

⊕**25** 1M S of Ák Áy Dhimítrios
(Kíthnos)
37°17'.1N 24°21'.9E
⊕**26** 1M N of Ák Volos (Sérifos)
37°13'.8N 24°29'.5E
⊕**27** 1M W of Ák Kíklops (Sérifos)
37°07'.4N 24°23'.7E
⊕**28** 0·2M W of Ák Amino
(entrance to O.
Livadhiou/Sérifos)
37°07'.66N 24°31'.68E WGS84
⊕**29** 1M N of Vrak Tsoukala
(Sífnos)
37°03'.9N 24°38'.0E
⊕**30** 0·4M W of Ák Karavi (N.
Kitriani/Sífnos)
36°53'.50N 24°42'.91E WGS84
⊕**31** 1M S of Ák Vlikadhi
(Andímilos)
36°45'.1N 24°14'.6E
⊕**32** 0·5M W of Nds. Akrádhia light
(Mílos)
36°46'.9N 24°22'.7E
⊕**33** 0·25M N of Ák Pelekoúdha
light (Stenó Mílou-Kimolou)
36°46'.45N 24°31'.7E
⊕**34** 1M S of S end of N. Políagos
36°43'.6N 24°38'.9E

Navtex

The following stations operate in Greece

Nav area	Station	B1 char	Transmission time	Language	Position	Freq	Country
III	Kérkira	K	0140, 0540, 0940, 1340, 1740, 2140	English & Greek	39°37'N 19°55'E	518kHz	Greece
III	Iraklion	H	0110, 0510, 0910, 1310, 1710, 2110	English & Greek	35°20'N 25°07'E	518kHz	Greece
III	Limnos	L	0150, 0550, 0950, 1350, 1750, 2150	English & Greek	39°52'N 25°04'E	518kHz	Greece

For coastguard stations for the sea area covered in this book see the map opposite.

About the plans

The plans which accompany the text are designed to help those cruising in the area to get in and out of the various harbours and anchorages and to give an idea of where facilities are to be found. It is stressed that many of these plans are based on the author's sketches and therefore should only be used in conjunction with the official charts. They are not to be used for navigation.

Waypoints

Waypoints are given for all harbours and anchorages. The origins of the waypoints vary and in a large number of cases the datum source of the waypoint is not known. Where I have taken waypoints for a harbour or anchorage it has a note after it reading WGS84. All these waypoints are to World Geodetic Survey 1984 datum which, it is intended, will be the datum source used throughout the world. Most GPS receivers automatically default to WGS84.

It is important to note that plotting a waypoint onto a chart will not necessarily put it in the position shown. There are a number of reasons for this:

WEATHER FORECASTS ON THE INTERNET

There are a number of good sources for weather on the internet. If there is a cyber café around half an hour should be plenty to get a forecast.

Mediterranean sailing

http://www.medsail.nildram.co.uk

Rod Heikell's site for sailing in the Mediterranean with a weather page and links to those sites he considers most useful in terms of content and download time. Includes 36 hour surface charts from NEMOC, satellite loops, wind and sea forecasts from a number of sources. Benefits from actually being used on board in the Mediterranean. Includes forecasts for Greece.

Nemoc (Naval European Meteorology and Oceanography Center)

http://www.nemoc.navy.mil/about1.htm

This is the US navy site based in Rota which has the best unclassified forecasts and maps for the Mediterranean. Many other private sites use the forecasts and maps from NEMOC (often without a source signature) so this is a good place to go first. Here you can get excellent text forecasts, surface analysis maps showing lows, highs and wind strength for next 36 hours, surface maps showing wave height and surface currents for next 36 hours, Meteosat photos updated hourly, satellite loop mpegs, wind and sea warnings, and much more. Excellent site which is quick to load.

Poseidon weather for Greece

http://www.poseidon.ncmr.gr/weather–forecast.html

Up to 72 hour surface wind forecasts for Greece. The best source of weather for Greek waters. The chart gives wind direction with colour coding for the wind force in Beaufort (the colour bar is on the right hand side of the chart) On the left hand side is a table for current and up to 72 hours forecast. Choose the one you want and press DISPLAY

University of Athens

http://weather.noaa.gov/weather/GR–cc.html

Weather observations at Greek Airports.

DWD Mediterranean Forecast

http:www.dwd.de/forecasts/seemm.htm

3-day text forecasts for a number of Mediterranean areas including the eastern Mediterranean. In German only, but easily read in table form. Forecast areas on a clickable map come up for: Alboran, Golfe de Lion, Balearics, Ligurian, West Corsica, Tyrrhenian, N Adriatic, S Adriatic, Ionian, N Aegean, S Aegean, Rhodes/Cyprus, Biscay.

The tables are arranged by column for Day (MO = Monday/DI = Tuesday/MI = Wednesday/DO = Thursday/FR = Friday/SA = Saturday/SO = Sunday)/Time (UTC+)/Wind direction/Wind force (Beaufort)/Gusts (Beaufort)/Wave height (m).

1. The chart may have been drawn using another datum source. Many of the Imray-Tetra charts use European datum 1950 (Europe50). There are many other datum sources that have been used to draw charts.

2. All charts, including those using WGS84, have errors of various types. Most were drawn in the 19th century and have been fudged to conform to WGS84 (the term 'fuzzy logic' could aptly be used).

3. Even when a harbour plan is drawn there is still a significant human element at work and mistakes easily creep in, as I know to my cost.

The upshot of all this is that it is important to eyeball your way into an anchorage or harbour and not just sit back and assume that all those digits on the GPS display will look after you. In the case of waypoints I have taken and which are appended WGS84, the waypoint is indeed in the place shown. In the case of other waypoints it can be derived from the light position, from reports in my files, or from other sources.

In this edition I have also included useful waypoints which are listed at the beginning of the relevant chapter and included on the location maps. As above, any that are appended WGS84 are from my own observations using the radar for distance off and a compass bearing for the direction. Given that some radar distance off readouts can be a bit of a guesstimate, these should be used with every caution. In most cases I have endeavoured to keep a reasonable distance off so that an error of say, 50m, should be unimportant when the waypoint is 0·5 NM from the land. There are other occasions when I have shaved a cape or islet and the distance off is considerably less.

All waypoints are given in the notation:

degrees   minutes   decimal place of a minute

It is important not to confuse the decimal place of a minute with the older 60 second notation.

I. The Attic Coast
Corinth Canal to Rafina

Corinth Canal to Sounion

If ever a coastline was drenched in ancient history this is it. The obvious image of the Parthenon jumps out of every second postcard and travel brochure like a token of Greece itself. From Akrocorinth to the Temple on Sounion are names resonant with a roll call of ancient battles, ancient seers and sages, heroes and tyrants, lovers and loveless suicide, names and monuments embedded in marble or lying in marble ruins on the ground. It is all too much. You can have ancient history and marble monuments with overkill. Even the dedicated philhellene will weary of it and seek refuge in a bar or taverna to escape the onslaught of old rock and ancient history.

And in truth modern Athens and its environs has little to do with its ancient precursor.

Useful waypoints
⊕1 Eastern entrance to Corinth Canal
  37°54'·9N 23°00'·5E
⊕2 0·5M S of Ák Kónkhi (Salamís SW end)
  37°52'·0N 23°27'·2E
⊕3 Marina Alimos (Kalamáki/Athens)
  37°54'·8N 23°42'·1E
⊕4 0·5M S of W end of Gaïdhouronisís
  37°38'·45N 23°56'·04E WGS84
⊕5 0·25M S of temple on Sounion
  37°38'·63N 24°01·31E WGS84
⊕6 0·15M S of S end of Makrónisos
  37°38'·56N 24°06'·25E WGS84

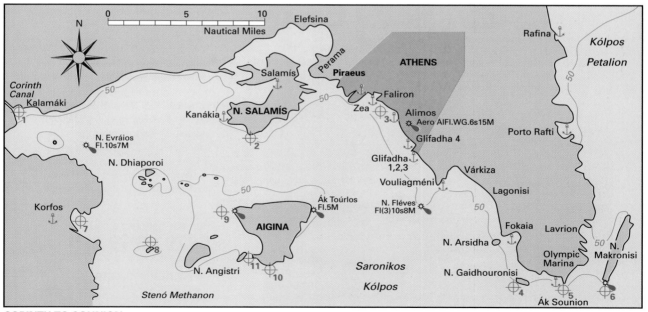

CORINTH TO SOUNION

PREVAILING WINDS

The prevailing wind in the Saronic Gulf is the *meltemi* blowing from the N to NE. To get to the marinas around Athens from the Corinth Canal it is best to stick close to the Attic coast. Gusts can be fierce off the coast but the sea is generally fairly flat. Heading down towards Aígina and Póros from Corinth you will be close or beam reaching and as you get towards Póros the wind usually moderates and may even turn to the S to SE.

If you are heading towards the Cyclades from Athens then stick to the Attic coast until Sounion before departing for the islands. It can get very windy and bumpy around the Kéa Channel and will get no better further E if the *meltemi* is at full strength. When I used to skipper charter boats from Athens it was not unusual for charterers who just had to visit the Cyclades to get as far as Kéa and change their minds and enquire if there was somewhere a little less windy to go to.

Quick reference guide

	Shelter	Mooring	Fuel	Water	Provisions	Eating out	Plan
Corinth Canal		B	O	O	O	C	•
Isthmía	B	A	O	B	O	C	•
Órmos Kalamáki	C	C	O	B	C	C	•
Ák Sousáki	C	BC	B	B	O	C	
Nísos Salamís							
Órmos Salamís	A	AC	B	A	B	B	•
Órmos Kanákia	B	C	O	O	O	C	
Kolones	C	AC	O	O	O	C	
Aias	C	C	O	B	O	C	
Órmos Peranis	C	C	O	B	C	C	
Kaki Viglia	C	C	O	B	O	C	
Ambelakia	B	BC	A	A	O	C	
Attic coast							
Pakhi	A	AB	B	A	B	B	•
Elefsina	A	AB	B	A	B	A	•
Zéa Marina	A	A	A	A	A	A	•
Mounikhías	A	AC	B	A	A	A	•
Faliron	A	A	B	A	A	A	•
Alimos Marina	A	A	A	A	A	A	•
Glifadha 4	A	A	A	A	A	B	•
Glifadha 1,2,3	A	A	A	A	A	B	•
Voula	A	A	B	A	B	B	•
Vouliagméni	A	A	A	A	A	A	•
Várkiza	AB	ABC	A	A	B	B	•
Áy Marina	B	C	O	O	O	C	
Lagonisi	B	AC	O	O	O	C	•
Órmos Anavíssou	B	C	O	B	B	B	•
Órmos Legraina	B	C	O	B	O	C	
Sounion	B	C	O	O	O	C	•
Órmos Paşalimani	C	C	O	O	O	C	
Órmos Pigadhi	C	C	O	O	O	C	
Olympic Marina	A	A	A	A	C	C	•
Lavrion	A	A	B	A	B	B	•
Órmos Thoriko	B	C	O	O	O	O	•
Porto Rafti	B	AC	A	A	B	B	•
Loutsa	A	A	B	B	O	C	•
Rafina	C	AB	B	B	B	B	•

After the Golden Age, Athens declined in the Middle Ages to a dusty little village under the shadow of the Parthenon. It did not become the capital of a unified Greece again until 1834 and was not even the first, nor the second, choice for the base of the new government. The small village of perhaps a few thousand souls and the fishing village at Piraeus were catapulted to the centre of life and commerce in the newly unified Greece and the population exploded. Although some attempt was made at town planning, it did not touch the anarchy of the suburbs where houses and buildings were thrown together in a vast sprawl around the centre. It is this sprawl of uninspired buildings strung along the coast and around the centre that makes it difficult, almost impossible, to believe that Attica and Athens are at the root of what we like to call western civilisation. Somehow we expect it to be different, to be an extension of the Parthenon, and when the awfulness of the place hits you it is like an assault on deeply held beliefs.

The geography of the coast is there as are the place names, but all around the Attic coast the real symbols of western civilisation are obvious, from the oil refinery belching noxious gases near Corinth through to the unbridled spread of reinforced concrete apartment blocks around Athens and its industrial suburbs, to yet more reinforced concrete dotted with TV antennas spreading towards Sounion. Homer's wine dark sea is stained with industrial effluent and flotsam and jetsam of every description. On top of it all sits the dreaded *nefos*, the polluted cloud which hovers over the capital and on bad days is worse than anything Los Angeles can produce. All this needs to be said, especially for the first-time visitor to the capital, who can be easily misled about the 21st century presence of the city and its surroundings by books which dwell exclusively on the sights and ancient monuments without telling you what you've got to get through to get there. Once this is understood you can get down to enjoying what Athens has to offer as a bustling modern city with its ancient ruins as a bonus.

I am not going to dwell on what to see and do in Athens. The obvious things, the Parthenon and the other ancient buildings around it, the

Archaeological Museum housing some of the finest ancient Greek sculpture in the world, the buzz of Plaka which was the original dusty village back in 1834, the cosmopolitan buzz of Syntagma and Omonia, the *evzones* in white kilts and stockings with pompom shoes, a few meals and a few drinks, will occupy more than the few days anyone passing through on the water will stay here. If you are here longer there is a plethora of guide books on what to do and see, and how to do so, on sale in Athens.

Outside Athens the Attic coast is nearly everywhere steep-to mountainous terrain, except for the large nearly circular Attic plain on which the capital sits. Around the narrow coastal strip the suburbs of Athens have spread in an unbridled sprawl, so that now modern Athens really extends from the industrial suburbs around Nea Perama to the far urban suburbs of Vouliagmeni and Varkilas. Today there are some three and half million living here, around one third of the population of Greece, and it is still growing as the young, the ambitious and the dispossessed home in on the magnetic attraction of a capital city. The infant industries of Greece have largely grown up here, and it said that over 70% of all the industry in Greece is based around the perimeter of Athens, mostly around Elevsis and Perama. It certainly seems like it when you sail into the greeny-brown waters off Athens.

For water-borne travellers Athens is the yachting centre of Greece, the equivalent of the Riviera or the Solent. There are more yachts, private and charter, based here than anywhere else in Greece and all of them are chasing a permanent berth somewhere along the Attic coast. Although this area has the greatest

concentration of marinas anywhere in Greece, still it can be next to impossible for a visiting yacht to find a berth. Anyone bringing a yacht to Athens will have to be persistent and insistent if they are going to find a berth. Unless you are chartering a yacht from an Athens based company, I personally think the best way to see Athens is by getting a ferry or hydrofoil from one of the nearby islands like Aígina or Póros, where a yacht can be left safely for a day or two.

Getting around inland

For information on moving around Athens, see the Introduction and simplified map of the area for getting to and from the new airport at Spata. Bus services run on regular routes: blue buses are the normal buses, yellow buses are express services, yellow trolleybuses operate around the centre, and orange buses are from outside Athens. The underground runs virtually north to south through the city centre. Taxis are everywhere and as long as the meter is running are the easiest way to get about. Hire cars and motorbikes can also be found everywhere, but unless you are going outside Athens don't bother. Like all capital cities it is choked with traffic and the traffic jams here are every bit as bad as in other large European cities.

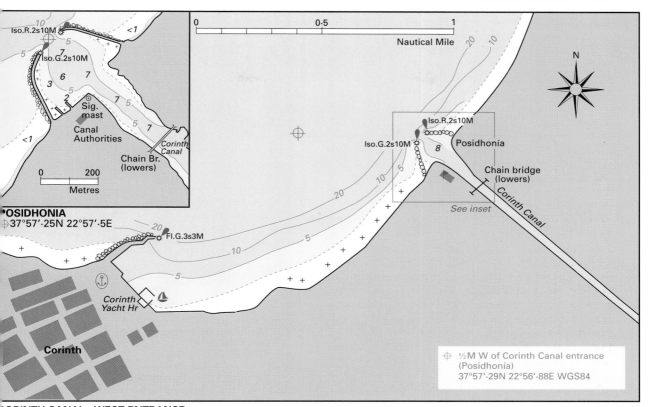

Iso.R.2s10M

Iso.G.2s10M

6 7

3 5 7 7

Sig. mast

Canal Authorities

Corinth Canal

Chain Br. (lowers)

<1

0 200
Metres

0 0·5 1
Nautical Mile

N

Iso.R.2s10M

Iso.G.2s10M

Posidhonía

8

Chain bridge (lowers)

Corinth Canal

See inset

⊕ ½M W of Corinth Canal entrance (Posidhonía)
37°57'·29N 22°56'·88E WGS84

POSIDHONIA
⊕ 37°57'·25N 22°57'·5E

Fl.G.3s3M

Corinth Yacht Hr

Corinth

CORINTH CANAL - WEST ENTRANCE

Corinth Canal

The idea of cutting a canal across the narrow waist connecting the Peloponnese to Attica was mooted by the ancient Greeks and many who came after. The present canal was started by the French and completed by the Greeks in 1893. It greatly reduces the distance between the Ionian and the Aegean and can be transited by yachts on payment of what is probably one of the highest canal fees per mile in the world.

First the facts: The canal is just over 3NM long, 25m (81ft) wide, the maximum permitted draught is 7m (23ft) and the sides of the canal rise to 76m (250ft) at the highest part of the cut. A current of 1–3 knots can flow in either direction depending on the direction and duration of the wind on either side and this can make passage through the canal difficult. I have encountered at least a 2-knot current which can make manoeuvring difficult. If you happen to be behind

Left Corinth Canal heading east　　　*Lu Michell*

a large ship, the wash from its and the attendant tugs propellers create a washing machine effect which can also cause problems when manoeuvring. Keep as far back from a ship in front as possible. There are chain bridges at either end which are lowered to let yachts and ships through.

At the western end of the canal (Posidhonia) the entrance is protected by breakwaters. Iso.R.2sl0M and Iso.G.2sl0M (actual range probably less) are exhibited at the entrance. In the summer westerlies often blow down onto the canal and the head of the gulf, causing a lumpy swell. It is possible to anchor inside the southern breakwater, but I don't recommend it as the holding is bad and the authorities are not happy about it. Just potter outside keeping the bows into the swell until the authorities signal you to enter.

At the Aegean end a breakwater protects a small harbour, but you go alongside on the quay by the Canal Authority building just inside the canal to pay. All paperwork is carried out here and the canal fees must be paid before transiting through to the Gulf of Corinth or vice versa. Care

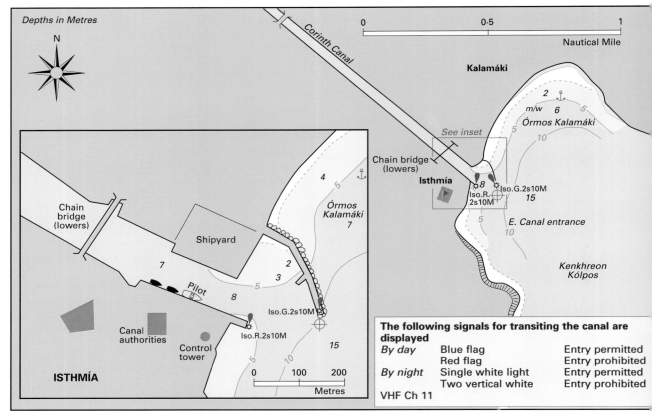

CORINTH CANAL - EAST ENTRANCE
⊕37°54′·9N 23°00′·6E

Map labels:

Depths in Metres

N

Corinth Canal

0   0·5   1
Nautical Mile

Kalamáki

2
m/w 6   5
Órmos Kalamáki
10

See inset

Chain bridge (lowers)

Isthmía

Iso.R. 2s10M

Iso.G.2s10M
15

4   5

Órmos Kalamáki
7

E. Canal entrance
10

5

Kenkhreon Kólpos

Chain bridge (lowers)

Shipyard

7

2
3

Pilot
8

5

Iso.G.2s10M

Iso.R.2s10M

15

Canal authorities

Control tower

ISTHMÍA

0   100   200
Metres

The following signals for transiting the canal are displayed

By day	Blue flag	Entry permitted
	Red flag	Entry prohibited
By night	Single white light	Entry permitted
	Two vertical white	Entry prohibited
VHF Ch 11		

is needed when going alongside the quay at Isthmía because although there is rubber fendering, it is very hard and any wash from the pilot boats or other craft will knock you about. You also need to pay attention to your mooring lines if a ship comes through after you or enters at Isthmía when you are tied up here. Any large ship sucks the water away from the canal sides, generating a considerable strain on your mooring lines and I have seen small craft badly damaged as a result. If someone stays on the boat instruct them to motor ahead or astern as required to ease the strain on the mooring lines.

The canal zone authorities use VHF channel 11. The canal is closed on Tuesday for repairs.

Caution Violent gusts can blow off the high land at either end of the canal. Both NW and NE winds gust off the land and as winds from these directions are common in the summer, care is needed.

Note For pilotage and harbours down the Peloponnese coast and towards Aígina and Póros see Chapter II. This chapter covers the mainland Attic coast to the east of the canal.

Órmos Kalamáki

The bay immediately N of the eastern end of the canal. There are numerous laid moorings in the bay for local boats so you need to anchor with care so as not to foul the ground tackle. Anchor in 4–10m on mud, sand and weed, mediocre holding so make sure your anchor is well in. Good shelter from northerlies although there are strong gusts into the bay off the hills. The bay is open to the S although southerlies are said not to blow home.

Tavernas ashore. The coast road from Athens to Corinth runs around the head of the bay and the rumble of traffic is incessant.

Ák Sousáki

Around the shores of the blunt cape there is a large oil refinery conspicuous by day because of its chimneys and by night by its flares. There are numerous jetties and quayed areas, but this is no place for a yacht to be.

In a bight on the W side of the cape there is a boatyard. A yacht can anchor off here on the north side of the bight in 5–10m on mud and weed. Good shelter from the *meltemi* but open S. There is a café in the boatyard.

I mention this as an anchorage in case you need it for some reason, but apart from the boatyard there is every reason not to come here. The oil refinery belches a miasmic fog into the air and the coast road is noisy day and night.

Nísos Salamís

Salamís is the largest island in the Saronic yet it is little visited by land or water-borne travellers. One of the reasons it is little visited by yachts becomes obvious if you study the regulations prohibiting navigation and anchoring around the northern coast of the island. Add to this the island's proximity to the grubby industry on the nearby mainland coast and a relative lack of usable anchorages, and its unpopularity is not too surprising. Perhaps also it is just too close to Athens and anyone leaving the capital is more tempted by the other islands a little further away, Aígina and Póros, and the coast of the Peloponnese.

Despite the associations between the name of the island and the famous Battle of Salamís, there is little on the island to give you the feeling that here one of the decisive moments in ancient history was settled in favour of the Greeks and so enabled the civilisation we base our own ideals on to continue to exist. For a summary of the essentials of the Battle of Salamís see the section in the Introduction.

The island itself is arid in the N and E but well wooded in the SW. It has a sizeable population, mostly in Salamís town, who are said to be predominantly of Albanian origin. There is a fair amount of agriculture on the island, numerous market gardens producing vegetables for Athens, and a growing number of pistachio groves following the success of pistachio cultivation on Aígina. On the NW corner of the island is the monastery of Faneromeni, the Apparition of the

Getting around

Buses run regularly from Paloukia, the ferry terminal on the east coast to Salamís town, the capital of the island. A less regular service runs from Salamís to Faneromeni where an irregular ferry service operates to the mainland. Regular ferries run from Paloukia to Perama on the opposite mainland shore. A less regular service operates from Paloukia to Piraeus. There is also a limited service from Faneromeni to Néa Perama.

Virgin, the centre of spiritual life on the island and a popular place of pilgrimage. Buses run from Salamís town if you want to visit it.

Prohibited areas

1. In Órmos Salamís navigation is prohibited within ½M of the shore between one and two miles E of Ák Petritis (the southern entrance point of the bay).
2. Navigation is prohibited around a small area off Elefsina in the NE of Kólpos Elevsinos.
3. Except for a narrow channel in the fairway, navigation is prohibited between the E side of Nísos Salamís and the mainland coast opposite. Navigation at night is prohibited. Anchoring is prohibited everywhere in the channel between Nísos Salamís and the mainland from Perama to Kólpos Elevsinos.

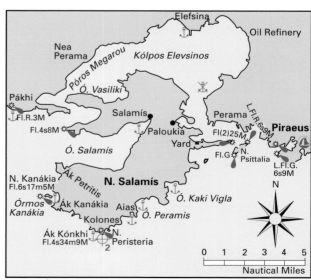

SALAMÍS TO PIRAEUS

⊕2 0·5M S of Ák Kónkhi (Salamís SW end)
37°52'·0N 23°27'·2E

Órmos Salamís

Pilotage

Approach The large bay on the W side of the island has no obvious distinguishing marks but the general location of the bay is easily ascertained. From the S the light structure on Nisís Kanákia will be identified when closer in. Once into the bay the cluster of houses of Salamís town will eventually be seen. When the *meltemi* is blowing there are gusts into the bay though little sea is generated across the bay.

Mooring Anchor off the village in 2–5m or go stern or bows-to in the small basin if you can find a space. These latter berths are usually crowded with fishing boats and you are unlikely to find a vacant spot. If you are going to the boatyard W of the town anchor off the yard in 4–10m. The bottom is mud, sand and weed, good holding once through the weed. Good shelter from the *meltemi* and open only to the S across the bay and to the W – westerlies are said not to blow home.

Facilities

Services Water in the basin and fuel nearby.

Provisions Good shopping for provisions in Salamís town.

Eating out Tavernas in Salamís town and a taverna near the boatyards.

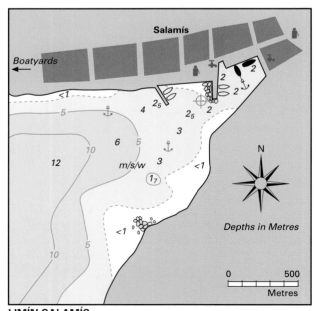

LIMÍN SALAMÍS
⊕37°57'·7N 23°29'·6E

Other Bank. PO. OTE. Ferry service from Paloukia to Perama and to Piraeus.

General

Salamís town, also known as Koulouri, cannot lay any claims to architectural distinction, but it has a dusty chaotic appeal to it and the locals are a friendly lot. In the town there is a small archaeological museum with some Mycenean artefacts recovered on the island.

Anchorages around the SW end of Salamís

Órmos Kanákia Nisís Kanákia light 37°54'·3N 23°23'·5E. The bay is partially sheltered by Nisís Kanákia. In the approach care needs to be taken of the reef extending northwards from Nisís Kanákia and southwards for a shorter distance from the south of the islet. Anchor in the N or S part of the bay taking care of a reef fringing the shore in the middle part of the bay. Beach ashore and wooded slopes behind. A taverna opens in the summer.

Kolones 37°52'·6N 23°26'·5E
A miniature harbour on the SW corner of Salamís. It is really too shallow for yachts and in any case the approaches are encumbered by shoal water. You can anchor off the harbour in calm weather.

Aias 37°53'·4N 23°28'·9E
This small bay affords good shelter from the *meltemi*. Anchor off the beach in 4–6 metres on sand. Care is needed of a reef running out from the shore. There is a short mole in the NE corner used by local fishing boats but there is really no room here for yachts although there are 2–3 metre depths on the outer end of the mole. Some provisions and tavernas ashore.

Órmos Peramis 37°53'·7N 23°29'·4E
The large bay E of Aias. Care needs to be taken of the reef fringing the shore and around Nisís Pera in the bay. Good shelter from the *meltemi*, although with strong winds from any direction some swell tends to roll into the bay. Some of the bay has now been developed as a sort of home-grown resort and there are tavernas on the beach in the summer.

Kaki Vigla 37°54'·6N 23°30'·7E
The large bay under Ák Tourlos. Mediocre shelter from the *meltemi* here and if it blows strongly a swell rolls into the bay. Anchor on the N side. Tavernas ashore.

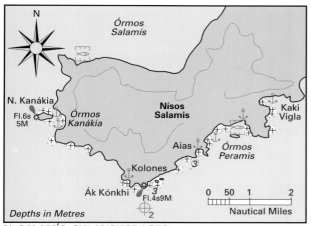

N. SALAMÍS: SW ANCHORAGES

⊕2 0·5M S of Ák Kónkhi (Salamís SW end)
37°52'·0N 23°27'·2E

Ambelakia 37°57'·1N 23°30'·7E

The inlet on the E side of Salamís opposite Perama. There is a boatyard in here with a quay and short pier where you can go alongside. Water and electricity and a taverna ashore. The boatyard has a 100 ton travel hoist and is well equipped to handle all manner of repairs.

Néa Perama to Perama

The mainland coast around the top of Salamís is not one which many yachts visit and there are good reasons for this. By and large it is an industrial wasteland with belching chimneys and the hulks of ships dotted around it. There are also many prohibited areas and you should study the chart of the area before proceeding up and around the north side of Salamís. Unless you are going to the boatyards at Perama there is little point in entering this polluted stretch of water and there are only a few really good places for a yacht to bring up for the night. There are two harbours here where you may find a berth.

If you want to explore the area where the Battle of Salamís took place (see the section in the introduction on the battle) take good care to stay out of the prohibited areas and in the channel permitted for navigation – I know of at least one yacht which was escorted out of the area when it strayed out of the permitted area.

Pakhi

A small fishing harbour on the mainland coast under Nisís Pakhi off the western entrance to Kólpos Elevsinos. It is usually crowded with fishing boats and you will just have to negotiate a berth wherever you can. Good all-round shelter inside. If you don't manage to find a berth here it is not far across to Órmos Salamís where there is always room to anchor.

Water on the quay and provisions and tavernas ashore.

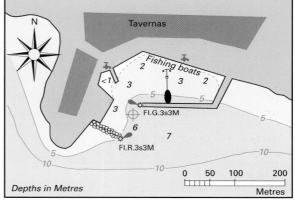

PAKHI
⊕37°58'·4N 23°21'·7E

Elefsina

A small fishing harbour off the suburb of Elefsina on the north side of Kólpos Elevsinos. Like Pakhi the harbour is always very crowded and you will have to negotiate a berth wherever you can. Good shelter inside. With northerlies you can anchor off in the bay to the W of Elefsina harbour in 4–5 m on mud.

Water on the quay and provisions and tavernas ashore.

Piraeus

The commercial harbour of Piraeus is solely devoted to commercial shipping and the numerous ferries running to destinations all over the Aegean. A yacht should not make for the harbour and it is in any case usually suicide to do so, with ships of all descriptions roaring in and out of the entrance at speed.

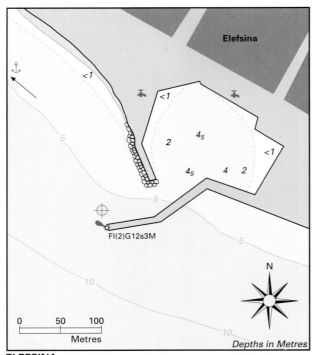

ELEFSINA
⊕ 38°02´·2N 23°32´·2E

Note

Off the eastern end of Nísos Salamís and under Voi Skrofes and Nisís Atalándi and Nisís Psittalia are the anchorage areas numbers 1 and 2 for commercial vessels waiting to enter Piraeus. This cluster of ships at anchor is conspicuous in the approaches to Piraeus and the marinas around the coast when approaching from the S and W.

Zéa Marina (Pasalimani)

Zéa Marina sits just around the corner on the E side of the headland from Piraeus commercial harbour. It is difficult to pick out from the distance for the first time and you will need to concentrate on the various marks identifying bits of the skyline and the coast.

Pilotage

Approach VHF Ch 09. From the S and SE the cluster of large ships at anchor off Piraeus commercial harbour will be seen and you need to keep a careful watch for ships getting underway from the anchorage or the commercial harbour. The blank wall of concrete of the apartment blocks spread along the coast makes it difficult to identify exactly where Zéa is, but the sketch of the approach

identifies the conspicuous objects on the skyline: the tall chimney at Piraeus and the stadium at Néa Faliron stand out well. The breakwater of the marina does not show up well, although once close in it will be seen as well as the masts of the yachts in the outer basin. Care is needed of hydrofoils entering and leaving the outer basin.

Mooring If you have not already made prior arrangements for a berth you will usually be directed to a berth on the outer breakwater. Shelter in the inner basin is excellent, but in the outer basin southerlies can cause a reflected swell which makes berths on the outer breakwater uncomfortable. A charge is made.

Facilities

Services Water and electricity at every berth. Shower and toilet block on the quay near the marina office. Fuel on the quay near the marina office.

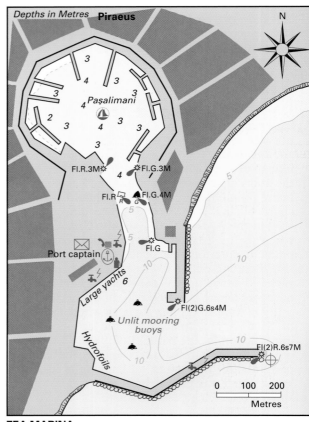

ZEA MARINA
⊕ 37°56´·0N 23°39´·2E

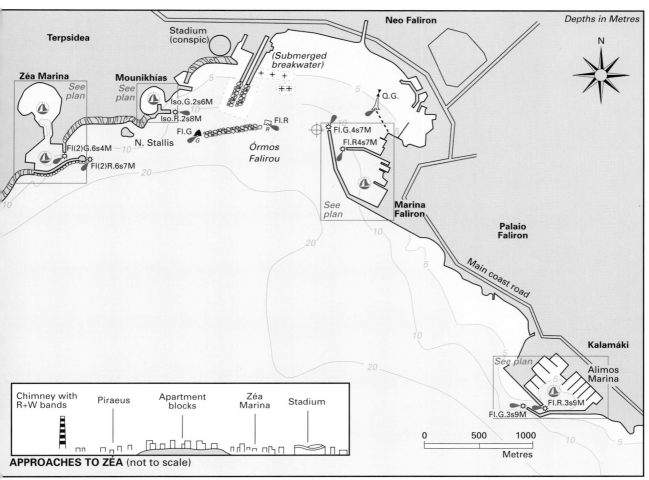

Terpsidea

Stadium (conspic)

Neo Faliron

Depths in Metres

N

Zéa Marina

See plan

Mounikhías

See plan

(Submerged breakwater)

Iso.G.2s6M

Iso.R.2s8M

Q.G.

Fl.G

N. Stallis

Fl.R

Fl.G.4s7M

Fl.R4s7M

Fl(2)G.6s4M

Fl(2)R.6s7M

Órmos Falirou

Marina Faliron

Palaio Faliron

See plan

Main coast road

Kalamáki

See plan

Alimos Marina

Fl.R.3s9M

Fl.G.3s9M

0   500   1000
Metres

Chimney with R+W bands | Piraeus | Apartment blocks | Zéa Marina | Stadium

APPROACHES TO ZÉA (not to scale)

ZÉA TO KALAMÁKI
⊕37°57´·1N 23°40´·8E

Provisions Provisions and ice can be delivered to the boat. Good shopping for all provisions near the marina.

Eating out Tavernas and restaurants of all types near the marina. You can eat Chinese, Italian, French or straight Greek. It is worth wandering around to Mikrólimani where you can eat well looking out over the small harbour.

Other Banks nearby. PO and OTE in the marina office. Doctors and dentists. Hospital. Hire cars and motorbikes Ferries from Piraeus to most destinations in the Aegean. Hydrofoils from Zéa to destinations in the Saronic and eastern Peloponnese

Paşalimani in Zéa Marina

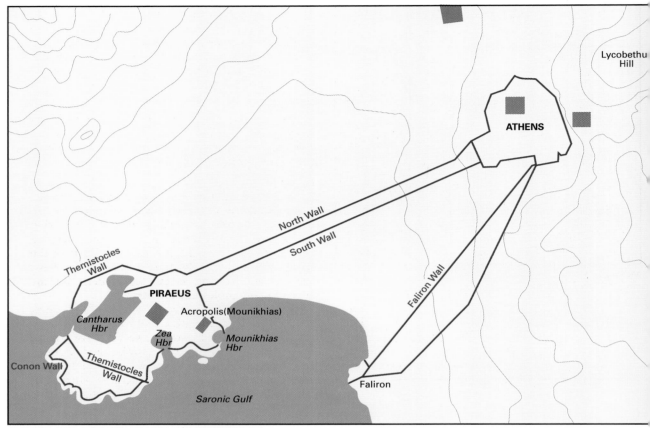

ATHENS AND PIRAEUS IN THE 5TH CENTURY BC

General

Zéa is one of the oldest small craft harbours, not just in Greece, but in the world. It was originally the harbour for ancient Zéa and was ringed by some 196 ship-sheds. The inner circular basin was surrounded by a stone wall about 15 metres (50ft) back from the water. A line of columns dividing the sheds off extended down to the water and the whole was roofed over. Slipways ran from the sheds into the water. Boats of this era were hauled regularly to dry out or they became so water-logged they could not be rowed or sailed. On a voyage the boats would be hauled onto a sandy beach, presumably on rollers and using manpower. Only a few remains of the ship-sheds will be glimpsed amongst the subsequent rebuilding which has gone on at Zéa. The inner circular basin is much the same shape as it was in ancient times, but the outer basin is new and formerly the ancient harbour would have opened straight onto the sea.

Zéa is arguably one of the best places to be close to Athens. It at least has the charm of being an established marina with all facilities nearby. It is easy to get into Athens from here and the streets behind the marina and over the ridge into Piraeus house shops and workshops selling and repairing just about anything you can think of. It is easy to spend half a day just wandering around looking at everything and is possibly as interesting as jostling with the crowds for a snapshot of the Parthenon (not that you shouldn't go there as well). In the cinemas the latest movies will be showing and these are usually sub-titled so that the original English dialogue remains.

Mounikhías (Turkolimani, Mikrólimani)

The almost circular harbour just E of Zéa. It is administered by the Royal Hellenic Yacht Club and others and you should enquire in advance to see if a berth is available.

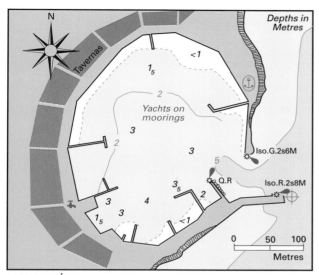

MOUNIKHÍAS
⊕37°56′·3N 23°39′·7E

Pilotage

Approach VHF Ch 09. The entrance lies ½M ENE of Zéa. The new detached breakwater just E of the harbour shows up well and closer in the masts of the yachts inside will be seen.

Mooring Berth where directed if you have permission. Numerous yachts are kept on fore and aft moorings in the middle of the harbour and navigating through them can be difficult. In calm weather it may be possible to go alongside the outer mole.

Facilities

Water and electricity on the quay. Provisions nearby. The harbour is ringed by numerous and relatively expensive restaurants, many of which specialise in seafood. Yacht club on the S side.

General

Like Zéa this was also an ancient harbour surrounded by ship-sheds with slipways for an estimated 80-odd triremes. Originally two long moles provided additional protection with a lighthouse tower on the end of each. Parts of the ancient harbour can be seen around the present harbour and serving as the foundations for the present short moles at the entrance.

Although you are unlikely to find a berth here, the harbour is well worth a visit by land. Sitting in a natural amphitheatre by the sea, it is something of an oasis away from the noise and frenetic atmosphere pervading most of Piraeus and Athens. Treat yourself to a meal in an almost Italianate setting, looking out over the harbour and the sea beyond.

Mounikhías looking ESE

Faliron (Phaleron, Flísvos)

The large harbour on the east side of Órmos Falírou.

Pilotage

Approach VHF Ch 09. The outer breakwater is high and easily recognised. There are usually numerous large motor yachts (read small ships) berthed under the outer breakwater.

Mooring Go alongside or stern or bows-to where directed or where convenient. This is not really a harbour for a visiting yacht, with most of the space occupied by permanent berth holders or reserved for the yacht club. A charge is made.

Facilities

Water and electricity on the quay. Good shopping and numerous tavernas and restaurants nearby in Palaio Faliron.

General

It is a pity there are not more berths available here. You are close to Palaio Faliron and its

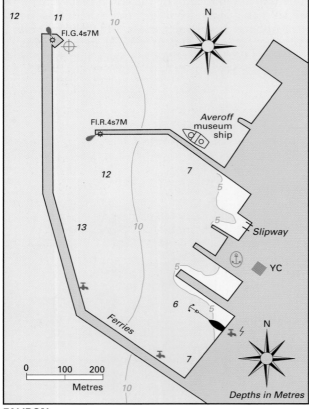

FALIRON
⊕37°56′·1N 23°40′·8E

The Tower of Winds

If you wander around Pláka, the old quarter of Athens, you will come across the Tower of Winds standing just outside the site of the Roman market place. Built in the first century BC by the Macedonian astronomer, Andronikos of Kyrrhos, the octagonal tower is remarkable for a number of reasons. On each of the eight marble sides there is a relief of a winged figure representing the wind that blows from that direction. Originally the tower was capped by a revolving bronze Triton holding a wand which pointed to the prevailing wind. It was also a clock-tower. Beneath the figures of the winds are eight sundials. Within the tower a water clock registered the hours, fed by a reservoir on the south side of the roof.

But what is most remarkable is that each of the eight sides of the tower faces the cardinal and half-cardinal points of the compass, although the compass in its most rudimentary form was not introduced from the east until over a thousand years later. Moreover, the figures depicting the wind fly around the tower in an anticlockwise direction, which is the direction in which any cyclonic system entering the Mediterranean also revolves, with the winds of a depression following the same pattern and sequence as that shown on the tower.

The figures

North Boreas, the violent and cold north wind, represented by a bearded old man wrapped in a thick mantle with the folds being plucked by the wind.

Northeast Kaikias, a cold bitter wind represented by a man holding a vessel from which olives are being scattered, representing the valuable olive crop being destroyed by this wind.

East Apeliotes, a handsome young man, carries flowers and fruit, depicting the mild and kindly nature of the wind.

Southeast Euros, represented by an old man with his right arm muffled in his mantle, heralds the stormy southeast wind.

South Notios, a sour-looking figure, empties an urn, implying rain and sultry weather.

Southwest Lips, represented by a figure pushing the prow of a ship, signifies the wind that is unfavourable for ships leaving Athens.

West Zephyros, the mild west wind, is represented by a handsome youth showering a lapful of flowers into the air.

Northwest Skiron, represented by a bearded man with a vessel in his hands, is interpreted in various ways. Either he is carrying a vase denoting occasional rain showers, or a charcoal vessel with which he dries up rivers.

shops, while not too far away is Athens centre. The *Averoff* museum ship is permanently berthed in Faliron and you can visit it most days. The *Averoff* was financed by a wealthy Greek industrialist (not surprisingly called George Averoff) and built for the Greek navy in England in 1910. She is an armoured cruiser/pocket battleship of nearly 10,000 tons with four ten-inch guns and eight six-inch guns. She served as a training ship until well past her sell-by date and was only recently turned into a museum ship. The ship is open Mon, Wed, Fri in the evenings (1900–2100 summer, earlier in the winter) and 1100–1500 on Sat and Sun.

Alimos Marina (Kalamáki)

A marina about 1½M SE of Faliron harbour. It is usually very crowded with permanent berth holders and even they do not know if their own paid-up berth will be free when they return.

Pilotage

Approach VHF Ch 09, 16. The harbour blends into the coast and is difficult to identify from the distance. From the W and SW the green lawn of a cemetery with a conspicuous white cross immediately W of the marina will be seen. Closer in the masts of the yachts inside and the breakwaters can be identified. The entrance is not apparent until you are right up to it.

Mooring Finding a berth is something of a lottery. If you have chartered a boat here then shore staff will direct you to a berth which they guard jealously for their own and no other. Visitors' berths are ostensibly under the W breakwater (berths A–E), but these are generally so congested with permanent berth holders that you will be lucky to find a spot here. Just shove and push until you find somewhere. There are laid moorings for most berths but many have been cut or lost. The Marina Office is generally not helpful in sorting out a berth. Good all-round shelter.

A charge is made.

Facilities

Services Water and electricity near every berth. Shower and toilet block near the office. Fuel on the quay. Yacht repair facilities.

Provisions Good shopping for provisions nearby on the main road. Provisions can be delivered to your yacht. A handcart and van comes

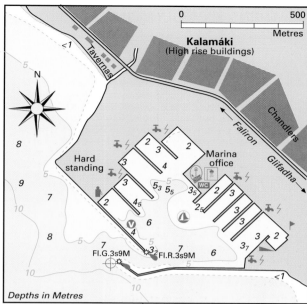

ALIMOS MARINA (KALAMÁKI)
⊕37°54'·8N 23°42'·1E

around with basic provisions and fruit and vegetables for sale in the summer. Ice available in the marina.

Eating out A few tavernas and restaurants along the main road. Better restaurants in Faliron.

Other PO, OTE, and banks in Palaio Faliron. Hire cars and motorbikes. Buses into Athens.

General

Kalamáki is a convenient marina close to Athens, but more than that you cannot say. The marina is a drab place in a drab suburb. At night a disco in the marina puts out a decibel level that rivals the road traffic just outside the entrance. For charterers it is a convenient base to pick up a yacht, but they should then head away from Kalamáki and Athens with all haste.

ATHENS 2004 OLYMPICS

Most people know the Olympics originated in Greece. The name comes from the site of the first Panhellenic games held at Olympia on the western Peloponnese near Katakolon in 776BC and many of the Greek heroes we know of proved their worth on track and field here. While the games were in progress a sacred truce, the *Ekeheira*, was observed for the duration and warring states put aside their differences to partake in the events, presumably returning to hostilities after the games. At the first games the prize for winning was purely symbolic, a palm leaf and an olive branch, but later some professionalism crept in and winners could expect monetary prizes and a lot of kudos from their home city-state.

The Panhellenic games were abolished in AD393 by the Emperor Theodosius as too pagan for the newly emerging Christian state. In 1896 Baron Pierre de Coubertin revived the games and the first modern Olympics were held in Athens in the same year. Now just over one hundred years later the modern Olympics have returned to Athens. Though fears have been expressed about the abilities of the Greek Olympic steering committee to get everything finished on time, it is likely that almost everything will be in place and that things will run with the sort of delightful organised anarchy that gets most other things in Greece done in a rush just minutes before opening time.

The map of where events will take place is pretty much self-explanatory. The sailing events will take place at the Áy Kosmas sailing centre.

Sailing was first introduced in the Paris Olympics in 1900 with just three classes. Today there are eleven sailing classes which will all be represented at the 2004 Olympics. The first Greek team to participate in Olympic sailing events was in 1948 and since then a number of sailing medals have been won by Greek teams. Former Crown Prince Constantinos skippered a Soling to a bronze medal in 1960, Ilias Hatzipavlas got a silver in the Finns in 1972, Anastasios Boudouris skippered a Soling to a bronze in 1980 and in the 1996 games in Atlanta Nikos Kaklamanakis got a gold in the Mistral sailboard class.

The eleven sailing classes at the 2004 games are

Board Sailing Men *Mistral One Design*
Board Sailing Women *Mistral One Design*
Single-handed Dinghy Men *Finn*
Single-handed Dinghy Women *Europe*
Single-handed Dinghy Open *Laser*
Double-handed Dinghy Men *470*
Double-handed Dinghy Women *470*
High Performance Dinghy Open *49er*
Multihull Open *Tornado*
Keelboat Men *Star*
Keelboat Women *Yngling*

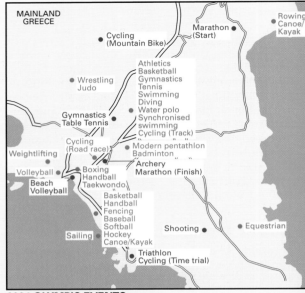

2004 OLYMPIC EVENTS

Áy Kosmas Olympic Sailing Centre

Work has begun on a yacht harbour at Áy Kosmas, to be used in the Athens Olympics in 2004. Work is not well advanced at the time of writing but the planned harbour is shown below. It is likely that after the Olympics it will become a yacht marina to provide the berths so much in demand along this coast.

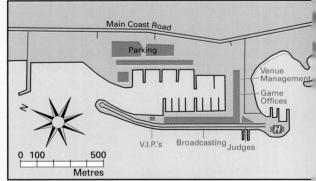

AY KOSMAS OLYMPIC SAILING CENTRE (Planned)
37°53′·6N 23°42′·7E

Glifadha 4

The first of the Glifadha marinas you come to heading down the coast from Athens.

Pilotage

Approach VHF Ch 09. The marina is tucked into the north side of Ák Axionis. The marina is not too easy to locate from the distance but closer in the masts of the yachts inside will be seen.

Mooring Go where directed by the marina attendant. There are laid moorings which must be picked up. Good all-round shelter. A charge is made.

Facilities

Services Water and electricity near every berth. Fuel delivered by mini-tanker. Shower and toilet block.

Provisions Good shopping for all provisions nearby in Glifadha. Some of the supermarkets will deliver to the boat. Ice available.

Eating out Several restaurants near the marina and others in Glifadha. In my experience it is better to stick to those near the marina.

Other PO. OTE. Banks. Doctors. Dentist. Hire cars and motorbikes. Taxis. Regular buses into Athens on the main road nearby.

General

The marina is well run and efficient with helpful staff, in marked contrast to Alimos Marina. If you can get in here this is something of an oasis away from the dissonance of people and noise that is Athens.

Glifadha 1,2,3

The three small harbours just S of Glifadha 4. Although they are called marinas, they are really much too small to merit the title.

Pilotage

Approach A church with a blue cupola on the shore and the masts of the yachts inside will be seen. Closer in a hoarding on the extremity of the mole of Glifadha 3 will be seen.

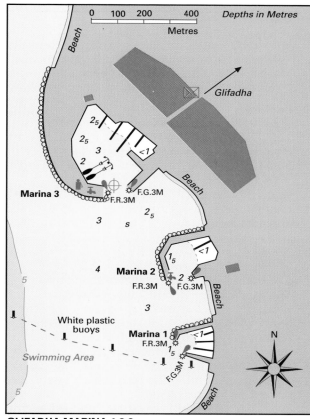

GLIFADHA MARINA 4
⊕37°52´·3N 23°44´·0E

GLIFADHA MARINA 1,2,3
⊕37°51´·8N 23°44´·6E

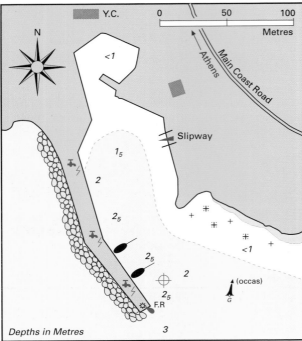

VOULA ⊕37°50´·3N 23°45´·7E

Mooring Go stern or bows-to where directed in Marina 3, the largest of the three small harbours. There are not normally berths available for visiting yachts. A charge is made.

Facilities
Services Water and electricity near every berth. Fuel in Marina 3.
Provisions Good shopping in Glifadha.
Eating out Tavernas nearby and in Glifadha proper.
Other PO and OTE. Banks. Hire cars and motorbikes. Taxis. Buses into Athens from the main coast road.

Voula

A small harbour about a mile south of Glifadha 3. The harbour is private and most berths are allocated so you cannot be certain of getting a berth here. An L-shaped mole provides reasonable protection behind. Care is needed at the entrance which is fringed by above and below-water rocks on the shore side. A small buoy marks the channel into the harbour. There are reasonable depths behind and yachts are kept here permanently. Tavernas and shopping nearby.

Vouliagméni

A marina tucked up on the W side of Órmos Vouliagméni.

Pilotage
Approach VHF Ch 09. Care needs to be taken of Vrakhonisos Kasidhis, an above-water rock

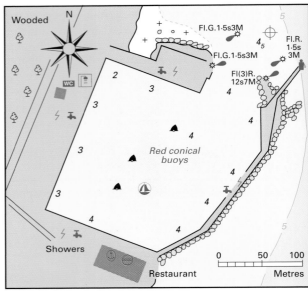

VOULIAGMÉNI
⊕37°48´·3N 23°46´·6E

fringed by a reef lying off the western entrance point of the bay. There is an inside passage but the prudent course is to keep to seaward of it. A large white hotel on the slopes behind the marina is conspicuous and closer in the marina breakwater and the craft inside will be seen.

Mooring Berth stern or bows-to where directed by a marina attendant. There are laid moorings to be picked up and you should not drop your anchor unless advised to. In the summer the marina is packed full of permanent berth holders and you will frequently be turned away. Good all-round shelter although southerlies can cause a reflected swell which makes it uncomfortable. A charge is made.

Facilities

Services Water and electricity near every berth. Fuel on the quay. Shower and toilet block ashore.

Provisions Most provisions available in

Voula, looking out to the entrance

Vouliagméni looking S into the entrance

Vouliagméni proper at the head of the bay. Ice available.

Eating out Several restaurants near the marina.

Other PO and OTE. Hire cars. Taxis. Bus service into Athens on the main road.

General

The marina was one of the first to be built in Greece and has a certain snobbish appeal situated next to the up-market real estate on the squiggly peninsula. If you can get in here it is something of an oasis with a wonderful feeling of calm away from the hubbub of Athens and the roar of traffic on the coast road. And you get to contemplate the millions of dollars worth of little ships berthed in here.

Órmos Vouliagméni

Technically it is illegal to anchor in the bay for some unknown reason, but in the summer yachts do anchor here. If the marina is full you can try anchoring off in the bay in 3–5m on mud and weed where there is good protection from the *meltemi*. Alternatively pop round to Varkilas where you can anchor off and get reasonable protection from the *meltemi*.

Várkiza

A small harbour in Órmos Varis, the large bay E of Vouliagméni.

Pilotage

Approach In Órmos Varis, Pondikonisi (Mouse Island) and the two rocks, Vrakhonisos Lito and Artemis, are easily identified. The harbour lies in the NW corner of the bay. Care is needed of the underwater rocks around the end of the breakwater.

Mooring Go stern or bows-to the outer mole or berth inside if there is room. Care is needed on the outer mole of the ballasting which extends underwater in places. In the inner basin local fishing boats usually occupy most of the berths in the southern corner and local boats are kept on the pontoon.

Anchorage A yacht can anchor off the beach to the NE or on the W side of the harbour. There is good shelter from the *meltemi* here although there are strong gusts down into the bay.

Facilities

Services Water on the quay. A mini-tanker can deliver fuel to the quay.

Provisions Good shopping for provisions near the harbour.

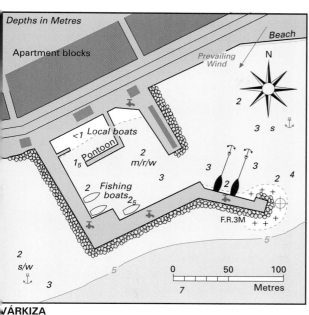

Depths in Metres

Apartment blocks

Beach

Prevailing Wind

N

2

3 s

<1 Local boats

Pontoon

1₅

2 m/r/w

3

3 3

2 4

2 Fishing boats 2₅

3

2 2

F.R.3M

5

2 s/w

5

3

0   50   100

7

Metres

VÁRKIZA
⊕37°49′.1N 23°48′.3E

Eating out Tavernas nearby and on the beach.
Other PO. Taxis and buses into Athens.

General

There is nothing special to bring you here to this outer suburb of Athens. The wide coast road runs behind the harbour and on the other side are the blank apartment blocks almost synonymous with an Athenian suburb. For all that, there is nothing really to drive you away either.

Várkiza looking E towards the entrance

Áy Marina

37°49′.0N 23°50′.1E

Approximately 1½M E of Várkiza there is a narrow inlet which provides good shelter from the *meltemi*. Anchor and take a long line ashore. At times the inlet is buoyed off for swimmers in which case you can anchor off in the bay immediately E of the inlet where there is still reasonable shelter from the *meltemi*. Care is needed of the reef running out from the shore on the E side of the bay.

Tavernas and bars ashore.

Lagonisi

A small harbour on the N side of Ák Thiniki. Care is needed of two reefs 1M SW of Ák Thiniki. Make the approach from the NW.

The mole is usually full of local boats so it is a matter of potluck whether you can find a berth here. Under the mole boats are also kept on laid moorings. In settled weather anchor clear of the laid moorings in 3–5m on sand and rock. Reasonable shelter from the *meltemi* but dangerous with strong southerlies.

Large hotel on the slopes above and tavernas a bit of walk around the shore.

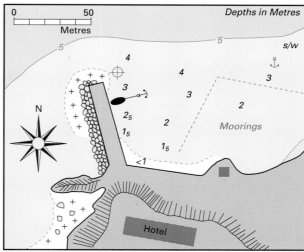

0   50

Metres

Depths in Metres

5

5

s/w

4

4

3

3

2₅

3

2

1₅

2

Moorings

1₅

<1

N

Hotel

LAGONISI   ⊕37°46′.8N 23°53′.3E

Vrákhoi Koudhounia

The above-water rocks and reef and shoal water of Vrak Koudhounia jut out from the coast about 1M N of Nisís Arsidha. The reef and shoal water extend in an ESE direction from the coast for 1M

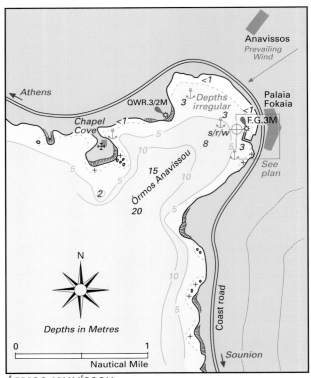

ÓRMOS ANAVÍSSOU
⊕37°43'·2N 23°56'·7E

Chapel Cove on the W side of Órmos Anavíssou. Some yachts are kept here on permanent moorings throughout the summer

so considerable caution is needed. A yacht should keep well to seaward. Although there is an inshore passage it is not recommended.

Órmos Anavíssou

The large bay E of Nisís Arsidha.

Pilotage

Approach Nisís Arsidha is easily identified and the channel between it and the coast has adequate depths. The above-water rock approximately in the middle of the channel is easily identified. Care is needed of a 2m shoal patch lying south of the N entrance point. In the entrance to the bay the village of Palaia Fokaia will be seen.

Mooring There are several places a yacht can anchor around the bay.

1. **Chapel Cove** On the W side of the bay. Good shelter from the *meltemi* and a number of boats are kept here through the summer on permanent moorings. Anchor clear of the permanent moorings where possible. A *cantina* opens in the summer.

2. In the NW corner where a number of local boats are kept on permanent moorings. The holding is reported to be poor so make sure your anchor is well in. Adequate shelter from the *meltemi*.

3. **Palaio Fokaia** Care is needed in the immediate approaches to the mole where there are uneven depths with rocks projecting up from the bottom to as little as 2–2·5m. There are adequate depths alongside the outer end of the mole and you may be able to find a berth here. Go alongside or stern or bows-to where possible. Make sure you are not taking a fisherman's berth or you will be unceremoniously evicted when the fishing boat returns. Care is also needed of floating mooring lines in the harbour.

Alternatively anchor off the mole in 3–6m. The bottom is partially composed of jagged coral-like rock that can snag an anchor so use a trip line or potter around until you find a patch clear of rock. The *meltemi* gusts off the land but there is adequate shelter here.

Water and electricity on the mole. Fuel nearby on the coast road. Good shopping for provisions and tavernas at the harbour and in the village.

A word of warning needs to be made about the tavernas here: touts flag down cars on the coast road and promise a world gastronomic occasion.

Looking S across Palaia Fokaia harbour to the anchorage outside

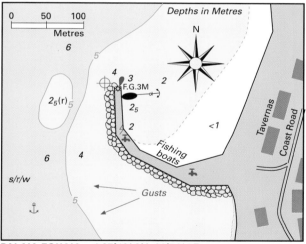

PALAIA FOKAIA ⊕37°43′·2N 23°56′·7E

In fact I have had one of the worst meals in Greece here at prices that would not disgrace London or Paris. I suggest you eat aboard or choose your taverna with care.

Nísos Gaidhouronisi (Patróklou)

⊕4 ½M S of W end of Gaidhouronísi 37°38′·45N 23°56′·04E WGS84

A high bold island lying ¼M off the coast 3M W of Ák Sounion. There are adequate depths in the fairway between the island and the coast but care

is needed of the isolated reef lying ½M off the mainland coast at the eastern end of the channel. Reefs also border the mainland coast for some distance at the eastern end of the channel.

Órmos Legraina

37°39′·7N 23°59′·6E

A large bay lying midway between Gaïdhouronisi and Sounion. You can anchor off on the E side of the bay in 3–5m where there is reasonable shelter from the *meltemi*. The W side of the bay is encumbered with reefs and shoal water. There is a small fishing harbour here but it has barely 1m depths in the entrance and mostly less than 1m depths inside.

Tavernas ashore and water at the camping ground. The bay is littered with caravans which don't do a lot for the place. It could be renamed 'Caravan Bay'.

Sounion

The cape on the SE corner of the Attic coast. It is commonly used by yachts waiting to go across to the Cyclades or back up towards Athens.

Pilotage

Approach The temple on the top of Ák Sounion is conspicuous from nearly everywhere. Closer in the islet of Arkhi in the entrance to the bay will be seen.

Mooring Anchor in the cove under the temple where convenient. The bottom is hard sand and weed, bad holding in most places and you should ensure your anchor is well in and if in doubt lay a second anchor. Good shelter from the *meltemi* although there are strong gusts into the bay. There are two mooring buoys in the cove although it is not certain why they are there – it may be worth taking a warp to one. If the cove is crowded yachts also anchor in the N of the bay and in fact all round the bay in the summer.

Facilities
Several tavernas ashore.

General
The temple on the cape is wonderful, an evocative place – and evidently most tourists in the vicinity of Athens think so, if the numbers of coaches lining the road in the summer are anything to go by. From lunchtime right up to

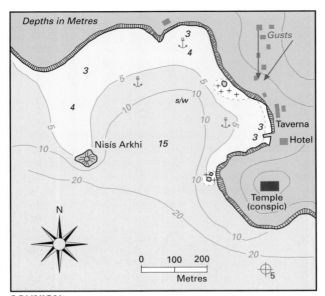

SOUNION

⊕5 0·25M S of temple on Sounion
37°38'·63N 24°01·31E WGS84

The Temple on Sounion

sunset coaches rumble to and from the cape and the temple. Luckily those travelling by water can nip up in the morning before the first coaches arrive and savour the atmosphere in comparative solitude.

The Temple to Poseidon was built around 444BC and stands on the foundations of an older temple. The temple did not exist in isolation but was linked to the small city of Sounion at the head of the bay. It was a wealthy little place, with its wealth garnered from the ships which stopped in here to shelter from the *meltemi* just as yachts do today. Grain ships bound for Piraeus from Evia would put in here regularly, and ships working their way from the Cyclades towards Piraeus would also stop here for a breather.

Sounion was evidently something of a tearaway city. Its wealth was legendary in the ancient world. It also had a reputation for looking after runaway slaves without too many questions being asked. Later it was a refuge for corsairs and pirates. It was here that William Falconer was wrecked in a Levantine trader and so acquired the material for his poem *The Shipwreck*. Falconer was both sailor and poet and an adventurer as well. He went to sea as a boy and though he wrote numerous poems, only *The Shipwreck*, published in 1762, was popular. Later Falconer moved from the Merchant Navy to the Royal Navy and

published *An Universal Dictionary of the Marine* in 1769, the same year he was drowned at sea. This extract tells of the fatal impact of the ship on Cape Colonna as Sounion was then called

'By now Athenian mountains they descry,
And o'er the surge Colonna frowns on high;
Where marbled columns, long by time defaced,
Moss-covered on the lofty Cape are placed;
There reared by fair devotion to sustain
In elder times Tritonia's sacred fane;
The circling beach in murderous form appears,

The anchorage under the temple at Sounion

Decisive goal of all their hopes and fears:
The seamen now in wild amazement see
The scene of ruin rise beneath their lee;
Swift from their minds elapsed all dangers past,
As dumb with terror they behold the last.'

It behoves me to mention that Byron also visited here and carved his name on a column, an act of vandalism that draws many to the cape to see where the bard visited. The temple is also at the apex of the giant isosceles triangle formed by Sounion, Aphaia on Aígina, and the Parthenon, temples all built around the same time – a surveying feat of some magnitude.

The Attic coast from Sounion to Rafina

From Sounion to Rafina the Attic coast runs north. Like much of the other Attic coast it is steep-to with the slopes dropping straight down to the sea except for the flat coastal strip between Porto Rafti and Rafina. This area is likely to become more popular now the new airport for Athens has opened at Spata, just inland from Vravrona above Porto Rafti. There are a number of harbours along this coast and a few anchorages. You feel a long way from Athens around the Sounion corner, but by Porto Rafti those awful anonymous apartment blocks make an appearance again and in fact you are not far from Athens itself via the new motorway built to link the airport and Athens.

PASSAGE TO THE CYCLADES

From Sounion many yachts will head across to Kéa or Kíthnos or further over to Síros or Míkonos. In the summer with the *meltemi* this means a brisk reach if you are lucky, or more likely a wet ride under much reduced sail. The *meltemi* tends to howl down through the Kéa Channel and over Kéa and Kíthnos. A confused sea is inevitably set up and for some charterers this is enough of an introduction to the *meltemi* at full blast and they then head west until the *meltemi* begins to peter out.

Charter boats which continue on downwind should remember they will have to bash back against the *meltemi* if the boat is based around Athens – and this can mean a wet and miserable end to a sailing holiday. At one time I made a living bringing charter boats back to Athens from the Cyclades in the *meltemi* season, but it is not something I would do again. There are better things to do than bashing back against the *meltemi* through the upper Cyclades. One tip: You can always head west towards Póros and then power up to Athens when the *meltemi* drops in the early morning.

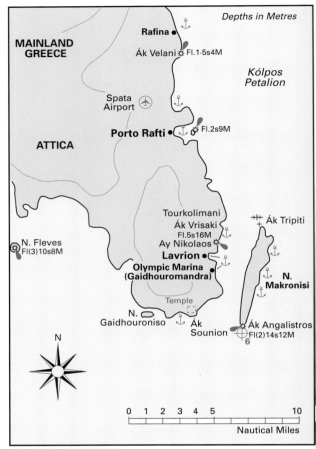

SOUNION TO RAFINA

⊕6 0·15M S of S end of Makrónisos
37°38'·56N 24°06'·25E WGS84

Increasingly it will be likely that yachtsman fly into Spata and head not for Athens, but for one of the harbours along this coast. The new marina at Gaidhourómandra and nearby Lavrion already attract many people who simply want to get off the plane and head for the islands.

Órmos Pasalimani and Órmos Pigadhi

These two bays between Sounion and Olympic Marina afford some shelter from the *meltemi*, although if it is blowing hard down the strait between the coast and Makronissos some swell rolls into the bays. Of the two Paşalimani affords the best shelter tucked up into the N corner.

Olympic Marina (Gaidhourómandra)

An inlet just around the corner from Sounion occupied by the Olympic Marina and yard.

Pilotage

Approach VHF Ch 09. From the S the inlet and the marina are difficult to identify until you are around Ák Fonias and at the entrance. Once into the bay the outer breakwater and the yachts in the marina will be seen. From the N you head on down past Lavrion for around a mile and then Olympic Marina will be seen.

Olympic Marina looking N

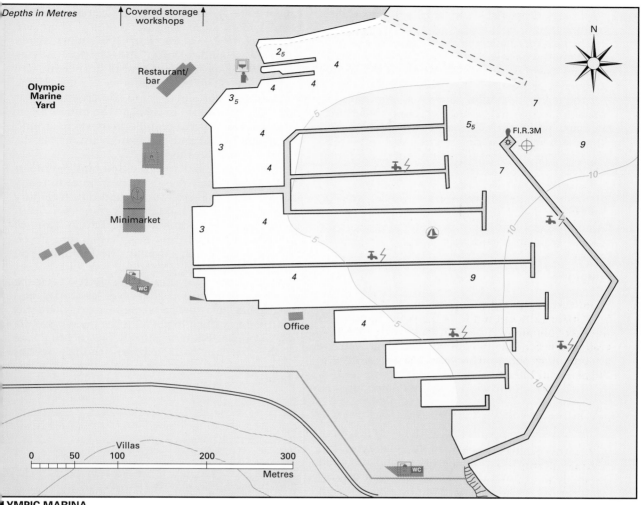

Depths in Metres

↑ Covered storage workshops ↑

Restaurant/bar

Olympic Marine Yard

Minimarket

WC

Office

Villas

N

Fl.R.3M

0   50   100   200   300
Metres

OLYMPIC MARINA
⊕37°41′·8N 24°03′·7E

With the *meltemi* belting down the coast it can be a bit bumpy in the approaches, but once inside it is flat.

Mooring Berth where directed. Laid moorings are tailed to the quay and you should pick up one of these and not use your anchor. All-round shelter inside. A charge is made.

Facilities

Services Water and electricity at every berth. Showers and toilets. Fuel quay.

Provisions Mini-market in the marina. Better shopping in Lavrion.

Eating out Taverna at the marina. Fotis, who used to have a taverna in the boatyard and whose food was renowned, now has a taverna outside the marina and yard a little way up the hill. He still cooks good food and will often come to pick you up if you phone (☎ 60875).

Other Bank office planned. Hire cars and a taxi can be ordered. Intermittent bus to Athens.

General

The newly opened marina has been planned for years and after numerous false starts has finally been finished. The Olympic yard behind the marina has existed for years and many of us have hauled yachts out here. In the 60s and 70s the yard used to build yachts including the Carter 33, 37 and 39 and the Olympic 45. There were even some ferrocement Endurance 45s built here. Today the yard hauls yachts and can carry out a wide range of specialist services including osmosis treatment and repaints.

The new marina will probably capture a pool of yachtsmen who want to fly into the new airport and get down to the yacht and off to the islands as quickly as possible. It is conveniently situated for the nearby Cyclades, but apart from that the marina seems to lack a certain something. Perhaps when there are a few more bars and shops around the marina it will come to life – at the moment you need to get into Lavrion for a bit of that.

Lavrion

A commercial harbour with some quay space for yachts lying approximately 1M N of Olympic Marina.

Pilotage

Approach From the S the buildings of the town are easily located and closer in the breakwaters will be seen. From the N the twin chimneys in Frangolimani will be seen and Lavrion lies 2M further S. Like Olympic Marina it can be bumpy in the approaches when the *meltemi* is blowing, but once inside the breakwaters it is flat although the wind still gusts down into the harbour.

Mooring Space is at a premium here as a number of charter companies base their yachts here. Try to negotiate a space on the town quay. Go stern or bows-to. The bottom is mud and good holding. If there is no space here you can try the other places indicated on the plan and if all else fails then anchor in the NE corner. Good shelter in the harbour.

Facilities

Services Water and electricity on the quay. Fuel can be delivered by mini-tanker.

Provisions Good shopping for provisions.

Eating out Tavernas and bars on the waterfront and in the town. There is not a lot to choose between the different tavernas so just go on instinct.

Other Bank. PO. OTE. Hire cars. Ferry to Kéa and Kíthnos.

General

Lavrion looks like a mining town with slag heaps, the old loading gantry and a dusty hinterland. And so it has been for 3000 years. Greece has little in the way of gold and other precious metals except here at Lavrion, where silver mines have been worked since at least 1000BC. There are estimated to be more than 2000 mine shafts scattered around Lavrion and classical Athens relied on the silver mined here to finance the city and its fleet. The mine shafts were sunk on the perpendicular or sloping into the ground and it was a capital offence to damage the mines. Silver Athenian coins were accepted everywhere around the ancient world and dominated currency in the way the dollar does today.

After the long war with the Spartans the mines declined, although they have been intermittently worked through the centuries. In the 19th century mining resumed, though this time for lead, manganese and cadmium. The Lavrion we see today largely dates from this period, and if you look past the grime covering the buildings you will see that there are some fine old houses scattered around Lavrion. In the last few years the waterfront has had a makeover and bars and restaurants have opened where formerly there was just the dusty dock road. With the opening of the new airport at Spata it is likely the yachting side of the harbour will expand, though it has competition just down the coast from Olympic Marina.

Looking across to Lavrion town quay from the yard

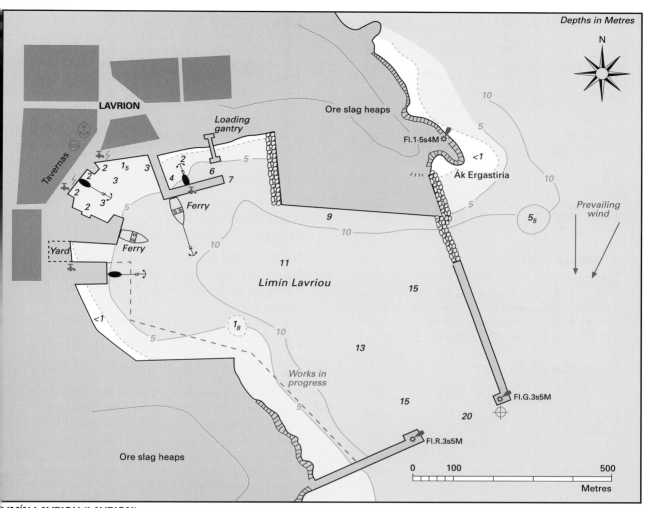

Depths in Metres

N

LAVRION

Loading gantry

Ore slag heaps

Fl.1·5s4M

Tavernas

Ák Ergastiria

Yard

Ferry

Ferry

Prevailing wind

Limín Lavriou

Fl.G.3s5M

Works in progress

Fl.R.3s5M

Ore slag heaps

0   100   500

Metres

LIMÍN LAVRIOU (LAVRION)
37°42′·7N 24°04′·0E

Órmos Thoriko and Frangolimani

One mile N of Lavrion lies the large bay of
Thoriko. When the *meltemi* is blowing you can
find good shelter in the north corner on either
side of the reef extending out from the coast.
Anchor in 3–5m on sand and weed. Good shelter
from the *meltemi* but open S.

To the N of Thoriko is Frangolimani
(Frankolimani = 'the harbour of the Franks') now
occupied by the power station whose twin
chimneys are so conspicuous. There is a long jetty
and docks, but these are not for yachts and you
should keep well clear of the bay.

The isthmus between Thoriko and
Frangolimani was the site of a harbour for ancient
Thoriko. This was an ancient Mycenean trading

post that acquired renewed importance during
the classical period to defend those all-important
silver mines at Lavrion and was substantially
rebuilt in 412BC. Probably ships berthed on
either side of the isthmus depending on the
weather. Around the slopes are the remains of a
theatre, defensive walls, some tombs and an ore
processing complex. When the *meltemi* screams
down from the N the place has a strange
poignancy, and you can imagine those ancient
sailors sitting around saying: 'I'm not going out
there in this weather'.

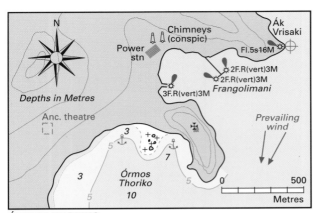

ÓRMOS THORIKO
⊕37°44'·7N 24°04'·9E

Tourkolimani

Around ½M N of Ák Vrisaki on the N side of Frangolimani there is Tourkolimani which affords some shelter from the *meltemi*, although it is not as good as that at Thoriko. Anchor on the north side of the bay. Open to the south.

Makrónisos

⊕6 0·15M S of S end of Makrónisos 37°38'·56N
24°06'·25E WGS84

This long skinny island lying parallel to the Attic coast has little in the way of good shelter from the *meltemi*. But in settled weather when the *meltemi* is not blowing it has a number of bays and coves that can be explored according to the wind direction. Those around the NE side look the most promising to explore.

Care is needed of Ifalos Tripiti off the NW end of the island. The reef is just awash and was usefully marked by the wreck of a coaster. Now the wreck has been pounded to bits and is mostly underwater, so care is needed to give the reef a wide berth.

The island was formerly called Helena or Eleni from ancient folklore that Helen rested here on her flight to Troy with Paris. More recently it was a prison island for a time after the Second World War, and after the civil war a large number of communists were incarcerated here to be 're-educated'.

Tourkolimani to Porto Rafti

Between Tourkolimani and Porto Rafti there are a number of bays and coves that can be explored in settled weather when the *meltemi* is not blowing. The *meltemi* tends to gust over the top of Evia and blow from the NNE down this coast, although the direction of the wind close to the coast can be modified by the actual topography. Remember the swell from the wind tends to curve around headlands and obstructions and consequently will roll into a bay from a more easterly direction on this coast.

Porto Rafti
(Raptis, Órmos Markopoulo, Mesoyaias)

A large bay with a significant built-up area around it lying approximately 10M N of Thoriko.

Pilotage

Approach The islet of Raftis with the statue atop in the middle of the entrance to Porto Rafti is easily identified. The villas and apartment blocks around the bay will also be seen from the entrance. Depending on the wind and sea make for Limín Mesoyaias on the N side of the headland separating the bay into two.

Mooring There are several places to moor.

Limín Mesoyaias Anchor in Limín Mesoyaias taking care of the numerous laid moorings in the bay. Care is also needed of the remains of a mole, now underwater, on the N side of the bay. Good shelter from the *meltemi,* and in fact boats are left here on moorings all through the summer.

Porto Rafti basin The basin at Porto Rafti on the N side of the headland is normally very crowded but you may be able to find a berth in the outer part of the basin on the E side. Go stern or bows-to if possible. Good shelter from the *meltemi*.

Rafti south bay In settled weather when the *meltemi* is not blowing you can anchor in the S of Porto Rafti or under the S side of the headland behind Nisís Prasho.

Facilities

Services Water and fuel at Porto Rafti basin.

Provisions Good shopping for most provisions near Porto Rafti basin.

Eating out Tavernas at Rafti and others scattered around the shores of the bay.

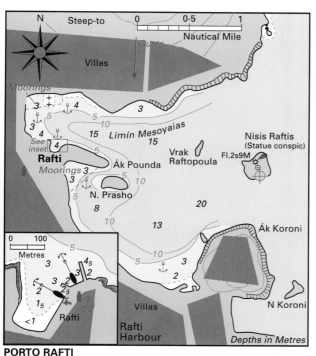

PORTO RAFTI
⊕37°53'·2N 24°02'·7E

Other PO. OTE. Bank. Bus to Athens.

General

Porto Rafti is surrounded by apartment blocks and villas which do little for the charm of the huge natural anchorage. The worst of the bland concrete apartment blocks which fringe Athens have been replicated here, and the place is indistinguishable from Kalamáki or Glifadha save for the steep-to slopes which surround most of this fine natural harbour. With the opening of the new airport at Spata it is likely even more buildings will erupt from the ground to disfigure the place.

The old harbour is the best bit of Rafti and here at least you can shut your eyes to the concrete surroundings. It is also the best place to eat, so even if you are anchored out it is worth bringing the dinghy across to here.

The place takes its name from the statue on the islet in the entrance. This is actually a Roman statue of a woman bearing fruit as an offering to the gods, but in middle ages it was thought the arm (now missing) held a pair of scissors and so the harbour was called Porto Rafti – the tailor's harbour.

Órmos Vravronas (Brauron)

37°55'·8N 24°01'·4E

A large bay just over 2M N of Porto Rafti. The bay shelves gently to a marsh at the head and you can creep in to anchor tucked as far into the N side as possible. A small islet should provide additional shelter if you can get behind it. When the *meltemi* is blowing a swell is pushed into the bay so it is really only suitable in calm weather.

On the S side of the bay are the ruins of ancient Brauron, now partially submerged in the swampy hinterland. The site was a sanctuary to Artemis and celebrated the mysterious 'cult of the bear'. In this young girls dressed as bears and enacted a ritual celebrating Artemis as goddess of fertility and childbirth. The Stoa of the Bears has been reconstructed and the whole waterlogged site has a wonderful serene feeling to it despite the proximity of the coast road.

Loutsa

Just up the coast from Vravronas is the small harbour of Loutsa, about midway along Órmos Loutsa. The harbour is a private nautical club and getting a berth here is something of a lottery. Only small yachts (up to 10m) should try to enter the harbour as there is little room for manoeuvring inside. In calm weather the best policy is to anchor and take the tender in to enquire if it is possible to get a berth.

Water and electricity on the quay and tavernas nearby.

In light northerlies or calm weather you can anchor under Ák Velani at the N end of Órmos Loutsa. The water is shallow for some distance off, so nose in carefully and drop the anchor in convenient depths. Care is needed of Vrak Kokkinonissa, an islet and reef off Ák Velani.

Rafina

A large ferry port lying 2½M NW of Ák Velani. There are few good places for a yacht to berth here and with a strong *meltemi* the place is best left alone altogether.

Pilotage

Approach The cluster of buildings around the port and on the slopes behind are easy to identify. Closer in the harbour breakwaters and the ferries themselves are easily identified. A yacht should make for the old fishing harbour.

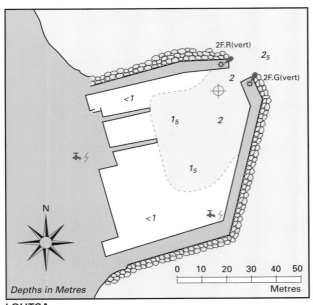

LOUTSA
⊕37°58′·4N 24° 00′·7E

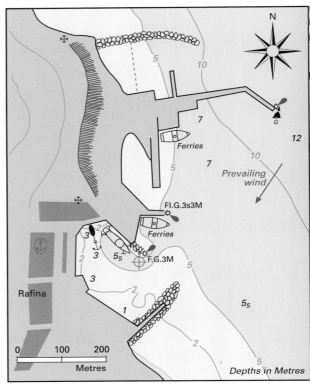

RAFINA
⊕38°01′·4N 24°00′·6E

Mooring Go stern or bows-to in the old fishing harbour if you can find a berth here. With a strong *meltemi* blowing there is a surge in here and it is not at all comfortable. In a moderate or light *meltemi* shelter is adequate. If there is not a berth in the old fishing harbour then you might try anchoring off in the northern basin above the ferry berths, though really the best policy is to head downwind to Porto Rafti where there is good shelter anchored in Órmos Mesoyaias.

Facilities

Services Water on the quay. Fuel can be delivered by mini-tanker.

Provisions Good shopping for provisions near the fishing harbour.

Eating out A range of tavernas around the old fishing harbour, some of which have good fresh fish.

Other PO. OTE. Bank. Bus to Athens and to Spata Airport. Ferries to many of the Cyclades and to Evia opposite.

General

Rafina suffers from the same rash of pour-and-fill buildings that blight Porto Rafti and other parts of this coast. Couple that with a harbour that is often crowded and in any case affords poor shelter in a strong *meltemi*, and the place doesn't have a lot going for it as far as yachtsmen are

concerned. At least if you get into the old fishing harbour you are near the original village of Rafina, but don't stray too far or the illusion will be shattered.

The advantage is that it is near the new airport at Spata and it has good ferry connections to the islands. If you need to pick someone up or drop them off then Rafina is a good place to do so. Otherwise I'd give it a miss.

II. Aígina to Póros and the adjacent coast

Corinth Canal to Póros

This chapter covers the western side of Saronikos Kólpos, (the Saronic Gulf), and is the area where most yachts based in Athens make for if they are not off to the Cyclades. Consequently the stretch of water between Athens and Aígina and Póros is frequently busy at the weekends and all through July and August. Surprisingly there are still some tranquil and uncrowded places, mostly along the coast of the Peloponnese, off what charter skippers here call the 'milk run'.

The coast of the Peloponnese is mostly steep-to, rising straight up from the sea to a jumble of mountainous ridges that criss-cross the area with no apparent pattern. The highest peak near the coast is Ortholithi, opposite the peninsula of Methana, rising to 1115m (3625ft). Most of the other peaks are around 600 to 900m (2000 to 3000ft). While the upper slopes are barren and rocky, indeed forbidding in places, the lower slopes are often covered in pine.

The main islands of Aígina and Póros are lower gentler places making them more amenable to agriculture, principally those two mainstays of the Mediterranean, the olive and the grape. In recent years the area of land cultivated for the vine has decreased and wine is now largely imported from the mainland or the hinterland of the Peloponnese. The olive has also declined because collecting the olives is so labour intensive compared to collecting money from the ample crop of tourists in the summer

As might be expected of an area this close to Athens, there are rich historical associations. Troezen on the mainland opposite Póros was readied for the evacuation of Athens when Xerxes looked as if he would crush the Athenian forces. Ancient Aígina was once a prosperous trading

Quick reference guide

	Shelter	Mooring	Fuel	Water	Provisions	Eating out	Plan
Órmos Kenkhreon	O	C	O	O	O	C	
Órmos Linari	O	C	O	O	O	O	
Frangolimani	C	C	O	O	O	C	
Órmos Dimani	C	C	O	O	O	O	
Nísoi Dhiaporioi	C	C	O	O	O	O	
Korfos	A	AC	B	A	C	B	•
Órmos Selonda	B	C	O	O	O	O	•
Néa Epidhavros	B	AB	O	A	C	C	•
Palaia Epidhavros	B	AC	B	A	B	B	•
Psifti	O	C	C	O	O	O	
Isthmus Bay	C	C	O	O	O	O	
Órmos Pounda	C	C	O	O	O	O	
Vathí	A	A	O	A	C	C	•
Chapel Cove	C	C	O	O	O	O	
Áy Yeoryios	B	A	O	B	C	C	•
Methana	A	A	B	A	A	B	•
Nísos Aígina							
Limín Aígina	A	A	B	A	A	A	•
Souvalas	C	A	O	A	C	B	•
Ayía Marina	O	C	O	B	O	C	•
Southern anchorages	B	C	O	O	O	O	
Perdika	A	A	B	A	C	B	•
Nisís Moni	C	C	O	O	O	C	
Nísos Angistri							
Limín Angistri	B	A	O	B	C	B	•
Skála Angistri	C	AC	O	B	O	C	•
Dhoroussa anchorages	B	C	O	O	O	C	
Nisís Kirá	C	C	O	O	O	O	
Nísos Póros							
Limín Póros	A	A	B	A	A	A	•
Órmos Vidhi	B	C	O	O	O	O	
Ák Dana	B	C	O	O	O	O	
Russian Bay	B	C	O	O	O	C	
Órmos Neorion	B	C	O	O	O	C	
Órmos Aliki	C	C	O	B	O	C	
Monastery Bay	C	C	O	O	O	C	
Órmos Barbaria	C	C	O	O	O	O	

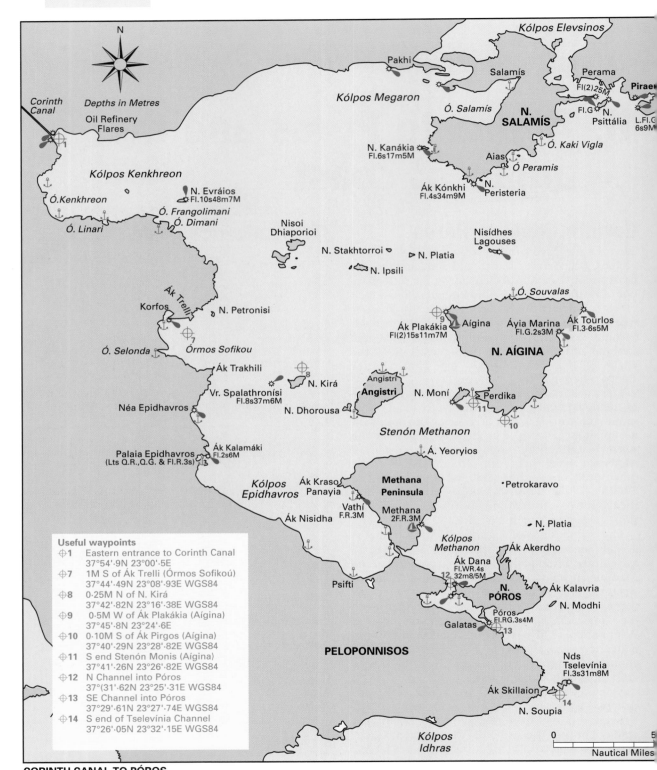

N

Kólpos Elevsinos

Pakhi

Salamís   Perama
Fl(2)25M   **Piraeu**

Corinth
Canal

Depths in Metres

Kólpos Megaron

Ó. Salamís   **N.**
SALAMÍS

Fl.G   N.
Psittália   L.Fl.G
6s9M

Oil Refinery
Flares

Kólpos Kenkhreon

N. Kanákia
Fl.6s17m5M

Ó. Kaki Vigla

Aias

Ó Peramis

Ó.Kenkhreon

N. Evráios
Fl.10s48m7M

Ák Kónkhi
Fl.4s34m9M

N.
Peristeria

Ó. Frangolimani
Ó. Dimani

Ó. Linari

Nisoi
Dhiaporioi

Nisídhes
Lagouses

N. Stakhtorroi   ▷ N. Platia

N. Ipsili

Ó. Souvalas

Ák Trelli

Korfos   N. Petronisi

Ák Plakákia
Fl(2)15s11m7M   Aígina

Áyia Marina
Fl.G.2s3M

Ák Toúrlos
Fl.3·6s5M

N. AÍGINA

Ó. Selonda   Órmos Sofikou

Ák Trakhili

N. Kirá

Angistri
Angistri   N. Moní   Perdika

Vr. Spalathronísi
Fl.8s37m6M

Néa Epidhavros

N. Dhorousa

Stenón Methanon

Palaia Epidhavros
(Lts Q.R.,Q.G. & Fl.R.3s)

Ák Kalamáki
Fl.2s6M

Á. Yeoryios

•Petrokaravo

Kólpos
Epidhavros

Ák Kraso
Panayia

Methana
Peninsula

• N. Platia

Ák Nisidha

Vathí
F.R.3M

Methana
2F.R.3M

Kólpos
Methanon   Ák Akerdho

Ák Dana
Fl.WR.4s
32m8/5M

Psifti

Ák Kalavria

N.
PÓROS

N. Modhi

Póros·
Fl.RG.3s4M

Galatas

PELOPONNISOS

Nds
Tselevínia
Fl.3s31m8M

Ák Skillaion

N. Soupia

Kólpos
Idhras

0   5
Nautical Miles

CORINTH CANAL TO PÓROS

PREVAILING WINDS

The prevailing summer winds in this area vary considerably. In Kólpos Kenkhreon W to NW winds often blow out from the Gulf of Corinth. These can be strong at times and often there are severe gusts off the coast of the Peloponnese down to Epidhavros. When the *meltemi* is blowing the wind is NE down over Aígina and Anghistri and curves to the E around Póros.

This area is on the limit of the *meltemi* and although it can sometimes blow strongly, it often dies out by mid-afternoon when a southerly sea breeze fills in. In the sea area between Aígina and Póros you will often be caught between the receding northeasterly and the advancing southeasterly.

There will sometimes be thunderstorms and an associated squall, though these are comparatively rare in summer.

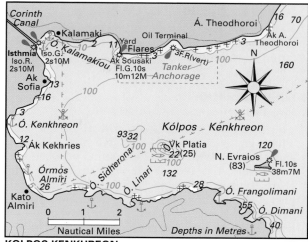

KOLPOS KENKHREON

⊕1 Eastern entrance to Corinth Canal
      37°54'·9N 23°00'·5E

centre and aroused the envy and wrath of Athens. Epidavros was the centre of ancient medicine and bequeathed a lesson in acoustics to our high-tech age in the shape of its perfect theatre. Aígina was the first capital of newly liberated Greece in 1833. Yet strangely enough it all feels a lot further from the glories of ancient Athens and the smog and pollution of the modern city than the actual sea miles suggest. At least for the latter that is a blessing.

Órmos Kenkhreon

37°52'·7N 22°59'·6E

The large bay 2M S of the Corinth Canal. It can be used in calm weather or in the westerlies which sometimes blow out of the Gulf of Corinth. Anchor in 3–10m where convenient on sand and weed. Taverna ashore.

It is here that ancient Corinth's second port, Kenkhreai, was built and parts of it remain on the sea bottom. There is some confusion over whether boats were loaded here to be dragged across the *diolkhos* or whether they were loaded at Kalamáki to the N of the present entrance to the canal. Ashore there are salt water springs called Helen's Baths where allegedly Helen of Troy once bathed.

Órmos Almiri is the large bay immediately south of Kenkhreon and is suitable in calm weather or westerlies.

Órmos Linari

37°50'·6N 23°04'·8E

Affords some shelter from the E and S, but shelter is not as good as it looks on the chart. When the *meltemi* is blowing a swell rolls into the bay. It is also deeper than shown with significant depths until close in.

Órmos Frangolimani

37°50'·7N 23°07'·0E

A large nearly circular bay that, like Linari, is not as good as it looks. It affords some shelter from the E and S but with strong easterlies a reflected swell enters. It is deeper than shown and you will usually have to anchor in 10 to 15m with a line ashore. Taverna ashore. A number of villas have been built around the slopes and the bay no longer has the isolated charm it once did.

Órmos Dimani

37°50'·3N 23°07'·8E

A bay about 1M ESE of Frangolimani. It affords some shelter from westerlies.

From here all the way round the coast until Korfos there are fish farms in every nook and bight. It could be renamed 'Fish Farm Coast'.

Nisidhes Platia and Evraios

Neither of these two islets in Kólpos Kenkhreon have usable anchorages. Both have large fish farms on the southern sides.

Nisoi Dhiaporioi

Nisoi Dhiaporioi channel 37°48'·9N 23°15'·5E

The group of islands lying 5M E of Dimani. There are two major islands: Nísos Áy Ioannis and Nísos Áy Thomas. The channel between the two islands has less depth than shown on the charts, with a reef connecting the two islands and only 3–4m depths closer to Áy Ioannis. Passage between the islands is possible in daylight, but have someone up front conning you through

There are two anchorages. On Áy Ioannis a yacht can anchor off on the E side though it is only really tenable in calm weather. On the S side of Áy Thomas a yacht can tuck under the chapel to get some protection from the *meltemi*.

Nisidhes Ípsilí, Stakhtorroi and Platia

This group of three islets lie E of Nisoi Dhiaporioi and off the NW corner of Aígina. There are no anchorages and in any case Nisís Ípsilí is used for target practice by the Greek navy. Already half of the islet is said to have been destroyed, so I suggest you stay well clear, especially if a few dull grey ships appear over the horizon moving at speed. I was once escorted out of the area by two destroyers during a combined forces exercise (it started just as I was passing Ípsili) and I hope it is the nearest I ever get to a military operation.

Korfos (Limín Sofikoú)

The large bay tucked around the corner from Ák Trelli. The houses of the village will not be seen until you are up to the entrance to the bay.

Pilotage

Approach There is little to indicate exactly where the bay is, but its general position is obvious. Nisís Petronisi and Nisís Kirá are easily identified. From the N considerable care is needed of the reef running out from Ák Trelli for nearly ¼M. Its danger is compounded by the fact that Ák Trelli itself is very low so it is difficult to see where the reef begins – give it a wide berth. There are also fish farms behind

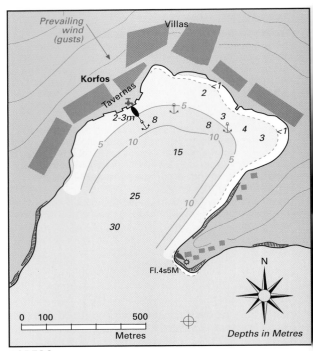

KORFOS
⊕37°45'·32N 23°07'·72E WGS84
(0·15NM S of light)

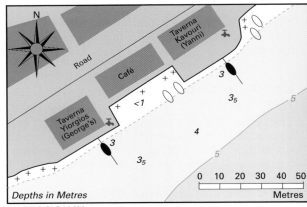

KORFOS QUAY

Nisís Petronisi and along the coast NE of Ák Trelli so the best thing to do is keep well outside both Petronisi and Ák Trelli and make the approach from the SE. Once up to the entrance of the bay the houses of the village will be seen and entry is straightforward.

Mooring Anchor where convenient. The bay is quite deep for anchoring and you will probably be dropping the anchor in 10–15m. There are

Korfos looking NE into the bay

laid moorings in the bay for yachts kept here on a permanent basis, but there is still plenty of room to anchor. A yacht can also go stern or bows-to on the concrete quays off two of the tavernas in the village, though care is needed as ballasting extends out in places. There are laid moorings off the taverna quays. The bottom in the bay is mud and weed, patchy holding in places. There is good all-round shelter although with westerlies there are strong gusts off the high land into the bay. With southerlies there is a bit of slop onto the quay at the village, more uncomfortable than dangerous. Passing boats, even small ones, also cause an inordinate amount of slop on the village quay.

Facilities
Services Water on the quay. Fuel can be ordered by mini-tanker.
Provisions Most provisions can be found nearby. Ice available.
Eating out Several tavernas along the waterfront, which is quite the most pleasant place to be. If you are berthed off one or other of the taverna quays then it is only politic to eat there or at least have a beer. Both Yanni and George serve pretty basic but good Greek fare and often have good fresh fish.
Other PO. Metered telephone. Hotels. Taxi.

General
The village is a nondescript sprawl of careless reinforced concrete houses, many of them left in the usual unfinished fashion with reinforcing rods pointing skywards, a ploy that avoids the tax on roofs. There are now also several sub-divisions on the steep slopes around the bay. The slopes about the village are rough folded rock covered in maquis and stunted pine bent by the westerlies which often howl off the hills. Despite the stunted architecture that goes with the pines, the waterfront is a convivial intimate place and one which grows on you the longer you stay. It is also a useful secure anchorage en route to or from the Corinth Canal.

Órmos Selonda

37°43'·8N 23°07'·8E

A deep inlet nearly 2M S of Korfos. The deep slit in the hills is reasonably easy to identify. The inlet is now partially obstructed by a fish farm, but there is still room to anchor although it is quite deep. Good shelter from all but easterlies. Even with the fish farm this is a spectacular spot, at the bottom of a deep ravine cutting through the steep slopes.

Néa Epidhavros

Pilotage

A small harbour lying approximately 2M S of Korfos.

Approach The small harbour is tucked into a bight under some low cliffs by the hamlet. The hamlet and harbour sitting at the bottom of a flood plain are easily identified in Órmos Néa Epidhavrou.

Mooring There is a limited amount of room in the harbour. Go stern or bows-to the pontoons off the taverna on the NE side of the harbour or alongside the end of the inner mole. You may also be able to negotiate a berth under the mole itself. Good shelter from the prevailing winds.

Néa Epidhavros looking out to the entrance

Anchorage If you cannot get into the harbour then in calm weather it is possible to anchor off the beach in 2–4m on sand and weed. There is usually some residual swell here, but at night it is usually calm.

Facilities

Services Water from the taverna.

Provisions Some provisions in the hamlet.

Eating out If you are berthed on one of the pontoons then it is only politic to eat at the *Taverna Agira* above. Besides, the view from the taverna is superb and the food is not bad either. In the hamlet proper there are several other tavernas and a bar.

General

Néa Epidhavros is not really that new. Until recently it survived on the extensive citrus groves on the flood plain behind the village and the sweet scent of orange and lemon pervades the place. The hamlet is perched next to the small river that formed the flood plain and now meanders down to the sea by the low cliffs on the N side of the harbour. From the hamlet it is an enchanting stroll around the beach and across the footbridge over the rivulet to the rocky path that leads to the taverna. The place has the feel of a secret place locked in under the cliffs and if you can get a berth here it is well worth tarrying for a day or two.

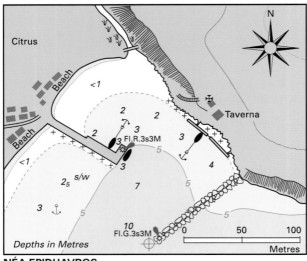

NÉA EPIDHAVROS
⊕37°40'·8N 23°09'·3E

Palaia Epidhavros

The village of Old Epidhavros lies tucked into a bay and out of sight from seawards. It is the logical place to make for to arrange an excursion to Epidhavros theatre and the Askeplion.

Pilotage

Approach The exact location of the bay is difficult to see from seawards, but a road scar S of the bay will be seen and closer in the light structure and a chapel on the N side of the bay will be seen. Once in the entrance to the bay everything falls into place: the buildings of the village will be seen and the two beacons marking the channel into the harbour are easily identified.

Mooring Go stern or bows-to the quay or anchor off where shown. The bottom is mud and some weed, generally good holding. Good protection from most winds. The bay is open E, and although the wind does not blow home it sends a swell in.

Anchorage It is also possible to anchor in the S or N of the bay. However, the local hoteliers do not like you anchoring too close to the beach, which is understandable given that most of their clients are here to snooze in the sun and swim in the sea. (And close that holding tank!)

Facilities

Services Water on the quay. Fuel can be delivered by mini-tanker.

Provisions Good shopping for provisions in the village. Ice available.

Eating out Numerous tavernas near the harbour and in the village. There is a good *souvlaki/kokoretsi* taverna in the main street and good pizzas near the waterfront.

Other Bank. PO. OTE. Hire motorbikes. Taxis who will usually tout around the harbour for excursions to Epidhavros theatre.

General

Though it is called 'old' Epidhavros, the hamlet at the head of the inlet is anything but old – a huddle of reinforced concrete houses, hotels, tavernas, bars and souvenir shops. In an attempt

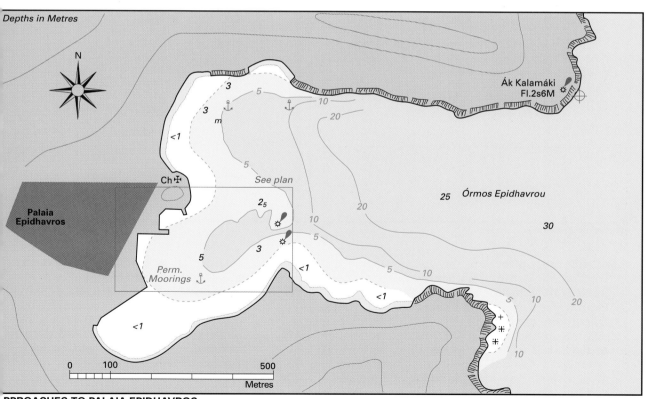

APPROACHES TO PALAIA EPIDHAVROS
37°38´.5N 23°10´.2E

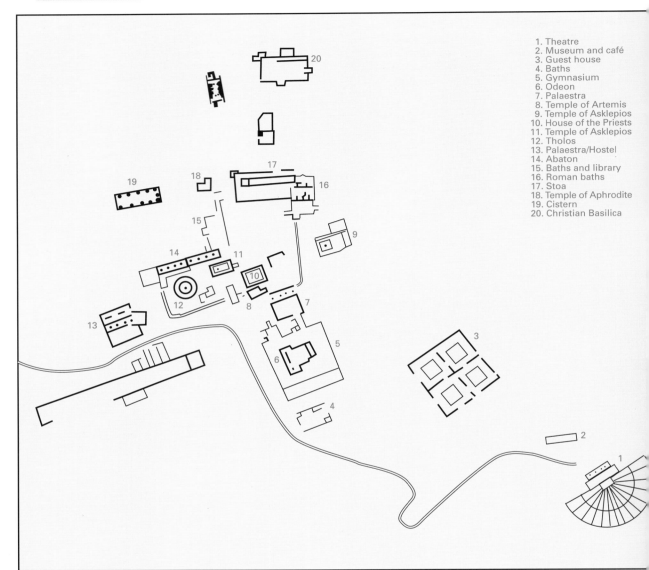

1. Theatre
2. Museum and café
3. Guest house
4. Baths
5. Gymnasium
6. Odeon
7. Palaestra
8. Temple of Artemis
9. Temple of Asklepios
10. House of the Priests
11. Temple of Asklepios
12. Tholos
13. Palaestra/Hostel
14. Abaton
15. Baths and library
16. Roman baths
17. Stoa
18. Temple of Aphrodite
19. Cistern
20. Christian Basilica

ANCIENT EPIDHAVROS

to tidy the place up the local council has constructed a strip of garden along the harbour front, presumably to hide the buildings. The 'old' tag refers of course to the Askeplion and theatre inland from the harbour.

It was in this bay that the patients and visitors to the Askeplion would arrive. From here it was normally a two-day trip up the steep winding gorge behind and into the valley of Epidhavros and the promised cure, around 12 kilometres altogether. Some would have travelled by donkey and some by sedan chair, but the majority would have walked up through the steep gorge. Along the way hostels and pilgrims' rest-places have been excavated and we can assume there were tavernas and fast-food vendors, stalls selling votive offerings, entertainers, indeed anything on which a drachmae or two profit could be made from the pilgrims.

In the Roman era the Askeplion was more akin to a health farm than a temple of healing and literally thousands arrived during the great

Epidhavros

Most people have heard of Epidhavros theatre. Its acoustics are legendary and everyone has heard the stories of how a piece of paper rustled or a coin dropped in the orchestra can be clearly heard in the top row of seats 22½m (74ft) from the orchestra. The stories are true and there is no doubt the acoustics are as near perfect as you can get for an outdoor stone construction. But in ancient times Epidhavros was not famed for its theatre, but as a place of healing.

At Epidhavros the simple rites of healing took the first steps towards systemic medicine. We know little of the ritual healing which took place here and to some extent must guess at what went on. Patients were first induced into a sleep, perhaps with the use of drugs burnt in vessels, and then left for varying periods until the sleep therapy (*encoemesis*) was deemed to have done its job. It is likely that some form of hypnotism or mesmerism was used, as appears to have been the case at the Temple to Hemithea in Asia Minor which had a good

success rate reducing pain during childbirth. This sort of holistic approach to healing can accomplish minor miracles and it is only now, a few thousand years later, that we are beginning to appreciate the power of mind over body and the body's own curative powers.

Empirical techniques were also used at Epidhavros. Frequent washing of the body was prescribed and old clothes, crutches, walking sticks and the like could not be brought into the sanctuary. Medical historians will tell you that simple hygiene practices are the greatest step forward we have ever made in medicine Diet and hydrotherapy were also considered important and the water at Epidhavros, like that at Lourdes, is still considered to have curative properties, even if it does come out of an old tap. Some surgery was also carried out at Epidhavros such as the opening of the abdominal cavity to remove parasites (recorded on a stele found nearby), but this was the exception rather than the rule.

Of Askeplius himself we know little. He seems to have been deified during or after his life and his genealogy smoothed out once he became popular. He probably lived around the 13th century BC and was later said to be the son of Apollo and Koronis. His symbol was the staff with a snake entwined about it, and according to some experts this is the harmless grass snake and not a poisonous species. The symbol is the one still used by the medical profession today. At first Askeplius was a local deity of Epidhavros and Thessaly, but as the fame of Epidhavros grew as a centre of healing his influence spread and it is likely that his deification occurred around this time.

The foundations of the Temple of Askeplius where the treatment took place, various other temples, the baths, the gymnasium, and the Katagogion (probably a hotel) are there. Only the theatre remains largely intact. It was designed by Polycleites the Younger and built in the 4th century BC. It seats 14,000 in 55 rows of seats arranged in a semicircle around the orchestra. Apparently the angle of incline of the theatre, around 26·5:1, provides the optimum angle for soundwaves to reach the top row of seats without any significant reduction in strength. Hitler copied the design of the theatre for the Olympic Games in Berlin in 1936.

One interesting point is that some music buffs claim that modern (from the last 500 years!) compositions played by orchestras here do not sound as they should because strings and woodwinds are distorted. This may be because the theatre was designed to throw the sound of the human voice and a few percussion and string instruments into the audience, and the sort of design needed for an open-air theatre to do that is different from the auditorium needed for a modern orchestra.

You can get to Epidhavros from Palaia Epidhavros (around 12 kilometres) or from Navplion (around 30 kilometres). In the summer a theatre festival is staged with ancient Greek drama (albeit in Demotic Greek) and excursions are arranged from Palaia Epidhavros and Navplion. It is worth going for the spectacle under the night sky even if you don't understand the play, but do take a cushion – those stone seats get awfully hard after an hour or two. The plays are staged on Fridays and Saturdays from June until the end of August.

Epidhavros theatre

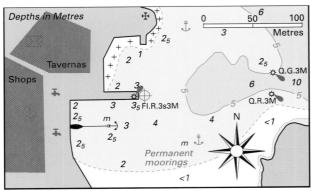

PALAIA EPIDHAVROS
⊕37°38′·3N 23°09′·5E

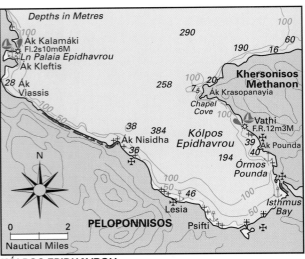

KÓLPOS EPIDHAVROU

festivals held in the theatre – it is difficult to imagine the little harbour crowded with ships and the hustle and bustle in the village and on the road leading up the gorge.

Kólpos Epidhavrou

From Palaia Epidhavros the Gulf of Epidhavros extends SE enclosed by the coast of the Peloponnese on the W and the Methana peninsula on the E. There are several anchorages around the gulf that can be used in calm weather

Epidhavros looking S into the bay

and in the summer there are often calms or light breezes here when it is blowing more strongly to the E.

Lesia A cove on the W side of the gulf off a small hamlet approximately 3M SE of Ák Nisidha. Anchor in 2–10m tucked in as far as possible.

Psifti In the SW corner of the gulf. A few fishing boats are kept on rickety wooden jetties here.

Isthmus Bay A bay in the SE corner of the gulf on the W side of the isthmus connecting the Methana peninsula to the Peloponnese. There is a small inlet immediately north which would be worth exploring.

Órmos Pounda The large bay under Ák Pounda. Anchor in 3–8m in the NE corner. There are irregular rocky depths immediately off the shore. A good barbecue spot, weather permitting.

Methana Peninsula (Khersonisos Methanon)

This triangular peninsula juts out from the coast of the Peloponnese connected only by a narrow isthmus at Taktikoupolis. Methana is as near perfect an example of the word peninsula (the Greek Khersonisos means literally 'nearly an island') as you are going to get. Its origins are volcanic, as even a cursory look at the jagged rubble-strewn slopes will tell you. The crater of the volcano is in the NW corner of the peninsula near the village of Kaimeni (properly Kaimeni

Byzantine castle, but to date no systematic excavation has been carried out. Pausanias in his 2nd century tour and commentary made the following observations on the volcanic nature of Methana:

'A little under four miles away there are hot springs; they say the water first appeared only when Antigonos was king in Macedonia: what appeared first was not water but fire blazing up above the earth, and when it died down the water sprang out. It still comes up hot nowadays and powerfully salty. But if you wash in it no cold water is available anywhere near, and if you dive into the sea the swimming is dangerous as there are numbers of marine monsters including sharks.'

Pausanias *Guide To Greece Vol 1* transl. Peter Levi.

This reference to an abundance of sharks where there are hot springs is an interesting one which I have heard before, both from ancient commentators and modern locals. Off Isola di Vulcano in the Lipari Islands in Italy similar stories are told and at Bençik in the Gulf of Hisarönü in Turkey sharks are said to be abundant where warm springs well up into the sea. I can't say I have ever noticed sharks in any of these locations, Methana included, but it would make sense that sharks would breed where hot springs increased the sea temperature.

There are three harbours yachts can use on the peninsula and several anchorages depending on the weather. If you go walking on the peninsula take stout footwear, a hat and water – the volcanic rock seems to intensify the heat and its sharp surfaces are hard on shoes.

Vathí

A small fishing harbour on the W coast of the Methana peninsula.

Pilotage

Approach The exact location of the harbour is initially difficult to determine, especially from the NW, but closer in the breakwater and the houses of the hamlet will be seen. The entrance is nearly impossible to make out until you are right up to it, although a white mast on the S side of the entrance and the light structure on the end of the breakwater will be seen. Care is needed in the entrance, which is very narrow and bordered by underwater rocks on both sides.

Mooring Go stern or bows-to on the S quay where there are good depths right up to the quay. The bottom is mud and weed and poor

Lesia anchorage to the south of Palaia Epidhavros

Khora – the 'burnt village') and Strabo (63BC–AD21) recorded a violent eruption here, although whether he witnessed it is not known.

Ancient Methana was not where modern Methana is today, as some guide books erroneously assume, but was on the W coast S of Vathi. There are extensive ruins here, some of which have been used in the construction of a

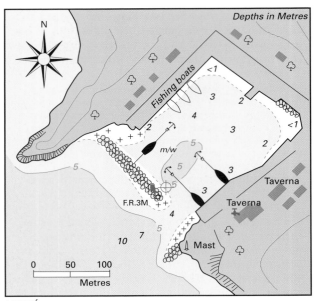

VATHÍ
⊕37°35´·7N 23°20´·3E

holding in patches. Good shelter from all winds now the new breakwater has been built.

Facilities
Water from the tavernas. Several tavernas which often have fresh fish, simply grilled over charcoal as it should be in a place like this. Other tavernas on the beach at Paralia a short walk S. Some provisions available at Paralia. Taxi.

General
The hamlet is a delightfully peaceful spot and is only now becoming popular with yachts. Apart from July and August it is little visited. Much of the coast nearby is covered in pine on the lower slopes, especially N of the hamlet. The upper slopes are strewn with jagged volcanic rubble, as is most of the peninsula.

Just S of the hamlet are the ruins of ancient Methana which received little more than a nod at its existence from ancient commentators. Pausanias mentioned a temple to Isis here: the Egyptian deity was Hellenised and then Romanised, and since the rituals dealt with fire and water it is perhaps not surprising the cult was introduced to this volcanic peninsula.

Vathi looking SE from the NW side of the harbour

Chapel Cove
37°36´·9N 23°18´·6E

N of Vathi a small white chapel on Ák Krasopanayia is conspicuous. With care a yacht can anchor in here or in the adjacent cove in settled weather. With a strong *meltemi* there are little whirlwinds in here and it is best avoided. It is deep for anchoring so if stopping just for lunch use the kedge rather than the bower anchor. The coves are quite deserted under steep pine-clad slopes except for a few local fishermen who potter around here. The chapel (Panayia Krasata) was apparently built by a wine merchant saved from shipwreck near here, and wine is said to have been used instead of water when the mortar was mixed.

Áy Yeoryios (Áy Giorgios, Kounopitsa)

Pilotage

Approach A small harbour here on the NE tip of the Methana peninsula. A large church on the shore is conspicuous. Care is needed as the entrance is rockbound and the harbour gets shallow quickly towards the shore. Have everything ready for berthing before entering.

Mooring Go stern or bows-to the mole where possible. Care is needed of underwater ballasting and variable depths off the quay. Good shelter inside.

Facilities

A couple of tavernas ashore.

General

If you can get into the harbour here it is an idyllic little spot. There is good swimming nearby and then you can stroll back to the taverna for a quiet beer looking out over the harbour. The mole was formed by sinking an old coaster (or perhaps it fortuitously came ashore here) and filling in the spaces.

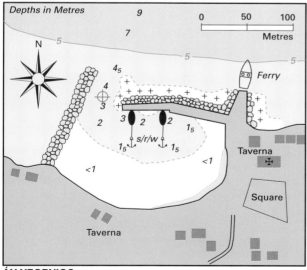

ÁY YEORYIOS
⊕37°38′·38N 23°23′·72E WGS84

Áyios Yeoryios (Kounopitsa) on the NE corner of the Methana peninsula

Methana

The main harbour and ferry port for the peninsula. The yacht harbour is S of the ferry pier behind a headland connected by a low isthmus to the peninsula.

Pilotage

Approach The buildings of Methana are spread along the shore on the SE side of the peninsula and are easily identified from the distance. The yacht harbour lies tucked away behind a headland to the S of the town and the entrance will not be seen from the N until you are around the headland. From the S the headland and entrance are easily identified. Care is needed in the narrow entrance which leaves little room for careless driving, especially if someone is coming the other way.

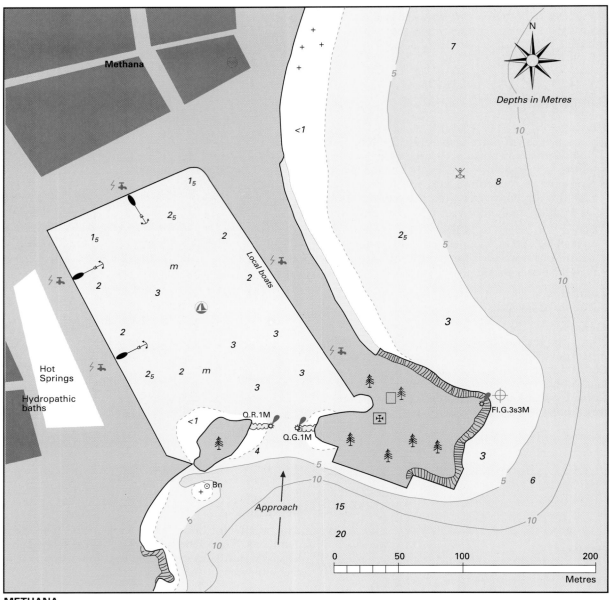

METHANA
⊕37°34´·6N 23°23´·5E

Mooring Go stern or bows-to the quay on the W side where convenient. There are shallow patches off the quay but it is all soft mud and you won't do any damage on it. The holding is good in the gluey black mud on the bottom, but when you haul the anchor up the goo deposits itself all over the boat and the crew and is damnably difficult to remove. Shelter in the harbour is all-round and numerous yachts are kept permanently here.

The harbour is classified as a marina and a charge is made, though not on the scale of the purpose-built marinas around Athens.

Facilities

Services Water and electricity on the quay. Showers and toilets. Fuel delivered by mini-tanker.

Provisions Good shopping for provisions in the town. Ice available.

Methana looking N into the entrance

Eating out Tavernas in the town, though none outstanding that I have tried.

Other Bank. PO. OTE. Ferries and hydrofoils to Aígina, Piraeus, Póros, and to Ídhra and other destinations south.

General

The hydropathic institute and your nose tell you immediately that this was once a spa resort utilising the sulphurous warm water that bubbles out of the ground and the sea. Presumably these springs are those mentioned by Pausanias and it is off here that 'marine monsters and sharks' were found. The village above the harbour is called Vromolimni which literally means 'stinking shore', a further reference to the sulphurous springs. The springs are said to be beneficial to those suffering from rheumatism, arthritis, dermatological complaints and nervous disorders and boats kept in the harbour are said not to suffer from fouling problems.

With all this going for it you might think Methana would be a bright and breezy place, but perhaps the miasma rising over the town envelops any euphoria, so most people find it a torpid and enervating spot and remember it only for the smell and the black mud in the harbour.

Nísos Aígina (Aíyina)

Aígina, lying only 12 miles from Piraeus, (though it is around 17 miles from Zéa and 18 miles from Kalamáki to Aígina harbour), is a popular weekend destination for Athenians escaping the smog of Athens whether by yacht, ferry or hydrofoil. It is not uncommon in the summer to find a nautical traffic jam between the island and Piraeus as everyone hurtles towards the harbour intent on finding a berth. Except in August and at weekends it is a remarkably tranquil spot and surprisingly little developed for such a popular resort.

The island has had its ups and downs. Its mythopaeic origins are derived yet again from the satyriac activities of Zeus, who bedded Aígina, loveliest of the daughters of the river god Asopos. To hide his sexual activities from his wife Zeus transported her to the island of Oinone which then became Aígina. I haven't counted the number of times Zeus transported his loves out of the sight and wrath of Hera, but it is a recurring theme. Aígina gave birth on the island to Zeus' son Aiakos, who though not well known in the pantheon of the gods, had two sons, Peleus and Telamon, who in turn sired Achilles (he of the vulnerable heel) and the courageous but rather challenged Ajax.

From excavations at Kólona to the N of modern Aígina town, numerous Neolithic remains have been found and occupation of this site continued through to the Bronze Age. There are several Mycenean sites around the island, indicating that it was important during this period, and Homer records that Aígina sent a fleet of 80 ships to Troy. The real period of prosperity for the island began in the 7th century BC and by the 6th century Aígina had established trading posts around the Aegean and up into the

Black Sea and down to the Nile. It even minted its own coins with the image of a turtle on them, one of the first Greek city-states to do, and established courts of law and an embryonic state health system.

It was inevitable that the proximity of Aígina to Athens would arouse the wrath of the Athenians, and so it did. Athens had difficulty persuading Aígina to send thirty ships to Salamís to fight with the Athenian fleet against the Persians, and although they eventually acceded to Athens' demands, it was a near-run thing as Aígina did not want to antagonise her trading partners in the E. As it was the ships from Aígina proved critical and distinguished themselves above others in the battle.

After the battle of Salamís relations between the two city-states deteriorated again – Pericles in Aristotle's *Rhetoric* demanded that the Athenians rid themselves of this 'sore spot in the eye of Piraeus' – and in 458BC Athens invaded the island, destroyed the city walls, confiscated most of the fleet and forced Aígina to join the Delian League. During the Peloponnesian war Aígina escaped from the Athenian yoke by siding with Sparta. Athens responded by expelling the

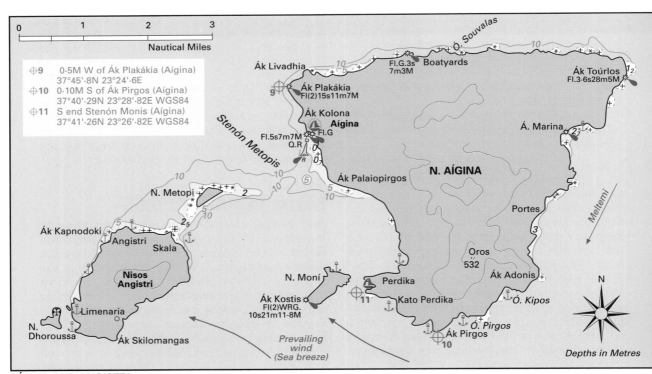

AÍGINA AND ANGISTRI

Getting around

Motorbikes and bicycles can be hired in Aígina town and this is the logical place from which to explore inland. Bicycles are probably best left for the cooler months if you are going any distance. The road system is basically a ring around the island and a road across the middle of the island from Aígina town to Ayía Marina.

It is well worth visiting Palaiochora in the middle of the island where the inhabitants retreated to in the Middle Ages. There are only the ruins of the houses left, but all the churches (twenty five of them) are intact and in good repair, although sadly not all the murals inside are – an attendant is normally on the site most mornings. Further on from Palaiochora stands the Temple to Aphaia on a wooded outcrop looking over Ayía Marina.

population and the island never recovered. The heavy-handed actions of Athens against upstart neighbours like Aígina reminds us that this, the city-state we so often cite for our democratic beginnings, was not above grinding down its enemies, real or perceived, with a lethal force which usually involved slaughtering the male population and enslaving the women and children: democracy with a jackboot, or at least a very thick sandal.

Aígina declined in importance during the Roman period and in the ninth century AD the capital was moved from the present port to Palaiochora in the middle of the island after repeated pirate attacks. Not until 1827 did it become prominent again when it became the first capital of newly freed Greece. The first modern Greek coins were minted here (a nice synchronicity with the 6th century BC) in 1829, though in the same year the capital was moved to Navplion. In recent years its proximity to Athens has aroused not envy but a thankfulness that there is somewhere away from the hubbub and pollution of the city to escape to.

Limín Aígina

The main ferry port and capital, situated on the W side of the island.

Pilotage

Approach From Athens the harbour will not be seen until you round Ák Plakákia, though houses spread from the town right up to the cape. The light structure on the cape is easily recognised and there is usually a hydrofoil or ferry heading to or from the cape. From the NW the town is easily identified and from the S it will be seen once you are past Nisís Moni. Closer in the single Doric column standing on Ák Kólona immediately N of the harbour will be seen, and the harbour breakwaters and entrance are easily identified.

Care needs to be taken of the shoal water extending from the harbour across to Nísos Angistri and of the shallows and reefs either side of Nisís Metopi. The shallows are only really a danger if you are coming from the W or headed from Aígina to Angistri. However from the S or when heading S from the harbour do not stray too close to Nisís Metopi. Close W of the entrance a red buoy marks a 2·4m rock and the buoy can be left to port or starboard. Another buoy marks a 3m shoal SW of the entrance.

In the immediate approaches care is needed of the car ferries and hydrofoils using the harbour and they should be given right of way in this bottleneck boat-jam.

Mooring Go stern or bows-to the town quay. In the summer the quay gets very crowded. Berths in the marina can be found, although many are occupied by local boats or yachts semi-permanently berthed here, and if you can find a berth in the marina use it. In the marina there are some laid moorings tailed to the quay. In the harbour proper the bottom is mud and weed, poor holding in places. Good shelter in the harbour and the marina from the *meltemi*, but westerlies cause a surge, more uncomfortable than dangerous, and southerlies send in a swell which with a strong blow can be very uncomfortable and possibly dangerous.

Facilities

Services Water and electricity on the town quay and in the marina. Fuel near the quay and a mini-tanker will deliver.

Provisions Good shopping for provisions in the town. There is a large supermarket on the coast road going S out of town (turn left at the Miranda Hotel). Several caïques on the town quay sell fruit and vegetables. Ice available from the fish market near the quay.

Eating out Good tavernas on the waterfront including the *Lekkas* and the *Flisvos* next to the Hotel Plaza. On the west side of the town is the 'Chicken Shop' serving spit-roast chicken and

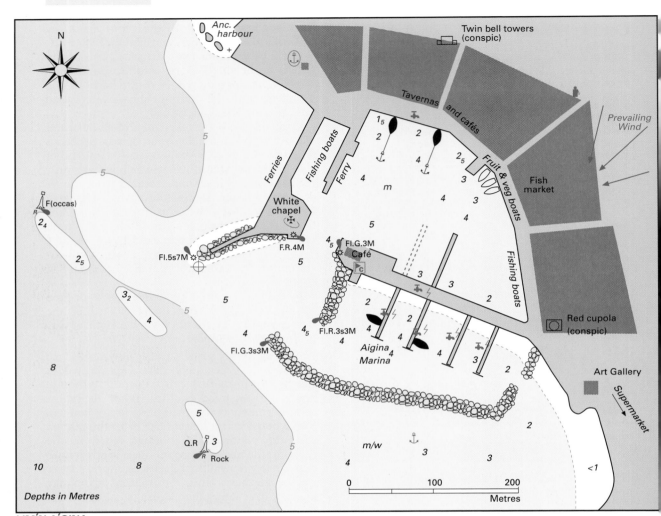

N

Anc. harbour

Twin bell towers (conspic)

Prevailing Wind

Tavernas and cafés

Fishing boats

Ferries

Ferry

Fruit & veg boats

Fish market

1_5
2
2
2_5
4
4
5
m

2
4
3
4
3
4
3

Fishing boats

White chapel

Fl.5s7M

F(occas)
R
2_4

2_5

3_2

4

5

F.R.4M

5

Fl.G.3M
Café

c

Fl.R.3s3M
4_5
4

Aigina Marina

4_5

Fl.G.3s3M

4

8

5

Q.R
3
R Rock

8

10

Red cupola (conspic)

Art Gallery

Supermarket

2

4
2
4
4
4
4
3

2
2

3
2

3
2

2

m/w

3
3
3

4

<1

5

Depths in Metres

0   100   200
Metres

LIMÍN AÍGINA
⊕37°44°′·7N 23°25′·5E

Entrance to Aigina harbour looking NE

pork which is good value. Behind the fish market is the *Psarotaverna Agora* with good Greek food.

Other Bank. PO. OTE. Hire motorbikes and bicycles. Ferries and hydrofoils to Piraeus and south to Methana, Póros, Ídhra and other destinations S.

General

The difficult approaches to the harbour were well known and commented on by Pausanias, though he goes a bit too far in his caution.

'Aígina is the most unapproachable island in Greece, there are rocks underwater or just breaking the surface all around it. They say Aiakos contrived it like this deliberately, for fear of sea pirates and to make it dangerous to enemies'.

Pausanias *Guide To Greece Vol. 1* transl. Peter Levi

In fact the approach was more dangerous in ancient times when there were two harbours, the present one (much rebuilt) which was the commercial harbour and the military harbour NW of the present harbour, which was reputed to have a secret entrance between the rocks known only to trusted Aiginites.

The present town is largely a result of its elevation as capital of the infant Greece in 1827, when most of the prominent buildings were planned and constructed. Although the capital was transferred to Navplion in 1829, the prominent public buildings and the grid layout of the town remained and were added to in later years with prosperous merchants' houses – fortunately the 19th century core of the town has altered little since.

On the flat plain S of Aígina town there are numerous stands of pistachio trees which were introduced to the island on a commercial basis in the early 20th century to boost the flagging agricultural economy and now Aígina pistachios (*fistikia Aiginis* – literally 'peanuts of Aígina') are known all over the Aegean. They are on sale everywhere in the town.

Souvalas

A small harbour situated approximately midway along the N coast. Reasonable shelter can be found tucked behind the mole if there is room amongst the local boats. Go bows-to the outer end of the mole where there are mostly 2–3m depths. Further into the harbour depths are

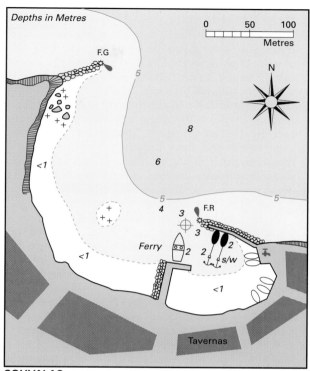

SOUVALAS
⊕37°46′·4N 23°29′·3E

irregular and shallower. Keep well clear of the pier on the S side where the ferry berths.

Reasonable shelter from the *meltemi* although with strong northerlies there is a surge in the harbour.

Tavernas ashore. To the W of the harbour there are several boatyards.

There are hot springs nearby, said to be beneficial for the usual range of ailments, rheumatism, arthritis and so on, but most of the population seem to be here not for the spa but for the clear air and sea away from the noise and pollution of Athens.

Ák Toúrlos

The cape forming the NE corner of Aígina. Care is needed of the Toúrlos reef and shoal water lying approximately 250m off the cape. Keep well clear of the cape when rounding this end of the island.

Ayía Marina

The large bay on the E side of the island. A large hotel and several smaller buildings around the bay are conspicuous. The anchorage in the bay is not the best with northerlies and is untenable with a healthy *meltemi* blowing. It is also open S so is only really tenable in calm weather or westerlies. Anchor in the NW of the bay clear of the ferry pier in 4–10m on sand, rocks and weed, not everywhere the best holding. The pier is for tripper boats bringing people here and you will be unceremoniously evicted if you berth here. At night you may be able to find a berth when the tripper boats stop running. Tavernas ashore.

If the weather is not suitable for a stop here a yacht can always go to Aígina town and visit the temple by bus or taxi. Several tavernas on the beach and at the temple site.

The Temple of Aphaia deserves a visit for its elegant simplicity and for its position in the mysterious temple triangle. It is dedicated to Aphaia, a Cretan deity popular in Mycenean times, whose cult was later dedicated to Athena. It was built on the site of a more ancient temple in 490BC and thus predates the Parthenon by a few years. The style of the temple is Doric and 24 of the original 32 columns are standing after being re-erected in 1960.

This temple completes the almost perfect isosceles triangle that can be drawn between the Parthenon, the temple on Sounion, and here. The mystery is a real one, since the initial construction of a temple on Sounion was interrupted by the Persians in 490BC (the present temple on Sounion dates from 444BC), as was the construction of the Temple of Aphaia. The Parthenon was begun in 447BC so it ties in with the later completion dates of the other two temples. Thus all three temples are of the same era, but is it likely they would describe a perfect isosceles triangle by coincidence – or was the geometry of the ancient Greeks more sophisticated than we credit them for? A small isosceles triangle is one thing, but one with sides 24 miles long is another.

Southern anchorages

⊕**10** 0·10M S of Ák Pirgos
37°40'·29N 23°28'·82E WGS84

Around the S end of the island there are several anchorages that can be used in northerlies or with light westerlies or easterlies.

Órmos Kipos Lies under Ák Adonis. Care is needed of above and below-water rocks fringing the coast. Anchor in 4–10m where convenient.

Órmos Pirgos Lies immediately W of Ák Pirgos. Anchor in 4–10m.

Kato Perdika The large bay immediately S of Perdika. Anchor off in 5–10m on sand and weed.

Perdika

A small fishing village and resort on the SE of Aígina. There is little room in here for yachts so you will have to squeeze in where you can.

Pilotage

Approach The hamlet and inlet are not easily seen from the N or S until you are up to the entrance. However, the location is obvious opposite Nisís Moni.

Mooring Go stern or bows-to either side of the inside short pier, the first pontoon or basically wherever else you can get into. The little harbour is popular in the summer and gets very crowded. You can also anchor with a long line ashore to the short pier on the SE side. Leave the end of the middle pier clear for the water tanker which comes alongside. The bottom is

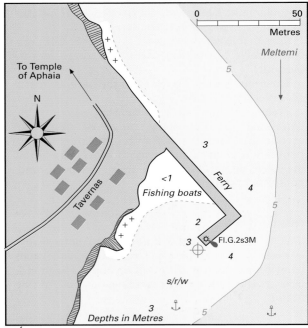

AYÍA MARINA ⊕37°44'·7N 23°32'·4E

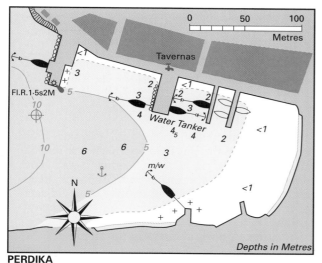

PERDIKA
⊕37°41´·43N 23°27´·06E WGS84

mud and weed, patchy holding in parts. Good shelter from all but strong westerlies.

Facilities

Water on the quay. Provisions available ashore. Numerous tavernas along the waterfront several of which usually have locally caught fish. The taverna immediately above the pier or the prosaically named *No 10* are as good as any.

General

Perdika was once a small fishing village, but it is

Perdika pier

Perdika pier looking SW

now about half and half tourism and fishing. Most of the tourism arrives on the water with charter yachts and others en route to or from Athens. It retains a pleasant shambolic sort of charm, with the houses seemingly piled on top of one another along the waterfront. There always seems to be something going on here, with boats chugging in and out, wives yelling at husbands not to stay too long at the taverna, and tourists on the waterfront watching it all happen.

Perdika

break their eggs before they be hatch'd; otherwise, by their multitudes, they would so destroy, and eat up the corn, that they would inevitably bring a famine every year upon the place. But they say, there are no hares at all in this island.

George Wheeler *Journey Into Greece* 1682

Nisís Moni

The island immediately opposite Perdika. It is conspicuous in the southern approaches to Aígina and when heading S from Aígina town. The passage between the island and Aígina is deep and free of dangers in the fairway. On the N side of the island yachts can anchor off the camping ground ashore. Here there is good shelter from southerlies. A taverna opens in the summer.

On the SE side of the island there is a cove surrounded by cliffs that can be used in calm weather. It is very deep and you will need to take a line ashore to the N side. The bottom is strewn with boulders so use a trip-line on the anchor.

The island is called Moni simply because it was once owned by the Monastery of Chrysoleontissa (Moni = monastery) in the middle of Aígina. It is now owned by the Touring Club of Greece, who run the camping ground set amongst the pine trees. There are said to be numbers of peacocks on the island.

Nisís Petrokáravo and Nisís Platía

South of Aígina are two small islets lying in the sea area between Aígina and Póros. Nisís Petrokáravo is a line of high jagged rocks, easily

Perdika means 'partridge' and although there don't seem to be many around these days, they were once a pest and were culled annually to prevent them eating the corn growing on the island. George Wheeler gives us this description from the time of the Turkish occupation.

'Aígina hath great plenty of corn, cotton, honey and wax; also abundance of almonds, and keratia, or carobs. It abounds also with a sort of red-legged partridges, that by order of the epitropi, or the chief magistrates of the town, all, both young and old, women and children, go out yearly, as the pygmies of old did against the cranes, to war with them, and to

Petrokáravo looking N with Nísos Aígina behind

identified and looking something like their name – the 'stone ship'. Nisís Platía is a low flat islet less easily identified.

Metopi Shoals

Between Aígina and Angistri lies Nisís Metopi, a low flat islet, with shoal water extending from either side. Between Metopi and Angistri there is a passage with 2·5–3m least depths on a course of approximately N–S around the mid-channel point. This passage is not recommended and in general a yacht should not attempt to pass in between Metopi and Angistri, where the depths are variable and there are numerous underwater rocks either side of the passage. Between Metopi and Aígina the channel has 8–9m depths approximately one-third of the way across from Aígina.

Nísos Angistri

The island of Angistri sits just 3½M from Aígina town connected to it by shoal water and sometime in the past Aígina and Angistri must have been one island. Despite its proximity to Aígina and to Athens it is little visited by tourists or for that matter by yachts.

The main town and capital is Milo (or Megalokhorio or Angistri) on the north of the island. The small port for the island is Limín Angistri on the northeast. There is also a harbour at Skála Angistri on the east side of the island south of the Metopi Shoals. The only other settlement of any size is at Limenaria in the south and, naturally enough, the only roads on the island are between these three settlements. Much of the island is wooded in pine and there are some good walks through the interior and around the coast.

Little is known about Angistri in ancient times. It was called Kekryfalia and may have had some association with Kekrops, the mythical first ruler of Athens who is often depicted as being a serpent from the waist down, though this may simply be a vague relegation of the island to the mists of time, a position it still holds if you listen to Aiginites talking about the backwardness of the islanders. Much of the present population are said to be of Albanian extraction, but I find this is usually just a name for Greeks in this region who are not from Attica.

Limín Angistri

Pilotage

Approach The harbour should be approached from the N side of the Metopi shoals. The buildings around the harbour are easily identified, but care is needed in the approaches because of the reefs and shallows extending out from the coast.

Mooring Moor bows-to the outer end of the quayed area if there is room or anchor off with a long-line to the breakwater. Keep well clear of the ferry berths and the area where the ferries must manoeuvre. With a strong *meltemi* the harbour is very uncomfortable and with strong southerlies may become untenable. Use in settled conditions with light northeasterlies or southeasterlies.

Facilities

Basic provisions can be found here and there are several tavernas in the summer. Ferry to Aígina.

General

It is well worth visiting Milo, where the narrow streets and old houses on the water's edge make it an enchanting and friendly place.

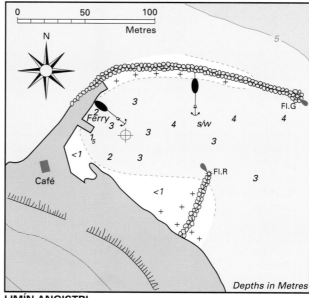

LIMÍN ANGISTRI
⊕37°42'·8N 23°20'·9E

Skála Angistri

A small harbour (also used by ferries) on the E side of the island and S of the Metopi shoals. The approach is best made from the SE so that you avoid the Metopi Shoals. From the N it is possible to enter through Stenón Angistri between Nisís Metopi and Angistri, though considerable care is needed. There are least depths of 2·5–3m in the fairway. You may be able to berth on the ferry pier after the ferries have stopped running, or try the fishing harbour N of the ferry pier where you will have to anchor with a long line ashore if you can find a berth. Shelter here is not good when the *meltemi* blows strongly and you should only use the place in calm weather.

Skála is the new Angistri, and from the harbour a rash of concrete buildings spread towards Milo. Tavernas and cafés in Skála.

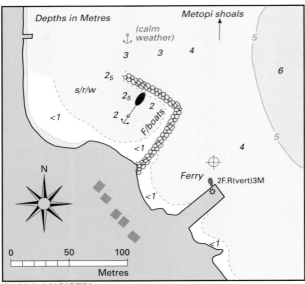

SKALA ANGISTRI
⊕37°42'·5N 23°22'·1E

Limenaria

A small fishing village on the SE side of the island. The cove off the village is nothing more than a cleft in the cliffs, but just NE there is a shallow patch which can be used in calm weather only.

Nisís Dhoroussa anchorages

N end of Dhoroussa Channel
37°41'·08N 23°19'·18E WGS84

On the SW tip of the island opposite Nisís Dhoroussa are several bays affording better shelter than might be evident from the chart. The channel between Nisís Dhoroussa and Angistri is deep and free of dangers in the fairway. The slopes around here are thickly wooded in pine and it is an idyllic spot that can be reached only by water. The southerly bay is the most popular and is well sheltered from the prevailing winds (NE and SE). It is fairly deep for anchoring. The fish farm is no longer here.

A taverna opens in the summer on the rocky spit opposite Nisís Dhoroussa.

Nísos Póros

Póros means a 'strait' or a 'crossing', a name that fits perfectly once you have seen the approaches to Póros town. At its narrowest, off the town proper, the island is separated by a mere 300m or so from the mainland and much of this is shallow so that the navigable channel is only 100m wide. Pausanias described how you could walk right across in the 2nd century AD, though he didn't say if he tried it. The approach to the town from the sea is one of the most attractive in Greece and Henry Miller provides one of the best descriptions in his classic *The Colossus of Maroussi*.

'. . . suddenly I realised we were sailing through the streets. If there is one dream which I like above all others it is that of sailing on land. Coming into Póros gives the illusion of a deep dream. Suddenly the land converges on all sides and the boat is squeezed into a narrow strait from which there appears to be no egress. The men and women in Póros are hanging out of the windows, just above your head. You pull in right under their friendly nostrils, as though for a shave and a haircut en route. The loungers on the quay are walking with the same speed as the boat; they can walk faster than the boat if they chose to quicken their pace.'

Never mind that ferries and hydrofoils speed in and out of the strait, that landing-craft ferries churn across to Galatas, that bars compete for the highest decibel level and the most banal offerings, that villas now spread out like a canker from the old town and sub-divisions indicate there will be more; never mind all that, because the essence of Miller's description is there and those of us who have spent some time here have a fondness for the

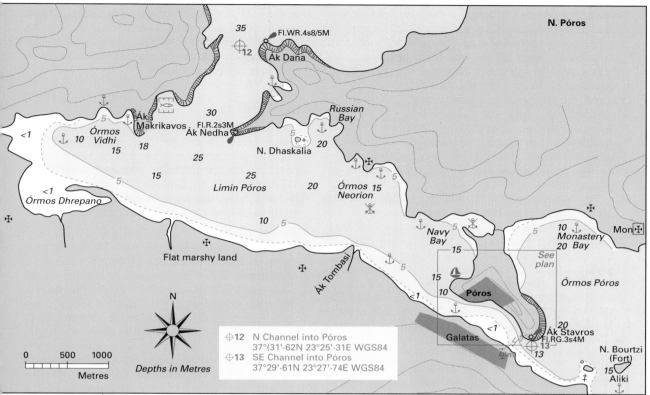

APPROACHES TO PÓROS

place that eclipses all this and endorses his words. And it has something else other than the appearance of a little Greek Venice, it has a sensuality, a calm (especially during siesta time), and what can only be described as a conviviality despite the constant coming and going of ferries and hydrofoils that makes life awkward for yachts on the quay.

Póros today is composed of two islands, joined by a narrow isthmus, which were described separately in ancient times. The small island on which the present day town stands was called Sphaeria and the larger island Kalauria or Kalavria which means 'good breeze', probably a reference to the mild and comparatively gentle version of the *meltemi* which blows across the island. Today this version of the *meltemi* which tends to blow in from the ENE is called the *boukadhoura*. Ancient Kalauria was built above the bay of Órmos Barbaria or Vagyonias on the N of the island, though little remains today except the foundations of the Temple to Poseidon.

The temple was well known as a sanctuary in ancient times and it was here that Demosthenes (384–322BC), arguably the greatest orator in Athens, sought safety after his politics could no longer be tolerated. To save his honour he committed suicide with poison concealed in the quill of his pen. Ancient Kalauria must have been of some importance as it was the headquarters of the Kalaurian League of the 7th century BC, a fairly loose association between Kalauria, Troezen on the mainland, and Aígina, designed to keep pirates at bay.

Little more of historical note occurred here until the 19th century when the island became involved, along with Ídhra and Spétsai, in the Greek Revolution against the Turks. The Greek fleet and foreign sympathisers used the sheltered anchorage off Póros as the fleet anchorage to regroup and take on supplies.

Towards the end of the revolution enmities began to surface and when Capodistrias, President of the Assembly, secretly signed an edict that would effectively end the brigandage the Idhriots had traditionally occupied themselves with, trouble was brewing. The edict specifically detailed a blockade of the Port of Ídhra and measures to prevent boats without valid documents from sailing, which it was hoped would control the endemic piracy. It should be remembered that the fleets from Ídhra and Spétsai were as inclined to attack British, French or Russian ships (their ostensible allies) for booty as they were to attack Turkish or Egyptian ships for the cause of the revolution and the spoils of war.

The admiral of the Greek fleet, Miaoulis, an Idhriot and former brigand, upon learning of the edict immediately set sail with his ships to Póros and captured the largest ship of the Greek fleet, the frigate *Hellas*, and the fort on Aghios Konstandinos. The Russian navy was brought in to deal with the rebel admiral and Miaoulis, faced by superior forces, decided to blow up the *Hellas* and several other ships. The act was universally condemned, even by Idhriots. As if to forestall any further rebellion the main navy dockyard was installed at Póros until it was moved to Salamís in 1881. A naval college still remains and for many years the old coal-burning dreadnought *Averoff* was berthed off here until its removal, much to the anger of the locals, to Faliron. Today a destroyer, the *Arrow*, is berthed here. During the junta of the Colonels, the captain of the *Arrow* fled Piraeus and took his ship to Egypt. It was returned after the dictatorship had ended.

Today Póros is a popular resort for Athenians and foreigners alike. Nearly all of this attraction is centred on Póros town or the nearby coast and for the most part the island is rugged and unpopulated. The only roads on the island run W to Russian Bay, E to the monastery of Zoodhokos Pigi, or around a circular route via the Temple of Poseidon in the middle of the island. On the opposite shore Galatas is a more down-to-earth, less touristy place, serving the agricultural hinterland. The area is well known for its extensive citrus groves which spread out to the west from the village and are known locally as *limonodassus*, 'the lemon forest'.

Limín Póros

The main harbour for the island lies tucked away in the strait between the island and the Peloponnese. Neither entrance into the strait is obvious from the distance, although the ferries and hydrofoils apparently disappearing and appearing from the land in the summer gives a clue to the whereabouts of the entrances.

Pilotage

Approach From the N head past Methana town towards the slit in the low cliffs that will just be discerned. Closer in the small lighthouse on Ák Dana and the light structure on Ák Nedha will be seen. Once around Ák Nedha, Póros town will be seen and the approach is obvious. Care is needed of ferries and hydrofoils leaving Póros as they cannot be seen until you are around Ák Nedha, when you will encounter them heading for the channel at full speed – that means 30-plus knots in the case of the hydrofoils and catamaran ferries.

From the SE it is difficult to see the entrance, and the low land of the isthmus between Sphaeria and Kalauria is sometimes mistaken for the entrance. Nisís Bourtzi with a fort on it is easily identified and closer in the light structure will be seen. Once around the corner you are literally in the harbour. Like the N entrance care is needed of ferries and hydrofoils leaving the harbour and also arriving – don't forget to look over your shoulder occasionally.

Once into the narrow strait between the town quay and Galatas, care is needed of the shallow mud bank extending out from the SW side of the channel. It is not marked and can be difficult to see, if the numbers of yachts going aground in the summer is anything to go by.

Mooring Yachts berth either stern or bows-to the town quay just E of the ferry quay or on the N quay. Chunks of the town quay in the channel are reserved for the ferries and hydrofoils, caïque ferries to Galatas, fishing boats, and a number of charter companies. There can sometimes be a current in the channel of up to

Getting around

Given the limited road system it is questionable whether it is worth hiring a motorbike or car, yet they are available at Póros town. Hire bicycles are also available and these would seem to make more sense. Caïque ferries run everywhere as far as Russian Bay and Monastery Bay, and of course across to Galatas. At Galatas it is possible to hire motorbikes and the obvious place to make for is ancient Troezen and the Devil's Gorge to the W of Galatas.

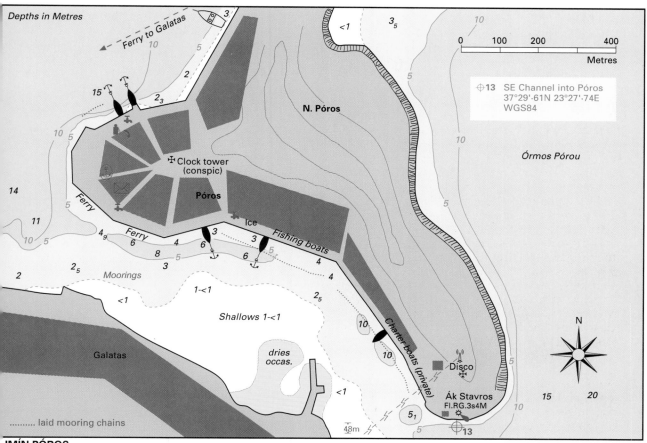

Depths in Metres

Ferry to Galatas

N. Póros

☩ Clock tower (conspic)

Póros

Ferry

Ferry

Ice

Fishing boats

Moorings

Shallows 1-<1

dries occas.

Galatas

.... laid mooring chains

Órmos Pórou

⊕13 SE Channel into Póros
37°29'·61N 23°27'·74E
WGS84

0   100   200   400
Metres

Charter boats (private)

Disco

Ák Stavros
Fl.RG.3s4M

48m

⊕13

LIMÍN PÓROS

1–1½ knots, usually in the direction the wind has been blowing. The bottom in the channel is soft mud and off the N quay mud and weed, not always the best holding in the latter. Care needs to be taken in the channel of sections of mooring chain lying approximately 20–30m off the quay. Shelter in the channel is excellent. Shelter on the N quay is good in the summer (the *meltemi* does not blow home), and in spring and autumn unless a strong northwesterly blows down off the hills.

The biggest problem in Póros is usually not the wind but the wash from the ferries and hydrofoils and inconsiderate motorboats. If you are in the channel the boat can be damaged unless you pay attention to warps and fenders – make sure you are pulled sufficient distance off the quay. It can also get a bit smelly in the channel in the hot summer months.

Facilities

Services Water on the N quay and the town quay. The 'waterman' usually comes round several times a day. Fuel delivered by mini-tanker. Showers available in some of the bars.

Provisions Good shopping for all provisions around the waterfront. Ice available from some bars.

Eating out Numerous tavernas of all types and persuasions on the waterfront. At the SE end of the channel quay there is the *Prima Sera* which has some excellent original fish dishes. Next door is *Dimitros*, a simple grilled meat place where you can eat in or take away. *Karavolos* behind the cinema on the N quay is also recommended. In Galatas right at the SE end of the village is *Vlachos*, which though it doesn't have a very inspiring view (over the local football field), does have good food and local wine. I suggest you avoid anywhere that

The 'sleeping lady' at sunset

has 'brother' in the title, or anywhere that touts – the good tavernas in Póros don't need to have someone directing you to a seat. On the waterfront Stavros at the *Cafe Remezo* serves a good breakfast and is something of a local for yachties here.

Other Banks. PO. OTE. Doctor and dentist. Launderette on the N quay. Hire cars, motorbikes and bicycles. Ferries and hydrofoils N to Methana, Aígina, and Piraeus and S to Ídhra, Ermioni, Spétsai and other destinations S.

General

Despite the wash from the ferries and hydrofoils, despite the competition for quay space, despite loud music from some of the bars, despite the day-trippers that pour in every day, Póros emerges through it all as a convivial and intimate place that many end up staying in longer than they intended. It is a picturesque spot, and I know people who have lived and worked here for years stand and watch the sun go down over the 'sleeping lady' with a dreamy expression in their eyes.

The 'sleeping lady' is the shape picked out of the hills in the W by the setting sun and unlike many similar epithets, the shape of the hills really does take on the appearance of a sleeping lady complete with most anatomical detail – it is best seen from the S end of the channel looking to the NW. In a way it is the paradox of the place that gets to you, a picture postcard spot plagued by its very charm, a sort of Brighton-by-the-Aegean that somehow mysteriously retains its charm.

Anchorages around Póros

There are numerous anchorages to the W and E of Póros town that can be used in settled weather or as an overnight anchorage.

Órmos Vidhi. The large bay on the E of Limín Poros. Anchor off the hamlet of Vidhi or in any of the coves on the N. The easternmost cove on the N has a fish farm in it but there is still room to anchor. The bottom here is mud and weed, good holding once you are through the weed though this can take some doing.

It is assumed the ancient port of Pogon, the harbour for Troezen, was situated here. The Athenian fleet gathered here before the Battle of Salamís and it was to here the women and children of Athens were evacuated before the battle.

Ák Dana anchorage The cove immediately under Ák Dana affords good shelter from the prevailing winds and is comparatively free from ferry wash. Clear translucent water for swimming in.

Russian Bay The first bay on the N side once into Limín Poros. It is easily recognised by the small islet in the middle with a white chapel on it. Care is needed of the reef running out for approximately 50m from the E side of the islet. Anchor where convenient in 8–12m depths on mud and weed and take a long line ashore if necessary. Good shelter from the prevailing winds. A taverna opens in the summer.

The bay is so named from the War of Independence when the Russian fleet was based here. The small chapel on the islet is called Thaskalio and is dedicated to teachers.

Órmos Neorion The large bay to the E of Russian Bay. Anchor in 5–12m on mud and weed, good holding once through the weed. The best place to be is in the cove under the Villa Galini with a long line ashore. Good shelter from the prevailing winds. Care is needed of the ski/parascending platform in the bay. Hotels and taverna/bars ashore.

The Villa Galini on the edge of the bay is where Henry Miller and George Seferis spent some time, Miller writing his *The Colossus of Maroussi* and Seferis composing his poetry. Looking out from the villa Seferis wrote these words in his diary, which capture still moments not just of Póros but of the Greek seascape.

Póros town looking ESE towards the yacht quay on the N side of the peninsula

Órmos Neorion and the anchorage under the Villa Galini

'The sea was not beating, breathless. The pinetree needles were motionless like thorns of sea urchins at the depth of clear water. A black ship dragged along the line of the horizon little by little, like the cloth of the Karaghiozis theatre, underlined this amazing vision and disappeared.'

Navy Bay The bay immediately W of Póros town. It is prohibited to anchor in the N part off the naval college, though the prohibition seems to be breached more and more each year. Anchor off the town quay in 10–16m.

Galatas Yachts anchor off the mainland side just NW of Galatas up to Ák Tombasi. Although somewhat exposed to northerlies, the holding in mud is excellent and there is a limited fetch across from Póros. Yachts also anchor on the Galatas side of the W end of the channel, although there are so many permanent moorings here now that it can be difficult to find a spot. Care is also needed over depths.

Órmos Aliki The bay tucked in between Nisís Bourtzi and Ák Aliki. Care needs to be taken not to cut across between Nisís Lazareto and the coast as a reef just under the water connects the two. Entrance can be made between Lazareto and Bourtzi or Bourtzi and Ák Aliki. Anchor in 3–10m. Good shelter from the prevailing winds. Taverna and watersports centre ashore.

Órmos Askeli. The large bay between Sphaeria and Kalauria. Anchor off the N side in 5–15m on mud and weed, patchy holding in places. Good shelter from the prevailing wind. Taverna/bar ashore.

Monastery Bay The bay under the monastery of Zoodhokos Pigi. A large and spectacularly uninspired hotel is conspicuous on the W of the bay. Anchor in 5–10m on the NE side of the bay. The holding is not the best here so make sure your anchor is well in. Taverna/bar ashore.

The monastery of Zoodhokos Pigi (Virgin of the Life-giving Spring) above can be visited just a short climb above the anchorage. The monastery has a spring outside and the water is said to have curative properties.

Squiggle Bay 37°31'·6N 23°30'·4E
A bay on the NE coast 1M W of Ák Kalavria. In calm weather it is an idyllic spot, but normally a swell is pushed in by the prevailing NE–N wind. There are coves to the W and E which can also be used.

Órmos Barbaria (Vagyonias)
37°32'·1N 23°29'·2E
The next large bay NW of Squiggle Bay. Like the latter a swell is normally pushed into here, but in calm weather it is an idyllic spot with a beach at the head of the bay. This is assumed to be the ancient harbour of Kalauria. Perhaps it was later used by invaders from the N or pirates and hence acquired its name from the word *barbaros* ('non-Greek').

Órmos Áy Paraskevi The bay to the NW of Barbaria with the islet of Bisti in the entrance. The bay is very deep and also has a considerable swell pushed into it with the prevailing wind.

Órmos Voriarnia 37°32'·3N 23°28'·3E
An inlet on the W side of Póros. It is fringed by above and below-water rocks so care is needed. A swell is normally pushed into here by the prevailing winds.

Troezen

Near the village of Dhamalas approximately 10 kilometres from Galatas are the ruins of ancient Troezen. The city was an important one in antiquity, one of the Kalaurian League, and the city to which Athens evacuated the women and children before the Battle of Salamís.

Most of the ruins have been picked over for subsequent building work for centuries, it being much easier to collect ready-cut rock than to have to quarry it. Consequently the churches and other buildings nearby have much ancient masonry incorporated into them, a palimpsest of stone spanning the centuries. The chance recovery of the 'Troezen Stone' recording Themistocles' decree for the evacuation of Athens (see the section on the Battle of Salamís in the Introduction) was doing sterling service as a doorstep at the local school until it was identified.

Troezen was established in the 5th century BC, or possibly earlier. It was known as the birthplace of Theseus, who killed the Minotaur and unceremoniously dumped Ariadne on Naxos. It was at Troezen that Theseus was told to move a heavy rock under which he would find the sword and sandals left for him by Aegeus and, sure enough, there is a rock here which has been dubbed Theseus' Rock. The town declined when it sided with Sparta in the Peloponnesian Wars and was subsequently sacked by Athens.

Enough of the foundations remain to make a visit interesting and there is the added benefit of the Devil's Bridge nearby. Here a stream rushes down a low ravine shaded by plane trees in a scene somehow more redolent of Scandinavia than of the Devil's work. The water is deliciously cool and it is a pleasant place to sit and cool your feet after walking around in the heat.

III. Ídhra to Spétsai and the adjacent coast

Ídhra to Spétsai

This chapter covers Kólpos Ídhras (the Gulf of Hydra) and the island of Spétsai and the nearby coast to the N and W. Unlike the areas covered in the two previous chapters there are few ancient associations (I can hear sighs of relief already from those numbed by trying to make sense of scattered ancient masonry). There are more recent associations with the Greek War of Independence, but we will come to that in due course.

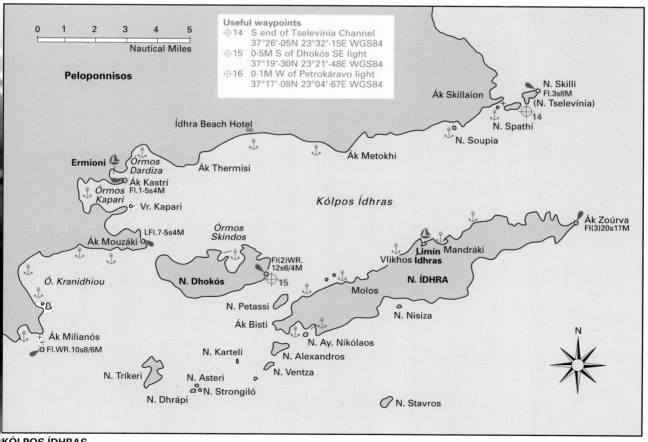

Useful waypoints
- ⊕14 S end of Tselevínia Channel
  37°26'·05N 23°32'·15E WGS84
- ⊕15 0·5M S of Dhokós SE light
  37°19'·30N 23°21'·48E WGS84
- ⊕16 0·1M W of Petrokáravo light
  37°17'·08N 23°04'·67E WGS84

KÓLPOS ÍDHRAS

PREVAILING WINDS

The E–NE winds blowing down onto Póros blow down to Nisidhes Tselevínia, where they bend to blow from the E into Kólpos Idhras. With strong northeasterlies gusts blow off the high land on the coast. Around Nísos Dhokós the winds are usually variable and may be from the E or the SE. Across to Spétsai winds are normally from the SE in the summer though northeasterlies may extend as far as Spétsai at times.

Around Kólpos Idhras the mountains rise steeply from the sea on the Peloponnese side and equally so around the coast of Ídhra. For the most part the mountains are barren rocky places, except for a few places on the Peloponnese coast where startling patches of green betray an underwater spring. The islands of Ídhra and Dhokós give the appearance of utter barrenness, though on closer inspection the SW end of Ídhra is clothed in pine on the lower slopes and I am assured by the locals that there is a patch or two inland where things can be grown. To the W the geography of the coast descends to more gentle outlines around Porto Kheli, and Spétsai also has a gentle aspect of rolling hills rather than craggy mountains.

The coast from Tselevínia to Ák Mouzaki

Nisidhes Tselevínia

These two islands, Nisís Skilli and Nisís Spathí, lie 4½M SE of Póros just where you 'turn the corner' into Kólpos Idhras. They are not easily identified from the distance if you are hugging the coast from Póros harbour, and you will not see the gap between Skilli and Spathí until up to Ák Spathí. The gap between the two islands is much used as a shortcut by yachts and by hydrofoils and ferries. The channel is deep and clear of dangers in the fairway, but considerable caution is needed to keep clear of the hydrofoils and ferries using it, especially as they seem to appear out of nowhere. Care must also be taken not to confuse the navigable channel with that between Nisís Spathí and the coast, which is obstructed by a reef – from the S this gap and not the navigable channel will often be the first you see.

Quick reference guide

	Shelter	Mooring	Fuel	Water	Provisions	Eating out	Plan
Tselevínia	C	C	O	O	O	O	•
Nisís Soupia	C	C	O	O	O	O	
Ídhra Beach Hotel	A	AB	O	A	C	C	•
Órmos Dardiza	O	C	O	O	O	O	•
Ermioni	A	AC	B	A	B	B	•
Ermioni south quay	C	A	B	B	B	B	•
Órmos Kapari	C	C	O	O	O	O	•
Órmos Kouverta	C	C	O	O	O	O	•
Nísos Ídhra							
Limín Ídhras	B	A	B	A	B	A	•
Mandráki	C	C	O	O	O	C	•
Órmos Molos	C	C	O	O	O	O	
Petassi	C	C	O	O	O	O	
Órmos Áy Nikólaos	C	C	O	O	O	O	
Nísos Dhokós							
Dhokós Cove	B	C	O	O	O	O	•
Órmos Skindos	C	C	O	O	O	O	•
Mainland							
Órmos Kranidhiou	C	C	O	B	O	C	•
Órmos Metokhi	C	C	O	O	O	O	•
Órmos Kosta	C	C	O	O	O	C	
Nisís Khinitsa	B	C	O	O	O	O	
Porto Kheli	A	AC	B	B	B	B	•
Nísos Spétsai							
Báltiza	A	AC	A	A	B	A	•
Dápia	C	A	B	B	B	A	•
Órmos Zoyioryia	B	C	O	O	O	C	•
Órmos Áy Paraskevi	O	C	O	O	O	O	•

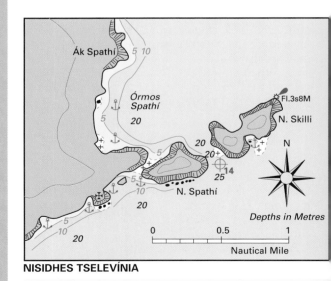

NISIDHES TSELEVÍNIA

⊕14 S end of Tselevínia Channel
37°26'·05N 23°32'·15E WGS84

Tselevínia looking into Kólpos Idhras from the channel between the islands

There are a number of anchorages around the islets depending on wind and weather.

On the S side of Nisís Spathí there is an isolated anchorage affording better shelter from the prevailing wind than appears on the chart. Anchor tucked in next to the islet and the mainland coast where convenient. You can also anchor under the headland with the small monastery or church close W which appears to be occupied. Both anchorages are open S.

On the S side of Nisís Skilli there is a cove affording good shelter from northerlies. Care is needed of the reef running out from the E side and the approach should be made from the SW with someone up front conning you in.

In southerlies you can anchor in the large bay under Ák Spathí with Nisís Spathí on the S side. Open to the N to E.

The coast W from Tselevínia

Along the coast between Nisidhes Tselevínia and Nisís Soupia there are a number of other coves and bights that can be used in calm weather. When the wind gets up in the afternoon they should be vacated.

Ák Skillaion, the cape reaching out to Nisís Spathí is presumed to be the cape where Minos, the first king of Crete (hence the Minoans) threw the besotted Scylla overboard. Minos defeated

the Megarans and Athens because of the treachery of the Megaran king's daughter Scylla who was in love with Minos. He ordered his Cretan crew to throw her overboard and it is here that she was washed up onto the cape – a not unreasonable place, as a great deal of flotsam and jetsam is carried by the wind and surface currents to this corner. The story ends on a macabre note as Pausanias relates that they 'show you no grave, her neglected body was torn to pieces they say by the sea birds'.

Pausanias goes on to give the following description of sailing from Skillaion to Ermioni.

> 'Sailing from Skillaion towards the city you came to the OX'S HEAD, another cape, and then to the islands beyond it, first SALT ISLAND which offers an anchorage, then PINE ISLAND, and thirdly LEFT HAND ISLAND. As you sail past them another cape called the OBSTACLE sticks out from the mainland, then comes THREE-HEADED ISLAND, and a mountain projecting into the sea from the Peloponnese, called the OX CROSSING, with a sanctuary on it to Demeter and her daughter and to Athene, Guardian of the Anchorage. Offshore lies an island called DECEIT, with another called WATER ISLAND not far away. From here the beaches of the mainland curve away in a crescent ending in Poseidonion (at Ermioni).'

Pausanias *Guide to Greece Vol 1* transl. Peter Levi.

Numerous explanations have been put forward to explain these navigation references. One (Leake) claims the ship Pausanias was in sailed right round Ídhra and arrived at Ermioni from the S. Another claims Pausanius was misreading the sailing directions of the time. None of these

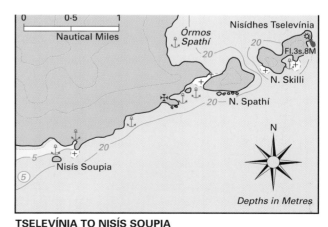

TSELEVÍNIA TO NISÍS SOUPIA
⊕ 37°25'·00N 23°29'·60E WGS84
0·2M S of N. Soupia

complicated solutions are necessary, as any sailor in a small boat navigating his way along the coast will quickly recognise. The prominent objects from seawards are not always apparent from looking at a chart, although retrospectively they can be identified. Thus the Ox's Head is the small prominent headland (now with a church on it) less than 1M after Spathí. Salt Island is Soupia, which does indeed have an anchorage behind it. Pine Island is probably Ák Metokhi which has silted and is now connected to the coast – there are lagoons around it and pine and other trees grow nearby sustained by a spring. Left-hand Island is Ídhra. The Obstacle (which it would be as you headed into the large bay on the coast and perhaps had to tack out in SE winds) is Ák Thermisi. Three-Headed Island is Dhokós with three conspicuous capes. The Ox-Crossing could be Ák Mouzaki, and the islands of Deceit and Water Island could be any of Trikeri, Spétsai or Spetsopoula. The crescent beaches could be either Dardiza or Kapari. Of course this is all as speculative as anyone else's guesses might be, but at this time we know there were primitive charts and I pin my faith on skippers of the time who would be very careful not to increase distance and danger by sailing around Ídhra to Ermioni. I'm fairly confident the route was a well known one and the skipper plugged along the coast by the shortest route to Ermioni.

Nisís Soupia

37°25'·00N 23°29'·60E WGS84
0·2M S of N. Soupia

An islet usually called Frog Island. It does indeed look like a crouching frog, though the name *soupia* actually means cuttlefish which I suppose it could also resemble. Behind the islet there is an anchorage that is reasonably well sheltered from the prevailing wind. Anchor in 3–10m where convenient. If you enter from the E side then care is needed of a rock off the mainland coast. On the W side depths are irregular and fairly shallow (3–5m) between the islet and the coast. Keep closer to the islet than to the coast. The bottom is covered in thick weed and is poor holding in parts. Tucked in behind the eastern entrance there is a minute cove with room for perhaps one or two yachts with a long line ashore or anchored fore and aft in idyllic surroundings.

On the slopes behind to the W a new villa development has been built and, although it is not overly intrusive, still it reminds us that the land along this coast is ripe for real estate development and that in the future there will probably be more blots on the landscape.

Ák Metokhi

A low sandy cape. In calm weather or light easterlies a yacht can anchor on the W side of the cape off the long sandy beach. The bottom shelves gently in. The water-boat for Ídhra has a jetty on the E side of the cape.

Nisís Soupia looking NE

Nisís Soupia and the anchorage behind looking S to Ídhra

Ídhra Beach Hotel

A hotel development near Plepi about 7M W of Nisís Soupia. It takes it name from Ídhra, no doubt to cash in on the charm and fame of the island across the water, though it bears little resemblance to the architecture on Ídhra.

The small harbour off the hotel is normally crowded with tripper boats and it can be difficult to find a berth. The harbour is private and whether or not you can stay here is really dependent on the goodwill of the hotel management. Care is needed in the entrance and in the basin which are very small. Only small yachts (10m or less) should attempt to enter and then only in calm weather.

In calm weather or light easterlies it is possible to anchor off the hotel complex. There is a restaurant and bar ashore. The hotel and bungalow complex appears to have been neglected somewhat in recent years and is desperately in need of a bit of mortar here and there and a lick of paint.

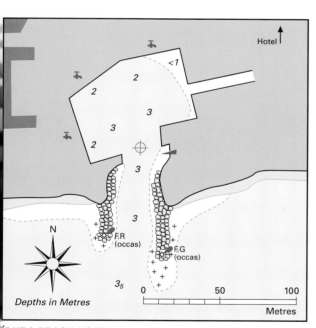

ÍDHRA BEACH HOTEL
⊕37°24′·8N 23°20′·4E

Órmos Dardiza

37°24′·3N 23°16′·4E

The large bay immediately NE of Ermioni. There is a rocky islet on the W side of the bay. In calm

weather or light easterlies a yacht can anchor off the beach. It is quite deep until close in and you will usually have to anchor in around 10m on mud and weed, patchy holding in places. Although it looks as if shelter should be good from even strong easterlies, in fact a swell is pushed round the corner into the bay. In the NE corner there is a disused loading gantry. A taverna opens in the summer.

Ermioni (Hermione)

The village in the far NW corner of Kólpos Idhras with a skinny headland sheltering the bay and harbour.

Pilotage

Approach The buildings of the village straddling the headland are conspicuous from both the E and the S. The headland and the light structure on the end are easily identified closer in and once into the bay the harbour will be seen. Care needs to be taken of the submerged ancient mole on the S side of the bay. Ferries and hydrofoils stop at Ermioni and a good lookout should be kept for them.

Mooring Go stern or bows-to behind the outer short pier. The bottom is mud and weed, good holding. Good shelter from all winds behind here. If it is crowded behind the pier it is possible to go bows-to the outer end of N quay under the breakwater. Care is needed as depths are irregular and rock ballasting extends underwater from the quay in places. It can be very uncomfortable here with easterlies which send in a swell side-on causing boats to roll badly and it may be better to anchor off N of the breakwater.

Anchorage Yachts can anchor in the N part of the bay in 2–4m. The bottom is mud and weed, good holding once the anchor is in, but the prevailing breeze tends to gust down into the bay and it can be uncomfortable until the wind dies in the evening.

Facilities

Services Water on the quay. Fuel delivered by mini-tanker.

Provisions Good shopping for all provisions nearby. Ice available.

Eating out Good tavernas on the waterfront and on the south side of the headland.

Other Bank. PO. Metered telephone. Hire

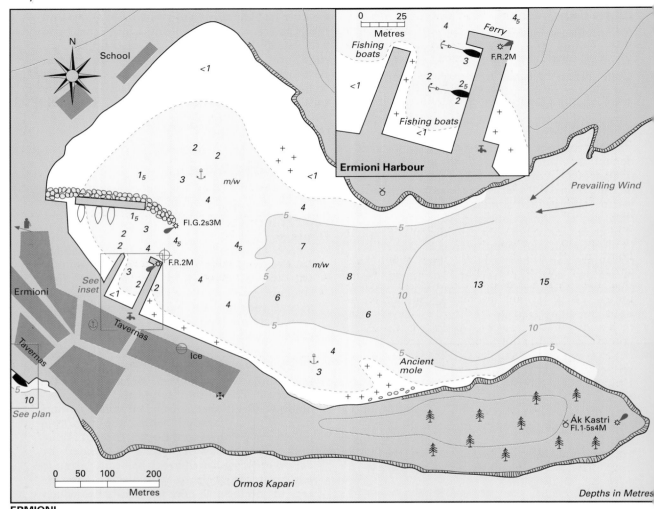

ERMIONI
⊕37°23′·2N 23°15′·0E

motorbikes. Ferries and hydrofoils to Piraeus and S and W.

General

The village is a quiet place after the bustle of the islands and well worth the slight detour off the nautical motorway linking the main islands. It has some tourism but not too much yet, though a number of the ubiquitous blank square concrete hotels of the 'pour-and-fill' variety have been erected. The headland on which the temples stood is now a pine-clad park which at sunset, with the scent of pine needles in the air, is the perfect place for a pre-prandial stroll. Over the saddle of the hill on the S side of the village the small local fishing boats are moored and there are

a number of bars and tavernas looking out over Órmos Kapari – the perfect place for a beer or ouzo or dinner.

Ancient Ermioni (or Hermione) was evidently a place of some consequence, if the number of temples and the space allotted to it in Pausanias' guide are anything to go by. It possessed three important temples and the city itself was ringed by a high wall. Little remains today of the city, although chunks of ancient masonry can be identified on the headland and built into some of the older buildings.

The temples had some strange rites recorded by Pausanias. At a small shrine to Aphrodite all virgins and widows intending to go with a man had to make a sacrifice – a sort of early version of church bans. On the headland there was a colonnade called Echo's Colonnade, where any word was repeated three times. In the temple to Demeter four old women resided, guardians of a shrine and statue inside which no one else, foreigner or resident of the city, was allowed to see. At the festival of Demeter four perfect heifers were driven into the temple and slaughtered with a sickle by the old women. The deities and the rites at Ermioni are significantly different to those in other cities and we can suppose this was a very ancient city embodying earlier gods and rituals.

Off the N side of the headland in a small bight are the remains of the ancient harbour. The city had numerous maritime links. The principal temple to Aphrodite on the headland was dedicated to 'Aphrodite of the Deep Sea and the Harbour'. Pausanias mentions that there were several harbours on the north side and it may be that the present harbour includes an ancient mole. There is an interesting reference in Pausanias to a unique festival held here every year in honour of Dionysus that included 'a musical contest in his honour, and prizes for a diving competition and a boat-race'. This is the earliest reference to a boat race that we have, and if true Ermioni was probably the site of the first recorded regatta in history. However there are problems over the translation of the word for 'boat race' and it may mean a swimming race. Still, it is a pleasant caprice on a sultry summer evening to sit on the headland and muse on what the boats might have looked like racing around the bay.

Ermioni south quay (Mandráki)

In calm weather or light easterlies it is possible to go stern or bows-to the S fisherman's quay. Enquire first that you are not taking a local boat's place. With southerlies or strong easterlies the quay becomes untenable and you should move around to the N side of the headland.

Órmos Kapari

In calm weather or light southerlies a yacht can anchor off the beach in Órmos Kapari. Anchor in 5–8m where convenient. Depending on the wind either the SW or the NW corner can be used. The bottom is mud and weed, good holding.

Off the southern entrance point of the bay care is needed of Nisidhes Kapari, an islet with some isolated rocks just above water to the E of it. In

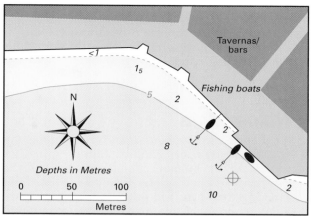

ERMIONI SOUTH QUAY
⊕37°23´·0N 23°14´·9E

calm weather there is a picturesque anchorage under the islet taking care of the reef to the W of it.

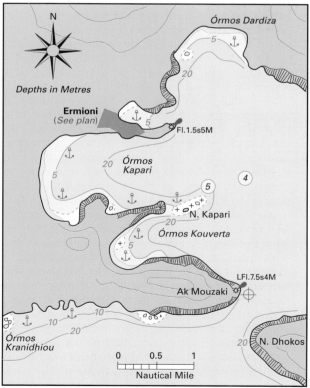

ÓRMOS KAPARI AND ÓRMOS KOUVERTA
⊕37°21´·0N 23°16´·4E

Órmos Kouverta

An indifferent anchorage S of Órmos Kapari. In calm weather anchor off the W or N side. With the prevailing winds a swell is pushed into the bay.

Nísos Ídhra

This stark mountainous island lying along the southern edge of Kólpos Idhras gives no indication of human habitation or even the possibility of it until closer-to you see a few white houses dotted here and there. It oozes prehistory although no prehistoric remains have been found and it was not until comparatively recent times, in the 18th century, that it worked its way into the history books. The ancient world effectively passed it by.

The barren precipitous slopes become friendlier on closer association. Houses and monasteries can be identified. At the southern end the lower slopes are clothed in pine. But the principal port and town of Ídhra, the only significant settlement, are hidden in a defile and cannot be seen until you are nearly up to the entrance. The closed book opens and the port and town are revealed suddenly and dramatically – especially to the navigator approaching it for the first time, who may have been wondering just where the harbour had got to.

The island has probably been a refuge for pirates and those on the periphery of society for a long time. Herodotus relates that Ermioni sold the island to refugees from Sámos in the 6th century BC, but they soon despaired of doing anything with the barren island and moved on to Crete. The name of the island is said to be derived from Hydrea, 'a watering place', but this is paradoxical as there are no significant springs on the island. Water is delivered to Ídhra by a tanker bringing it over from the mainland. In the 16th and 17th centuries refugees fleeing from the mainland settled at Kiapha on the hill above the harbour. These were probably of Albanian origin, as Kiapha is Albanian for a 'head' or 'summit'. The settlement flourished in its own modest way and soon the inhabitants began to indulge in modest trading voyages to the Peloponnese. The small vessels for this were mostly built locally and as the profits from the trading voyages increased, larger vessels up to fifty and sixty tons were built. The smaller vessels would have been lateen rigged but larger vessels were probably schooners or small brigantines.

The island was little affected by the Ottoman conquest of the Peloponnese and nearby islands, being of little significance or threat – or so it appeared. When an Ottoman fleet anchored off Ák Metokhi to take on water the Grand Vizier, Damed Ali, was surprised to receive a delegation from the apparently deserted island. The Idhriots pledged not to interfere in Ottoman matters and the Ottomans in turn were content to leave the Idhriots alone and to collect an annual tax. Idhriots served in the Ottoman fleet and Ottoman ships were repaired in the island shipyard.

The shipowners prospered and under Russian protection ran profitable cargoes of grain from the Black Sea to the Aegean. A little privateering on the side brought in nearly as much revenue and British captains cursed the piratical Idhriots and suggested in dispatches that Idhriot ships should be blown out of the water despite Russian protection. Most of the mansions around the port were built in this prosperous time at the beginning of the 19th century. Although Byron is often thought of as an out-and-out Philhellene, he had a canny understanding of the Greeks that these verses from *Don Juan*, though placed in an anonymous Aegean island, I think apply perfectly to Ídhra and the Idhriots of the time.

A fisherman he had been in his youth,
And still a sort of fisherman was he.
But other speculations were, in sooth,
Added to his connection with the sea,
Perhaps not so respectable, in truth.
A little smuggling and some piracy
Left him at last the sole of many masters
Of an ill-gotten million of piastres.
A fisher therefore was he, though of men,
Like Peter the Apostle, and he fished
For wandering merchant vessels now and then
And sometimes caught as many as he wished.
The cargoes he confiscated, and gain
He sought in the slave market too and dished
Full many a morsel for that Turkish trade,
By which no doubt a good deal he made.

Don Juan Lord Byron

The Idhriots were reluctant to join the Greek War of Independence – after all, they enjoyed good relations with the Ottomans and had prospered handsomely from it. In 1821 things came to a head when a group of unemployed sailors and captains caused the town council to resign and make over the Idhriot fleet to the Greek cause. The small ships carrying few cannon could not hope to take on the Turks wholesale and developed the art of the fireship to perfection. An old ship was covered in tar, littered with kindling and barrels of gunpowder and then sailed by a skeleton crew into the Turkish fleet, where it was set on fire, and the crew escaped in a small cutter towed behind. The Turks never found an answer to the fireship, and the small Idhriot fleet, along with the Spetsiots, caused disproportionate damage for all their few ships.

The end of the war spelled disaster for Ídhra. The fleet was decimated and the new Greek government clamped down on privateering. There were no blockades to run for big profits, new boats could not be financed and new technology in the shape of the steam engine was undermining old sailing skills. Ídhra declined and in 1842 there was only a population of 4,000 left from the 28,000 of the 1820s. The town and port were left a shell that remained much as it had been in the early 19th century until the trickle of tourism in the 1960s.

Limín Ídhras

The harbour and town are tucked into a cove approximately in the middle of the N coast of the island

Pilotage

Approach Though the harbour and the main part of the town cannot be seen until you are right up to it, the houses straddling the ridge on either side and up the slopes behind the town can be distinguished. The numerous ferries and hydrofoils entering and leaving the harbour provide good clues to its whereabouts. Closer in, the town and harbour mole will be seen. Care needs to be taken of the ferries and hydrofoils entering and leaving as well as tripper boats, water taxis and other boats. The entrance is quite narrow and care is needed of traffic jams in the entrance.

Mooring Ídhra is a popular destination and if you want to be assured of a berth in the summer, especially at weekends, you will need to be here by two or three in the afternoon or earlier. Go stern or bows-to the mole or the S quay. It is best to be on the N quay as, although shelter is normally good, with strong northerlies the harbour is like a washing machine and the only place to be is on the N quay under the mole. At the height of summer, boats are commonly banked three out from the quay and crossed anchors and cross tempers are commonplace. The bottom is mud and weed, good holding, although as indicated you will probably be over someone's anchor or they will be over yours.

Note Large yachts can anchor stern-to the outside of the breakwater in settled weather. They will have to drop anchor in very deep water, typically 30–40m, and take a long line to the outside rock ballasting. If it blows strongly from the N they will not be able to remain here.

Facilities

Services Water on the quay.

Provisions Good shopping for provisions. There is a small market just back from the S quay. Ice available.

Eating out Numerous tavernas of all types. In from the SE corner of the harbour *The Garden* is recommended for its country-style dishes, and close by is *Xeri Elia*. Further up the hill are *Krifo Limani* and *Yeitoniko* which have good food. I suggest you stay away from anywhere, especially the bars, on the waterfront, where excessive prices and false bonhomie are the rule. There are some good bars further into the town.

Other Banks. PO. OTE. Water taxis. Ferries and hydrofoils to Piraeus and W and S.

General

The trouble with Ídhra is that everyone wants to see it, and in the height of summer it is overcrowded. By day cruise ships and ferries pour

Limín Ídhras looking N   *Nigel Patten*

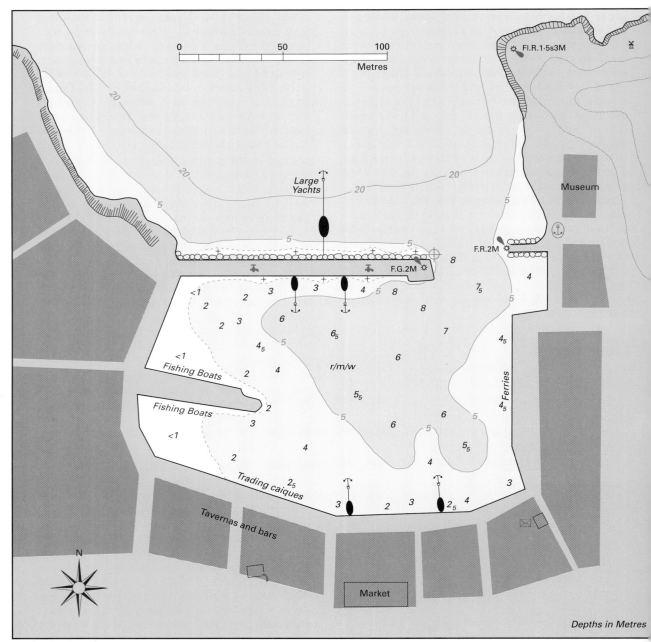

LIMÍN ÍDHRAS (ÍDHRA)
⊕37°21´·1N 23°28´·0E

people into the place; by night fenders pop and the amphitheatre of the harbour is choked with the fumes from the generators of large motorboats. There must be more souvenir-gift-gold-jewellery shops per square metre in Ídhra than anywhere else, and in the waterfront bars it is assumed any spare change is a tip after you have been charged New York prices for a drink.

And yet you must see it. It is a museum town that has changed little since its abrupt change of fortune in the mid-19th century. The mansions packed around the harbour are elegant examples of 18th and 19th-century shipowners' houses built before the age of the motor vehicle. Because there are so few places to go there are still virtually no motor vehicles on the island except the refuse truck and a couple of cars.

The majority of the mansions, known as *archontiki*, were to Italian designs though executed by Greek stonemasons, with the western slopes the favoured spot for the wealthy. One of the largest, the Tombazis house, is now part of the Athens School of Fine Arts. Any building work now is carried on in much the same way as in the past (thanks to a historical preservation order) with the raw materials brought in by caïque and unloaded onto the pier on the W side of the harbour, from where it is transported by donkey around the town and outskirts. If you want to get anywhere inland and feel disinclined to walk, then donkeys are the only alternative.

Ídhra harbour looking onto the waterfront quay

In the 1960s the town attracted the disaffected and disillusioned and also a few artists. One who combined disillusion with art was Leonard Cohen, who lived on the island for a while and composed his suicidal ballads here – he is said to still have a house here. Gradually the attractions of the place grew, and the numbers now visiting daily must run into thousands. Out of season in spring and autumn there are fewer visitors, the place is more amenable and you have a better chance of arriving late and finding a berth.

Mandráki

A bay approximately ¼M E of Limín Ídhras. It offers reasonable shelter from the prevailing winds. Anchor in 8–15m, keeping clear of the area buoyed off for swimming. The bottom is mud and weed, reasonable holding. Easterlies blowing down the gulf send some swell in here, more uncomfortable than dangerous, and the bay is open N.

19th century engraving of Ídhra

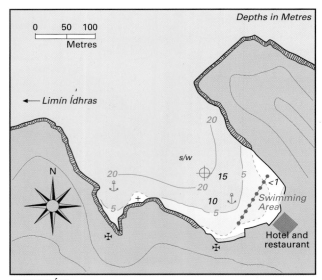

MANDRÁKI
⊕37°21'·5N 23°28'·8E

Ashore there is a small hotel and restaurant. Mandráki has one of the few sandy patches that can be called a beach on Ídhra and tripper boats run round to here from the town. Mandráki means a 'sheepfold' or a 'small enclosure' and in the 19th century this was an alternative port when the town harbour was full. It also had several boatyards building and repairing the sailing ships, and today a small boatyard for local caïques still survives.

Anchorages around Nísos Ídhra

Depending on the wind and sea there are a number of anchorages around Ídhra that can be used.

Órmos Panayía Zourvas 37°22'·0N 23°32'·2E
Nearly 3M NE of Mandráki there is a cove at the bottom of a steep ravine that can be used in calm weather. It is very deep here and you will need to anchor and take a long line ashore.

Órmos Molos 37°19'·6N 23°24'·8E
A small cove approximately 3M SW of Limín Ídhras. Anchor and take a long line ashore – normally to the W side. There is reasonable

Mandráki just E of Ídhra harbour

Órmos Áy Nikólaos 37°18'·0N 23°23'·5E

On the SW end of Ídhra there is a large bay bisected by a headland and Nisís Áy Nikólaos. A small chapel by the shore will be seen. Anchor in either bay, although the E bay is the favoured of the two. With the SE wind in the afternoon some swell rolls into the bay.

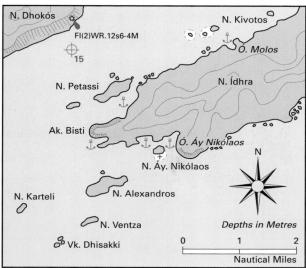

ÍDHRA SW CORNER

⊕15 0·5M S of Dhokós SE light
37°19'·30N 23°21'·48E WGS84

Nísos Dhokós

This high barren island lies between the SW end of Ídhra and the coast of the Peloponnese. If Ídhra appears bare and barren and uninhabited, then Dhokós is more so. On the S side the slopes drop precipitously to the sea leaving only a small rocky spur on the SE for the little lighthouse to sit on. On the N side the slopes are less steep, but only marginally so. The island belongs to a number of Idhriot families and was formerly used for quarrying marble. A derrick still sits on the W side of the entrance to the Órmos Skindos. There are a number of anchorages around Órmos Skindos, the large bay on the N.

1. **Dhokós Cove** The small inlet just inside the western entrance to Órmos Skindos. Anchor in 4–8m and take a long line ashore to the W or N side of the cove. Care is needed as the large

shelter from the prevailing winds in here, with the two outlying islets providing some additional shelter. Open to the N when a swell is pushed in.

Petassi anchorage 37°18'·4N 23°22'·6E

In calm weather there is a cove suitable for a lunch stop in a bight on the coast of Ídhra under Nisís Petassi.

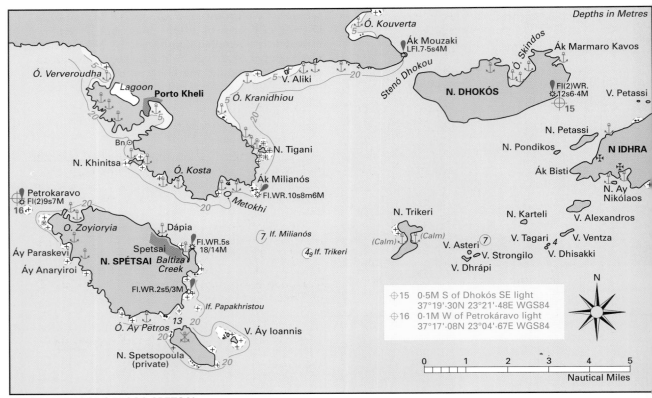

NISOS DHOKOS TO NISOS SPETSAI

Ák Mouzaki on the north side of Stenó Dhokou

mooring chains to which a buoy was formerly attached still lie on the bottom and if you foul the chain there is no chance of lifting it to clear it. Ashore is a hamlet, though only a few houses are occupied. The cove has wonderful clear water, a mottled turquoise and blue, and is a good safe place to overnight in.

2. ***Órmos Skindos*** In settled weather boats anchor anywhere around the large bay with a long line ashore or anchored free depending on the wind direction. Good shelter from the prevailing easterlies and in settled weather you can overnight here. A taverna opens in the summer at the NE end of the bay.

3. ***Wreck Cove*** In the very NE of Órmos Skindos is a cove sheltered by a thin finger of land. If approaching from the E care is needed of the reef and shoal patch off the outside of the finger. Anchor with a long line ashore. Good protection from the prevailing winds and a delightful spot. The area around has been excavated and is believed to be a Hellenic

Nisís Dhokós. Anchorage in the NW cove of Órmos Skindos

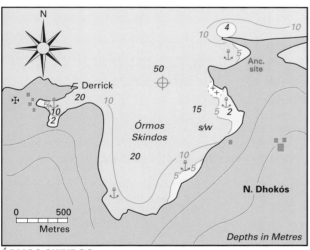

ÓRMOS SKINDOS
⊕37°20′·8N 23°20′·2E

Note In the sea area between Ídhra and Dhokós there is often a period of variable light winds or calm when on either side there is a good breeze blowing. It is best to motor through this patch and pick up the breeze on the other side.

Nisís Trikeri

0·5M S of S end of N. Trikeri
37°15′·05N 23°16′·46E WGS84

The island lying almost midway between Ídhra and Spétsai. Fishing boats will often be seen around it and in calm weather a yacht can anchor on either side of the isthmus joining the two halves.

Between Trikeri and Ídhra are several other islets and rocks. Proceeding W from Ídhra these are Nisís Alexandros, Nisís Ventza, Vrakhonisos Tagari and Dhisakki, Nisís Karteli and Vrakhonisos Strongiló, Asteri and Dhrapi just E of Trikeri itself.

The coast from Ák Mouzáki to Porto Kheli

Órmos Kranidhiou

Around Ák Mouzáki is the large bay of Kranidhiou. In calm weather and light southerlies or northerlies there are several places a yacht can anchor around the bay.

1. ***North side*** In calm weather anchor where convenient off the N side of the bay. The bottom shelves up nearly everywhere to convenient depths, but there are several small coves E of Vrakhonisos Aliki which are usually favoured. There are several large hotels on the N side around Petrothalassa.
2. ***Northwest head*** At the head of the bay the bottom shelves gently to the beach along the low-lying shore. In calm weather anchor off in 3–5m where convenient. In the SW corner off the beach some shelter can be gained from light southeasterlies. Tavernas on the beach in the summer.
3. ***West side*** Anchor off in any of the coves on the W side where there is some shelter from light southeasterlies. There is also an anchorage behind Nisís Tigani which is popular. Numbers of villas have now been built along this coast.

harbour, possibly of around the 5th or 6th century BC. Ashore there are remains from the Mycenean era including parts of a wall and houses. A ship from this era has been excavated here and at one time yachts were banned from anchoring in the cove. This prohibition appears to have been lifted, at least in practice.

4. In calm weather there is a cove on the E side of the island that can be used. When easterlies blow down the gulf it becomes untenable.

Ák Milianós (Áy Emilianós)

0·3M S of Vrak. Kounoupia
37°16'·96N 23°12'·04E WGS84

The cape with a chapel on it is easily identified. Now there is a light structure on the end of the reef (Vrakhoi Kounoupia) coming out from the cape fewer boats are tempted to cut the corner and come to a grinding halt.

Ifalos Milianós and Trikeri

Two reefs lying approximately 1·4M (If. Milianós) S of the cape and 2M (If. Trikeri) SE of the cape. Ifalos Milianós has 7m least depth over it and Ifalos Trikeri 4·9m least depth so they are really only of concern to deep draught vessels.

Órmos Metokhi

The bay immediately W of Ák Milianós. Care is needed on the E side of the bay which is bordered by shoal water and a small islet. Yachts can anchor around the bay where convenient as the water shelves up to the shore, though care is needed in one or two places where reefs border the coast. The prevailing wind will not always blow home into here and some yachts stay overnight. Ashore near the cape is the *Limanaki Taverna* which has honest food.

Órmos Kosta

The next bay approximately 1M W of Metokhi and the mainland terminal for the ferry to Spétsai. The prevailing wind normally pushes a swell into here, but in calm weather or light southeasterlies a yacht can anchor off where convenient.

Immediately W of Kosta is another bay which can be used in calm weather. Care is needed of the reef off the W entrance point.

Nisís Khinitsa

A low barren islet lying close to the E entrance point of Porto Kheli. Behind the islet a yacht can anchor in 3–5m depths on sand. Here there is good protection from the prevailing southeasterly blowing up the Spétsai Channel and consequently it is popular in the summer. You can also tuck into the coves on the mainland coast behind the islet, though care is needed of the depths in places.

Several large hotels nearby.

Porto Kheli

The large circular landlocked bay opposite Spétsai.

Pilotage

Approach It is difficult to determine exactly where the entrance is for the first time, although in the summer the numbers of boats coming and going and the hydrofoils and water taxis

Ák Milianós looking NE

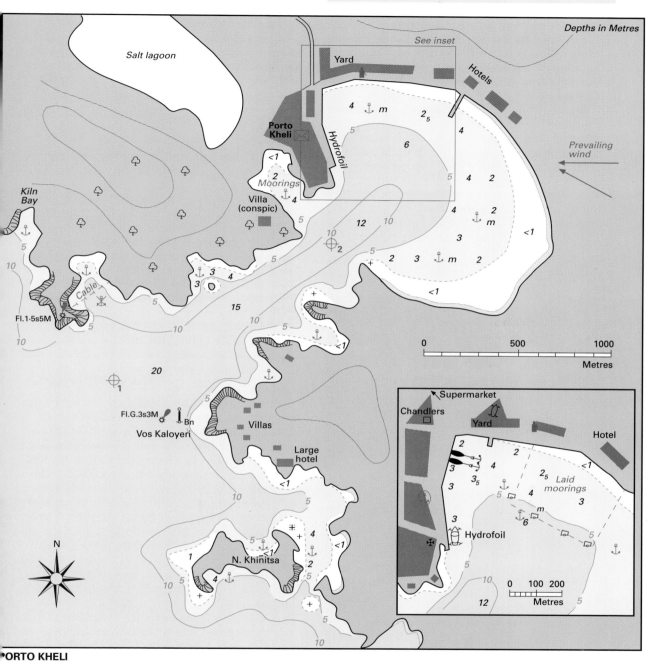

Depths in Metres

Salt lagoon

Yard

Hotels

See inset

Porto
Kheli

Hydrofoil

Moorings

Villa
(conspic)

Prevailing
wind

Kiln
Bay

Cable

Fl.1·5s5M

Fl.G.3s3M

Bn

Vos Kaloyeri

Villas

Large
hotel

N. Khinitsa

Metres

Supermarket

Chandlers

Yard

Hotel

Laid
moorings

Hydrofoil

Metres

PORTO KHELI
⚓1 37°18′·67N 23°07′·85E WGS84
⚓2 37°19′·07N 23°08′·56E WGS84

entering and leaving give a fairly good clue. Closer in the white light structure on the W side and the beacon marking the reef on the E side will be seen. Once into the entrance everything falls into place and entry into the bay proper is straightforward. Care is needed of the hydrofoils and water taxis and other boats using the bay and although it is perfectly feasible to sail in, keep an eagle eye out for other craft.

Mooring Go stern or bows-to the northern half of the quay or anchor off. In the N part of the bay there are numerous laid moorings for craft kept here on a permanent basis and the area is buoyed off by a line of small black buoys with Q lights on them, though these rarely work. There are also several buoyed areas for swimmers and water-skiers so care is needed when choosing a spot to anchor. Alternatively anchor in the SE corner. The bottom is gooey mud and excellent holding, though make sure your anchor is well in if going on the quay as the prevailing wind blows straight onto it. The bay is a 'hurricane hole' as far as shelter goes and shelter from all winds is good, apart from the fetch across the bay which can make it bumpy on the quay in strong southeasterlies and uncomfortable in the SE corner with strong northerlies.

Porto Kheli looking out to the W side of the channel

Porto Kheli anchorage and moorings on the NW side of the bay

Facilities

Services Water delivered by tanker and fuel by mini-tanker. The water on the quay is brackish.

Provisions Good shopping for all provisions in the town. There is a supermarket just in from the NW corner. Ice available.

Eating out Numerous tavernas in the town and around the northern shore. *Maria's* along the road towards the hotels serves good honest food and the *Paradise* in town is as good as any. Yachties often use the *Rendezvous* bar near the NW corner. There are other bars at the S end of the quay past the hydrofoil berth.

Other Bank. PO. OTE. Hire motorbikes and cars. Hydrofoils and catamaran ferry to Piraeus and points along the way and to the S.

General

Keli means eel, and presumably there were once lots of them here, though I suspect it is a reference to the lagoon immediately W of the port which is now a fish farm and was probably once connected on the E to the harbour. In the SE corner are a few ruins and a necropolis of ancient Alice (Halice or Aleis) of which little is known (and about which little is said) by ancient commentators. Presumably it was not of great importance, though you would have thought the natural harbour would have warranted a sizeable settlement. The quayed area and bulldozed strip and the small airport were initially built in the 1960s for a NATO base which was subsequently scrapped.

Porto Kheli is tailor-made for watersports, so it is no surprise that a number of hotels have been built around its shores and that the bay itself is a riot of fluorescent windsurfer sails, dinghy sails, water-ski and parascending boats. Swimmers take refuge in buoyed off areas and pedalos occasionally venture into the watersport maelstrom outside the buoys. Yachtsmen should take care not to run over dilettante windsurfers and wobbly skiers and in turn should take care not to get run down by gin palaces and hydrofoils.

Anchorages around Porto Kheli

1. **East side** of the entrance. There are two coves here in which yachts can anchor, although craft are sometimes moored here on a semi-permanent basis.
2. **West side** of the entrance. A bay with an above-water rock in it is often used. There is a wreck on the bottom near the above-water rock so care is needed. Anchor and take a long-line ashore.
3. **Light Structure Cove** The cove immediately E of the light structure at the entrance. Although in an area where anchoring is prohibited because of underwater cables, it has been used for a long time and no one seems to object. Anchor near the head of the bay to avoid the cable.
4. **Kiln Bay** The cove immediately W of the light structure. Reasonable shelter from the prevailing winds.
5. **Headland Bay** The cove just NW of Kiln Bay. The headland looks like an islet from some directions. Anchor in 2–5m on sand and weed. Good shelter from the prevailing winds in here. Just NW is another cove which also affords reasonable shelter from the prevailing winds.

Nísos Spétsai

This relatively low-lying island lies just S of Porto Kheli separated by a strait just over 1M across. It is nowhere very high, reaching just 276m (899ft) at its summit, with the outline softened even more by the pine forest covering most of the island. It was known as Pityoussa (the pine tree island) to Pausanias, a name thought somehow to give rise to the present one of Spétses or Spétsai. However, its present covering of pine is not ancient, but the product of a reforestation programme implemented at the turn of the 20th century.

In common with much of the surrounding area, Spétsai has no ancient associations that we know of. Like Ídhra it was not until the 18th century that migrants from the Peloponnese settled here and the island was little known, even to Greeks, until the War of Independence. Spétsai joined the war effort earlier than Ídhra, indeed it was the Spetsiot example which spurred Ídhra to adopt the cause, and committed the Spetsiot fleet to fighting the Ottoman navy, scoring some notable

successes under the direction of the island's heroine, Boubalina.

Born Lascarina Boubalina in Ídhra to a sea captain, she grew up with a passionate interest in the sea and ships. Not surprisingly, she married a sea captain from Spétsai and accompanied him on his voyages. She got through two more husbands before the War of Independence and managed to have nine children and accumulate a large fleet of ships courtesy of the three husbands. Her most daring exploit was to force the surrender of the Turkish garrison at Navplion and with hardly a shot being fired. She simply sailed up to Navplion and threatened to send fire-ships into the Turkish fleet. They promptly surrendered. She was fêted all over Greece and so

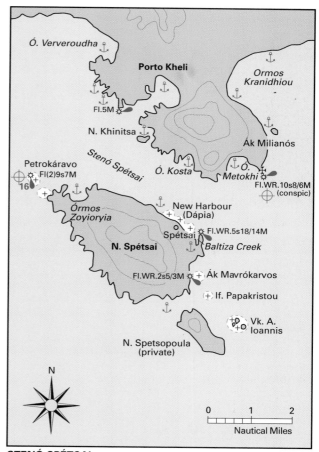

STENÓ SPÉTSAI
⊕0.3M S of Vrak Kounoupia
   37°16'·96N 23°12'·04E WGS84

⊕16 0·1M W of Petrokáravo light
      37°17'·08N 23°04'·67E WGS84

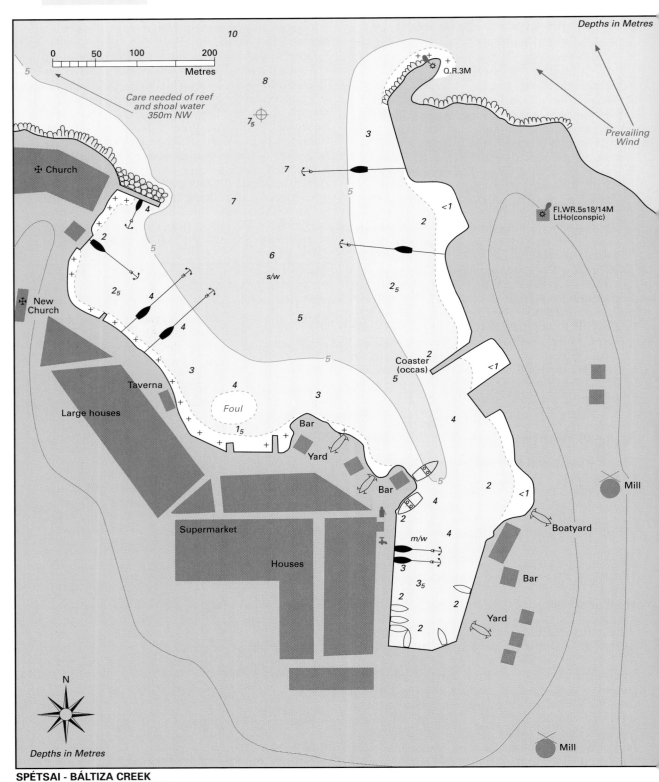

Depths in Metres

10

8

7·5

Care needed of reef
and shoal water
350m NW

Metres

0 50 100 200

5

✚ Church

4

2

✚ New
Church

2·5

4

7

6

s/w

4

4

5

Foul

3

4

3

Taverna

Large houses

1·5

Bar

Yard

Bar

Supermarket

Houses

m/w

Q.R.3M

3

7

5

<1

2

2·5

5

Prevailing
Wind

Fl.WR.5s18/14M
LtHo(conspic)

Coaster
(occas)

2

5

4

2

<1

2

<1

4

4

2

3

3·5

2

2

2

Mill

Boatyard

Bar

Yard

Mill

N

Depths in Metres

SPÉTSAI - BÁLTIZA CREEK
⊕37°15´·85N 23°09´·85E WGS84

many legends grew up about her exploits, especially her sexual appetite, that it is hard to separate fact from fiction.

With the war won, Spétsai declined and languished until the return of a native son at the turn of the century. Sotiros Anagyros was born on Spétsai, but left to make his fortune, which he did, returning a millionaire. Inspired no doubt by Pausanias' description of a pine-clad island (though we cannot be certain his description is of Spétsai), he embarked on a massive project to replant most of the island with Aleppo pine. He also built the first hotel on the island, the *Poseidonion*, and the exclusive boys' boarding school staffed by teachers from the British Council. Anagyros was generally not liked by the natives for his high-handed changes to the island, though his heart was in the right place. On his death the estate (most of the island) passed to a trust. Sadly, fire recently destroyed much of the pine forest on the western side of the island and the boys' school was closed down in 1984, though there is talk of turning it into a conference centre.

In the 1950s one of the teachers delegated to the school was the young John Fowles, and aficionados of his writing will know that Spétsai is the setting for *The Magus*. The House of the Magus or *Bourani* where much of the enigmatic action takes place is the large Villa Yasemia on the W coast above Áy Paraskevi. John Fowles has said that *The Magus* embodied more of what he was trying to get across than his later novels, and he later revised the ending in line with how he, rather than the publisher, thought it should be.

Getting around

Basically there is a single ring road around the island, with a few interconnecting tracks in the interior. If you want to do a circuit there are either bicycles or motorbikes for hire – the fit should take bicycles and boycott the motorbikes, which have only recently been allowed on the island, so that Anagyros doesn't get too restless in his grave. For getting back and forth from Báltiza and the Dápia, gharries can be used. There is an intermittent bus service running along the N side of the island, and a couple of taxis. I was here when the first bus was introduced to the island and to no one's surprise it mysteriously ended up at the bottom of the harbour. The town council were not amused and had every gharry driver on the island arrested. Not until they pledged not to interfere with the bus service were they released.

Today the island has a fair amount of tourism, though it is not overburdened by it. Despite the recent fire much of the island is still covered by pine, and there are pleasant walks or you can cycle around the island. The enlightened policies of Anagyros banned motor vehicles from Spétsai and though a few have crept in in recent years, most transport is still by horse-drawn gharry. There is something ineluctably old-fashioned and wonderful about clip-clopping back to the harbour after a good meal.

Báltiza Creek

The inlet on the NE end of the island where a yacht should make for, rather than the ferry port at the Dápia approximately halfway along the northern side of Spétsai.

Pilotage

Approach The houses of Spétsai spreading from the Dápia around and over Ák Fanári are easily identified. Closer in the lighthouse on Ák Fanári and several windmills (now converted to houses) will be seen. Care is needed of the reef running out from the coast for some 300m approximately halfway between Báltiza Creek and the Dápia. When proceeding along here shape the course in a semicircle from the Dápia to Báltiza or vice-versa. Care is also needed of the short reef and shoal water off the end of Ák Fanári. With the prevailing southeasterlies there is often a confused rolling swell at the entrance, though it is flat inside the outer harbour.

Mooring Anchor in the outer harbour with a long line ashore to the E or W side. There is room for half a dozen boats to go stern or bows-to the stubby mole on the NW end of the outer harbour, though care is needed of underwater ballasting. The bottom is mud, sand and weed, reasonable holding. The inner harbour is normally crowded in the summer, but you may find a berth double or triple-banked out. Crossed anchors are virtually unavoidable. Shelter in the outer harbour is reasonable, although strong southeasterlies cause a surge. Shelter in the inner harbour is excellent. The only proviso on shelter is that the water-taxis cause a lot of wash, which is not only uncomfortable but could damage a yacht berthed on the stubby mole in the outer harbour.

Báltiza Creek looking W towards the stubby pier at the entrance

Facilities

Services Water and fuel on the quay tucked just inside on the W side of the inner harbour.

Provisions Good shopping for provisions nearby or go into town.

Eating out Numerous tavernas nearby and in the town. A speciality of the island is *Psari Spetsiotiko*, 'Spétsai fish', which is a fish like bream cooked in a casserole with tomatoes, stock and cheese. Near the harbour *Haralambos* on the road around the outer harbour has good fish as does *Trehandiri* nearby. It is well worth the effort to grab a gharry and go to *Klimataria* inland at Analipsis – a wide variety of *mezes* are served and the best idea is just to ask for a selection and let everyone dip in.

Other PO. OTE. Banks. Hire motorbikes and bicycles. Ferries and hydrofoils to Piraeus and places along the way and S.

General

Báltiza is something of an oasis away from the bustle of the Dápia although at night some of the bars turn the volume up a bit too much. The various small yards around the harbour build and haul caïques which are reputed to be amongst the best in Greece. Tim Severin had his replica of an early Greek scouting ship built here for his voyages following the track of Jason and the Argonauts and the wanderings of Odysseus. It was built using traditional methods, starting with the outside planking and inserting the ribs afterwards, using wooden pegs joining the planks edge to edge, soaking the wood in the sea to bend it into shape, until finally a replica of a Homeric scouting galley was launched into Spétsai harbour. Don't believe the rumours about the epoxy tubes lying around during construction.

Above the harbour and lining the road into town are numerous *archontiki*, the rich merchants' houses like those on Ídhra, built during Spétsai's economic boom in the early 19th century. Above the outer harbour is the Monastery of Aghios Nikolaos, established as a monastery in the 17th century and now the cathedral of the island. The distinctive lattice work tower looks over a pebble mosaic square and the place has a wonderful peace to it, partly because the roads leading to it are stepped and inaccessible to gharries and motorbikes. Inside is a cell where Paul Bonaparte, brother of Napoleon, was kept pickled in a barrel of rum for five years after he was accidentally shot on board a British ship. The road towards the Dápia from the cathedral square is the pleasantest way to get into town, with views of the sea glimpsed across courtyards and lush gardens.

Dápia

The centre of town where the ferries and hydrofoils berth on the long pier. A yacht should not attempt to go on the ferry pier or use the small harbour at the root of the pier which is exclusively for caïque ferries and water-taxis. To the W of the ferry pier is a short mole where a yacht can go stern or bows-to if inclined to do so, alternatively you can anchor off to the W of the mole. Protection here is less than adequate and there is always a surge with the prevailing southeasterly wind making it extremely

uncomfortable, and on the mole you risk damaging your boat. The mole and the anchorage are of course open to the N.

In calm weather the Dápia is a possibility when Báltiza is full, although there can be a lot of wash from water taxis and the like. Just above the harbour bars and restaurants fairly hum, and you should find one to have a drink in at sunset to watch the hustle and bustle on the water and on the land around. Close W is the old private school founded by Anagyros which is now to be turned into a conference centre.

Órmos Zoyioryia

The large bay on the NW end of Spétsai. There is good protection from the prevailing southeasterly winds in the bay and in the summer it is popular. Anchor where convenient in 3–10m on sand, weed and some rocks, good holding. Some yachts take a long line ashore on the E side. If a northerly blows in the night the bay can become untenable. Taverna/bar ashore in the summer.

On the W side of the bay is Lazaretto Cove where there is better shelter. Anchor and take a long line ashore. Here there is better shelter from northerlies blowing down out of Argolikos Kólpos.

Zoyioryia is an attractive spot with a scrappy beach shaded by pine down to the water's edge. There used to be the wreck of a fairly large yacht here which, according to the locals, had belonged or been seized by the Commandant in charge of a German garrison on the island in the Second World War.

Petrokáravo

⊕**16** 0·1M W of Petrokaravo light
37°17'·08N 23°04'·67E WGS84

Off the NW tip of Spétsai is the rocky islet of Petrokáravo, connected intermittently with Spétsai by above and below-water rocks. The islet is unmistakable and crowned by a light structure which is also prominent. There is a deep-water passage (there are actually two but I will mention only one) between the reef lying approximately 300m off Ák Broumboulo and the rock just above water and a reef around it lying approximately 500m S of Petrokáravo. Care is needed and you should have someone up front conning you through. If in doubt go round Petrokáravo.

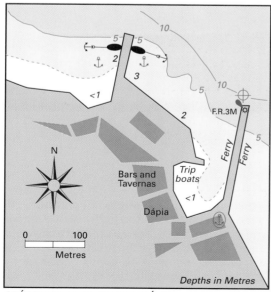

SPÉTSAI NEW HARBOUR (DÁPIA)
⊕37°16'·2N 23°09'·5E

Nisís Petrokárovo off the NW tip of Spétsai looking SE

Ormos Áy Paraskevi

A cove on the W side of Spétsai just over a mile from Ák Broumboulo. In calm weather or light southeasterlies a yacht can anchor off here, but with strong southerlies it becomes untenable when a swell is pushed in. On the southern slopes is the Villa Yasemia that figures so prominently in John Fowles' *The Magus*.

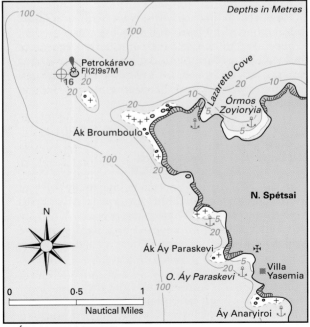

SPÉTSAI NW CORNER

⊕16 0·1M W of Petrokáravo light
37°17'·08N 23°04'·67E WGS84

Top Horse drawn gharry
Below Spetsiot caïque. Engraving on wood

Órmos Áy Anaryiroi

The bay immediately south of Órmos Áy Paraskevi. In calm weather or light southeasterlies a yacht can anchor off here, but like Paraskevi it becomes untenable in strong southerlies. It is popular in the summer with a lot of watersports activity, and consequently is well supplied with tavernas and bars ashore.

On the north side of the bay is Bekeris' Cave which, so the locals relate, was used by smugglers to hide from the authorities. It can be reached by a path along the beach, but formerly it was said that it could only be reached by swimming underwater and emerging into it that way.

Órmos Áy Petros

The long sandy bay on the S of Spétsai. In calm weather a yacht can anchor off here, but with the prevailing southerlies it becomes untenable. It is also popular in the summer.

Stenó Spetsopoula

The narrow channel between Spétsai and the small island of Spetsopoula lying off its SE tip. It is less than ½M across and bordered by shoal water and reefs. Care is needed of the reef and shoal water off the narrow headland off Spétsai and the reef (Ifalos Papakristou) lying to the E of it. The latter can be difficult to see with any chop on the water.

Nisís Spetsopoula

This small island is the very private property of Stavros Niarchos, one of the richest Greek shipowners (the late Onassis not excepted) around. It has a small harbour on the northern end which you can go and look at from a distance, but cannot enter. Ashore there is a large villa set in manicured parkland. Workers from Spétsai are ferried over daily.

You will often see one or other of Niarchos' yachts (i.e. little ships) moored off the island, though sadly the wonderful black three-masted schooner *Creole* has long been sold. This essay in grace and power, sculpted by Camper and Nicholson in 1927 (214ft long with 32,000sq ft of sail) was acquired by Niarchos when he was in the habit of competing with Onassis for status and media attention. It is said that the only question he asked before buying it was 'does anyone else have one like it' and when the answer was 'no' he bought it. In its later years under Niarchos' ownership it sat sadly neglected in Zéa Marina, slowly rotting until it was finally sold. It has now been restored for one of the large fashion houses in Italy and regularly competes in classic yacht regattas.

The distinctive lattice-work tower of Áy Nikólaos above the old harbour at Báltiza

IV. The Argolic Gulf and Eastern Peloponnese to Cape Malea

The Argolic Gulf to Cape Malea

This chapter covers Argolikós Kólpos, the gulf curving back northwards from Spétsai and Porto Kheli, and the eastern coast of the Peloponnese running from the head of the gulf right down to Ák Maléas. Compared to the Saronic islands it is comparatively little visited by yachts, with most of the Athens-based yachts stopping at Ídhra and Spétsai, at least for their weekend jaunts, and hardly ever venturing up into Argolikós Kólpos. There is no good reason for this as both the sailing and the scenery are magnificent, with the prevailing winds in the Argolic filling in like clockwork every day and dying down at night to peaceful evenings. Further down the eastern Peloponnese things are not so ordered wind-wise, but the imposing mountains bordering the coast and the magic and interest of the places along the way more than make up for this.

On the plain of Argos at the head of Argolikós Kólpos, and surveying some of the only flat land in this area, is Mycenae and the triangle of other ancient cities around it: Tiryns, Argos and Asine. In the period from 1500 to 1100BC the Myceneans conquered most of what is now Greece and spread into Asia Minor – indeed the Trojan War is seen as an attempt by the Myceneans to spread up into the Black Sea area. The Myceneans are the Acheaens of Homer's *Iliad* and *Odyssey* and Agamemnon was probably the King of Mycenae. The associations are powerful and vivid, though strangely the landscape is not, and it is the man-made artefacts rather than the setting which impresses one.

Around the eastern Peloponnese there are not many ancient associations at all, at least not on the coast. Sparta is so far inland from the coast it does not touch it, and the few ancient ruins on the coast appear to have been minor settlements.

It was in the Middle Ages that the architectural monument crowning Monemvasía was built, fortified by the Byzantines and added to by the Venetians and Turks. It exemplifies what this coast once was: an obstacle to the ancient Greeks, who preferred to tramp through its rugged interior, and a trade route for the Byzantines and Venetians who kept to the coast and spurned the interior (with the notable and unique exception of Mistra). At least for the yachtsman with a more handy vessel than his medieval cousins and an 'iron mainsail', the coast is not quite as forbidding as it must once have been – though it still pays to treat it with respect.

Useful waypoints
⊕16 0·1M W of Petrokáravo light
　　37°17'·08N 23°04'·67E WGS84
⊕17 1M W of Nisís Ípsili light
　　37°25'·9N 22°57'·1E
⊕18 1M W of Ák Megalí (Toló)
　　37°30'·6N 22°50'·3E
⊕19 0·25M E of Ák Yérakas
　　36°46'·17N 23°06'·90E WGS84
⊕20 0·25M E of Monemvasía headland
　　36°41'·52N 23°03'·89E WGS84
⊕21 0·75M S of Ák Maléas
　　36°25'·48N 23°11'·62E WGS84

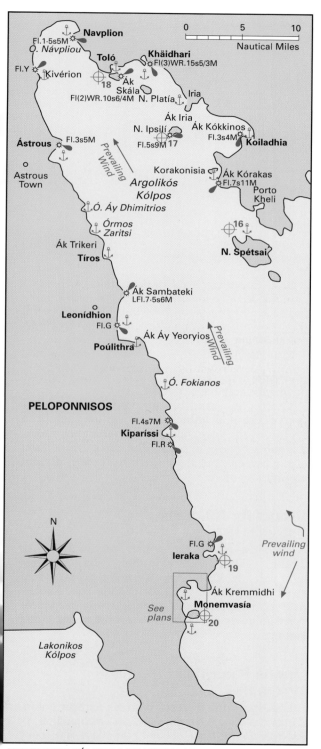

ARGOLIKOS KÓLPOS AND THE EASTERN PELOPONNESE

Quick reference guide

	Shelter	Mooring	Fuel	Water	Provisions	Eating out	Plan
Órmos Ververoudha	C	C	O	O	O	O	
Kórakonisia	B	C	O	O	O	O	•
Órmos Panayítsa	C	C	O	O	O	O	
Órmos Áy Spridhion	C	C	O	O	O	O	
Koiládhia	A	AC	B	B	C	C	•
Órmos Karterou	C	C	O	O	O	O	
Órmos Vourlia	C	C	O	O	O	O	
Iria Harbour	A	A	O	O	O	C	•
Khäidhari	A	AC	O	A	C	C	•
Toló	C	AC	B	A	B	A	•
Nisís Toló	C	C	O	O	O	C	
Órmos Karathona	B	C	O	O	O	C	
Navplion	B	AB	B	A	A	A	•
Míloi	O	C	B	B	C	B	
Kiverion	C	AC	B	B	C	C	•
Ástrous	A	A	B	A	B	B	•
Órmos Áy Dhimítrios	O	C	O	O	O	O	
Órmos Krionéri	C	C	O	O	O	O	
Órmos Zaritsi	O	C	O	O	O	O	
Tiros	B	AC	B	B	B	B	•
Leonídhion	B	A	B	A	C	C	•
Poúlithra	B	AC	O	B	C	C	•
Órmos Fokianos	C	C	O	O	O	O	•
Kiparíssi	B	ABC	O	B	C	C	•
Ieraka	A	AC	O	O	C	C	•
Órmos Kremmidhi	C	C	O	O	O	O	•
Órmos Palaio	C	C	O	O	O	O	•
Monemvasía	AC	ABC	B	A	B	B	•
Áy Fokas	O	C	O	O	O	O	

PREVAILING WINDS

In Argolikós Kólpos the normal summer wind blows up the gulf from the SE. This is a thermal sea breeze and it normally arrives like clockwork around midday and blows until the sun sets. It is normally Force 4–5, occasionally slightly more, and can be relied upon from June until September. Occasionally a strong *meltemi* will get over the hump of the Argolid and blow down the gulf, though rarely more than Force 4–5. In the morning there is usually a calm or a very light northerly land breeze. Occasionally a katabatic wind will blow down off the mountains at night from the NW and will sometimes get up to a Force 7 or so. Ástrous appears to be the worst spot for this, but fortunately it doesn't happen often.

From Kiparíssi down to Ák Maléas there may be a sea breeze from the E to SE though normally it is less than Force 4–5. Alternatively the *meltemi* may blow from the NE and though it is normally Force 4–5, at times in summer it will get up to Force 7. With a strong *meltemi* big seas are pushed onto the coast and there can be severe gusts around Palaio Monemvasía.

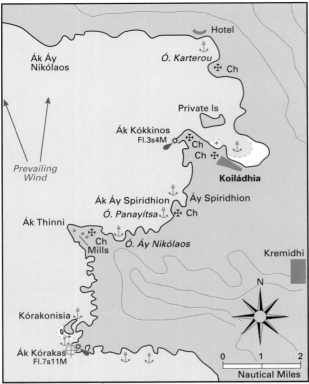

ÁK KÓRAKAS TO ÁK ÁY NIKÓLAOS
⊕37°21'·2N 23°04'·1E

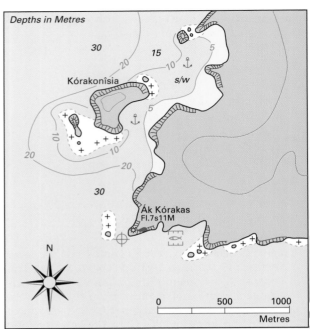

KÓRAKONISIA
⊕37°21'·2N 23°04'·1E

Órmos Ververoudha

37°20'·2N 23°07'·4E

The large bay backing onto the fish lagoon at Porto Kheli. A yacht can anchor in the southern end in 5–10m on mud and weed. In light southeasterlies the shelter is adequate, but with strong southeasterlies a swell is pushed around the corner into the bay. Northerlies also send a swell in.

On the northern side of the bay and along to Ák Kórakas are several coves which can be used in calm weather. Care is needed of reefs and rocks bordering the coast in places.

Kórakonisia

Immediately round the corner from Ák Kórakas is the islet of Kórakonisia sheltering a cove behind it. Entry can be made from either the SW or the NW, taking care of the numerous rocks and reefs around the islet and the coast. Good shelter from the prevailing southeasterlies and it is possible to

overnight here, though if a strong northerly blows down you may have to leave.

There is translucent turquoise water everywhere and although the solitude has been broken by the large villa built on the slopes above, it is still a wonderful place. The name means 'islet of the ravens', but there seem to be few of them around any more.

Órmos Áy Nikólaos

37°23'·4N 23°05'·0E

A bay just round the corner to the E of Ák Thinni. There is reasonable shelter here, although the SE afternoon breeze pushes some swell round the corner and into the bay. Anchor in 8–12m on sand and weed. Care is needed of permanent moorings here. A taverna opens in the summer.

Órmos Panayítsa

37°23'·5N 23°06'·0E

A large bay immediately SW of Ák Áy Spiridhion. There is a church on the shore and a chapel on Ák Áy Spiridhion. Care needs to be taken of a rocky shelf fringing the beach. Anchor in 5–10m on sand with some rock. Good shelter from the prevailing southeasterlies, although a swell sometimes creeps around the cape into the bay. Open to the N. Clear water and a beach ashore.

Órmos Áy Spiridhion

37°24'·1N 23°06'·6E

The bay immediately NE of Ák Áy Spiridhion. Anchor in 4–8m on sand and some rock. Better shelter than Panayítsa.

Koiládhia

An anchorage and fishing harbour tucked into the bay around Ák Kókkinos (Red Cape).

Pilotage

Approach A chapel on Ák Kókkinos and the large cathedral in the village are conspicuous. The entrance between Ák Kókkinos and Nisís Koiládhia will not be seen from the SW until you are close to it. Care needs to be taken of the reef running out from Ák Kókkinos and the final approach should be from the NW. In the

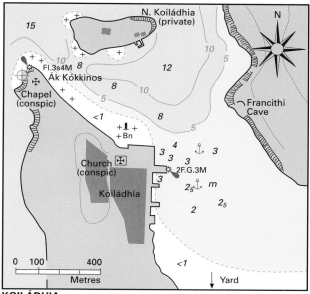

KOILÁDHIA
⊕37°25'.4N 23°06'·8E

channel under Nisís Koiládhia care is needed of the reef and shoal water fringing the coast with a reef marked by a stumpy beacon just NW of the quay. Entrance can also be made between the E side of Nisís Koiládhia and the coast.

Mooring Anchor off in 2·5–4m where convenient. Care needs to be taken of numerous permanent moorings in the bay. The bottom is sticky mud, excellent holding. Good all-round shelter. It is possible to go stern or bows-to or alongside one of the piers off the village, but these are usually occupied by fishing boats and the prevailing southeasterly tends to set up a slight chop across the bay making it uncomfortable until the wind drops at night.

Facilities

Services Water on the quay and a mini-tanker can deliver fuel by arrangement.

Provisions Most provisions can be found in the village. Ice available.

Eating out Several tavernas on the waterfront which may have fresh fish off the boats.

Other PO. OTE. Taxi.

General

The village would win no architectural prizes for its 'pour-and-fill' buildings, but it more than makes up for this with friendly inhabitants and a proper working atmosphere serving the large

Koiládhia looking NW towards the village and conspicuous church

Koiládhia quay

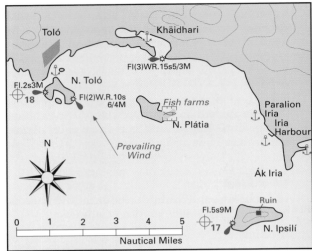

ÁK. IRIA TO TOLÓ

⊕17 1M W of Nisís Ípsili light 37°25'·9N 22°57'·1E
⊕18 1M W of Ák Megalí (Toló) 37°30'·6N 22°50'·3E

fishing fleet based here (caïques are built ashore) and the agricultural hinterland. It is unlikely to attract tourists as the water is muddied by silt whipped up from the bottom, so it is not the translucent blue expected in the Mediterranean. It has attracted a Greek shipping millionaire who owns the islet of Koiládhia in the entrance. A large house has been built on the islet and there is a small harbour where the owner berths his motor yacht – needless to say you cannot berth here unless invited.

Pausanias mentions an ancient city called Mazes in the vicinity which was probably here at Koiládhia, although nothing now remains. In fact the area has much older associations in the Francithi Cave prominent in the cliffs opposite the village where numerous prehistoric remains have been found. Apart from the bones of various animals, the skeleton of a stone-age man from the Mesolithic period was found, the oldest inhabitant of Greece so far discovered and a find important for the piecing together of early Neolithic life in Europe.

Órmos Karterou

37°26'·8N 23°07'·3E

The bay just above Órmos Koiládhia. A hotel is prominent on the slopes. In calm weather or light southeasterlies a yacht can anchor off the beach, but with fresh southeasterlies a swell is pushed into the bay.

Órmos Vourlia

A large bay on the mainland coast opposite Nisís Ípsili. In calm weather a yacht can anchor off in here although it is everywhere very deep. On the W side there is an inlet just NE of Ák Iria which looks worth exploring. On the W side NE of this inlet there are several fish farms.

Nisís Ípsili

⊕17 1M W of Nisís Ipsili light 37°25'·9N 22°57'·1E

A high, bold, dome-shaped island dropping straight down into the sea. There are considerable depths everywhere around it, with nowhere to anchor off. The inscription 'ruin' on the old Admiralty chart looks intriguing.

Iria Harbour

Just over 1M NNW of Ák Iria is a small fishing harbour. The houses of Paralion Iria will be seen and closer in the breakwater sheltering the

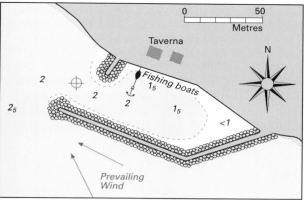

RIA HARBOUR
⊕37°28'·7N 23°00'·0E

Nisís Platía

0·25M E of E end of N. Platía
37°29'·6N 22°56'·6E

The low island lying off Órmos Valtou. It used to be possible to anchor off the N side of the island, but a fish farm now obstructs most of this anchorage and does little for the former charm and solitude of the place.

Khaïdhari (Vivari)

The deep slit of an inlet on the coast opposite Nisís Platía.

Pilotage

Approach The entrance is difficult to make out from the distance, although the cleft in the cliffs can be identified with a fair degree of certainty. Closer in the ruins of a small fort on the western side of the entrance and the light structure and a small stone hut on the eastern side will be seen. The entrance is deep and clear of dangers and entry is straightforward. Once into the bay care is needed of the fish farms on the S side.

Mooring Anchor off in 6–12m, taking care of the permanent moorings. Alternatively go stern or bows-to either side of the outer end of the pier on the N side. There are 3m depths at the end of the pier and 1·5–2·5m depths on the outer

harbour. An L-shaped breakwater with a snub breakwater at the entrance faces NW. There are 2–3m depths at the entrance and 1–2m depths inside. Care is needed of floating mooring lines used by the fishing boats. A small yacht can just squeeze in and berth with a long line to the quay near the entrance. Shelter is reasonable from the prevailing southeasterly wind. Ashore there is a taverna/bar.

In calm weather it is possible to anchor off the beach here, but with a fresh southeasterly a swell is pushed down onto the anchorage and it is most uncomfortable and may become untenable.

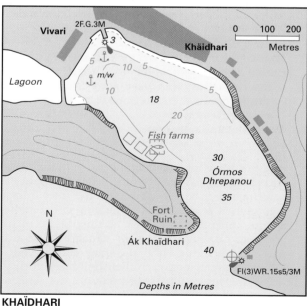

KHAÏDHARI
⊕37°31'·4N 22°56'·1E

Khaïdhari looking E to the pier

Khaïdhari

have been a useful one for a fleet anchorage and in 1714 built the little fort to guard the entrance. They also built shipyards at the head of the bay to haul and repair their naval fleet. One year later Pasha Khodja arrived with a fleet of 150 ships and destroyed the fort and seven ships hauled out in the yard. This push by the Turks was an attempt to drive the Venetians out of the Peloponnese for good, although they still retained other footholds in Greece.

Toló

A resort built behind the long sandy beach W of Khaïdhari and partially sheltered by Nisís Toló.

Pilotage

Approach From the E and W the buildings of Toló are easily identified, but from the S Nisís Toló obscures the view. However, the general location is easy enough to determine from the relative position of Nisís Platía. Closer in the channel between Nisís Toló and the village will be seen. Ifalos Toló, a reef lying just under a mile SSE of the SE of Ák Skála on Nisís Toló has a least depth over it of 3·7m, so will only be of concern to deep draught craft.

Mooring Anchor off the beach in 5–10m. Care is needed of the numerous permanent moorings on the bottom. The bottom is sand, good holding. The shelter here is better than it looks, as the prevailing southeasterlies do not blow home and although some swell is pushed in, it dies down at night. The small harbour is crowded with local boats and generally they do not like visiting yachts in here. You may find a berth on the outside of the mole or the quay on the S side of the harbour.

Facilities

Services Water on the quay in the harbour, but it is difficult to find someone to turn it on. Fuel in the town.

Provisions Good shopping for all provisions in the town.

Eating out Numerous tavernas on the waterfront and in the town, but prepare to be disappointed by the poor-quality tourist fare served up.

Other PO. OTE. Banks. Hire motorbikes and cars. Intermittent bus to Navplion. Hydrofoil to Piraeus.

end on either side. Care is needed as there is underwater ballasting along the sides of the pier and it may be best to go bows-to. The bottom is mud and weed, good holding. Shelter is all-round in the inlet, but a slight swell penetrates with the prevailing southeasterlies which can make the berths on the quay slightly uncomfortable until the wind drops.

Facilities

Services Water on the pier.

Provisions Limited provisions in the village.

Eating out Tavernas on the waterfront. The tavernas here often have good fresh fish. Try the *Delfini* or the easternmost taverna perched over the water.

Other Metered telephone. Taxi.

General

The fjord-like inlet is magnificent, with high land and cliffs rising sheer from the water except at the head, where a barrage separates the inlet from a lagoon used as a fish farm. The human habitation is not magnificent, with uninspired square concrete buildings of recent vintage. I like this place so much that I wish the locals had expended a bit more imagination in their building efforts.

On the western entrance point are the remains of a small fort which is probably of Venetian origin. The Venetians thought the harbour would

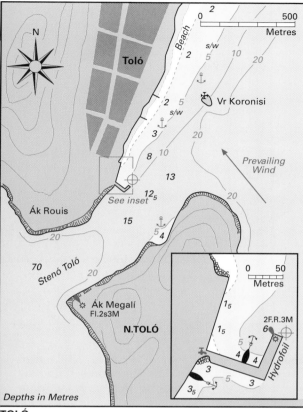

TOLÓ
⊕37°30′·9N 22°51′·5W

Depths in Metres

General

What was once a small fishing village has continued to expand as a tourist resort on the strength of the fine sandy beach stretching around the coast. Hotels and condominiums now line the beach, catering for package holidays. It is not my sort of place, too mercenary by half, and there is little to keep the visitor here apart from the plethora of tavernas.

Just north of Toló is ancient Asine which was an important city early on, but declined after it was sacked by the Argives. The inhabitants had sided with Sparta and after their allies left, the Argives attacked it. When it was apparent that all was lost, the Asinians packed up their women and children and chattels into their boats and sailed off to settle in the Gulf of Messinia in the Peloponnese closer to the Spartans. You can identify the coastal site as you sail up the coast to Navplion and really this is the best way to see it as there is little left of the ancient city and only the dedicated should go by land.

The island lying off Toló has several anchorages which can be used in calm weather.

Channel Anchorage Anchor off in the bight at the island end of Stenó Toló. Some protection from southeasterlies.

Nisís Dhaskalia With care a yacht can anchor in the bay under Nisís Dhaskalia, the islet on the south side of Nisís Toló. The most convenient depths will be found off the NE side of the islet as the bay proper on Nisís Toló is very deep. A swell is pushed in by the prevailing southeasterlies.

Órmos Karathona

37°32′·4N 22°49′·0E

The large bay on the N side of Ák Khondros. A breakwater has been built out from the southern entrance point nearly to the tiny islet in the bay. Anchor in 2·5–6m on the S side of the bay. The bottom is sand, mud and weed, good holding. Good shelter from the prevailing winds and under the breakwater there is nearly all-round shelter.

Ashore several tavernas open in the summer. The bay is an attractive place with steep rocky slopes above the tree-lined beach and is popular with Navplionites in the summer.

Toló looking SW to Nisís Toló

Navplion

The largest town in the gulf and the commercial harbour for the hinterland.

Pilotage

Approach The town, hidden by a low ridge, will not be seen from the S. A chapel on Ák Khondros is easily identified, and a large hotel on the saddle of the ridge is conspicuous. The fortress of Palamidhi is also conspicuous, though not as much as might be expected because the honey-coloured stone blends with the rock of the mountain. Closer in Nisís Bourtzi with a fort on it and the light structure on Akronavplia are easily identified. Once up to Akronavplia things are straightforward. Care is needed of occasional cargo ships entering and leaving.

Mooring Go alongside or stern or bows-to the E quay or on the W side of the stubby pier. The bottom is sticky mud and good holding. Good shelter from the prevailing southeasterlies, although dust off the quay is blown across your decks. Sometimes at night a northwesterly will blow, though it is normally more uncomfortable than dangerous. The E quay is very smelly with sewage emptying into the

Navplion quay looking NW to Nisís Bourtzi

harbour and berths on the W side of the pier are only marginally less so.

Facilities

Services Water on the quay when you can find the waterman. Fuel can be delivered by mini-tanker.

Provisions Good shopping for all provisions in the town, although most shops are off to the E.

Eating out Numerous tavernas of all types and numerous bars along the waterfront. Prices in Navplion are on a par with those in Athens and the reason for this may be that most of them are summer-only affairs run by Athenians. Stroll along the waterfront in the harbour looking at menus and also wander along the high street (Staikopoulou).

Other PO. OTE. Banks. Doctors. Dentist. Hire motorbikes and cars. Bus to Athens. Hydrofoil to Piraeus and stops along the way.

General

It is a great pity the harbour is so smelly. The old town is an enchanting place, with a mixture of Venetian, Turkish and neo-classical buildings from the early 19th century when Navplion was briefly capital of the newly liberated Greece. Buildings lean out at odd angles, wooden Turkish balconies perch over the streets, and then suddenly you come into the central square with the old Venetian arsenal, now a museum, looming over the square at the western end of

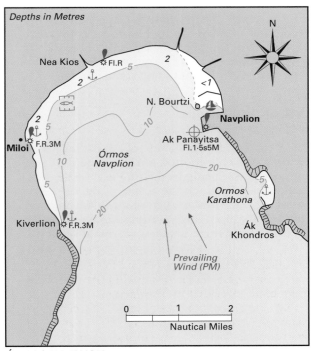

ÓRMOS NAVPLION
⊕37°33'·8N 22°47'·6E

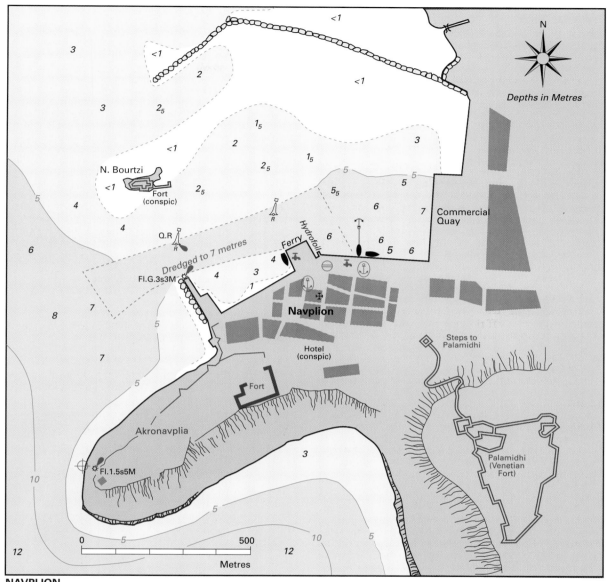

N

Depths in Metres

N. Bourtzi

Fort
(conspic)

Q.R

Dredged to 7 metres

Fl.G.3s3M

Ferry

Hydrofoil

Commercial
Quay

Navplion

Hotel
(conspic)

Steps to
Palamidhi

Fort

Akronavplia

Fl.1.5s5M

Palamidhi
(Venetian
Fort)

0   500

Metres

NAVPLION
⊕37°33'·8N 22°47'·6E

town. Bougainvillaea and clematis grow everywhere, concealing whole walls and covering ruins. An old Turkish fountain still runs; a Venetian lion grins inanely. Navplion has charm, and lots of it.

The town was quite probably a Mycenean naval base, though nothing remains of this. Its mythopaeic founder was Nauplius, a son of Poseidon. His son Palamedes gives his name to the steep rock behind the town and also to the

Venetian citadel on top. Palamedes is credited with a whole range of inventions, including the lighthouse, most of the Greek alphabet, weights and measures and the games of chess and dice – a busy man or god. The original Greek town was conquered and razed by Damocrates of Argos in 676BC and never recovered. It doesn't enter the history books again until AD589 when it is recorded as part of Byzantine territory. Its fortunes were to be an up-and-down affair

Mycenae

This is the city and the site that has given its name to the warrior race that subjugated much of Greece and provided the material for Homer's Acheaens. It is probably (and if not it should be) the city of Agamemnon, and the gold death mask found in a burial tomb is popularly said to be his. Perhaps from here the heroics and the pathos of the Trojan War captured in the *Iliad* and the *Odyssey* were set in motion, when Agamemnon declared his intention to avenge the wrongs of Paris and bring Helen back from Troy. And underneath all this is the brooding horror of the tragedy of the House of Atreus.

The tale begins with Tantalus, son of Zeus, who for some benighted reason served up his son Pelops as a gift for the gods. Not surprisingly they were horrified, and reconstituted poor Pelops complete with an ivory shoulder because the goddess Demeter had inadvertently eaten it. Pelops settled in the `island' now named after him, the Peloponnese (Peloponnisos). Tantalus was sent off to Hades where he was forever to be tormented by hunger and thirst.

The descendants of Tantalus were blighted with a curse for his foul deed. Pelops had two sons, Thyestes and Atreus, and when Thyestes seduced Atreus' wife he had the children of Thyestes killed and cut up to be served to their father for dinner. It doesn't end here. The progeny of Atreus included Agamemnon and Menelaus, husband of Helen (later of Troy). To appease the gods and help the campaign, Agamemnon sacrificed his daughter Iphigenia. While he was away Agamemnon's wife Clytemnestra had taken a lover and along the way Agamemnon had picked up a lover of his own, Cassandra. Cassandra predicted horror and blood, and so it was when Clytemnestra killed her husband Agamemnon on his return from the Trojan Wars.

This may seem convoluted, but after all I have tried to condense what Aeschylus packed into his dramatic trilogy, the *Oresteia*. Why it is called the *Oresteia* will become clear when you realise the horror is not over. Orestes was Clytemnestra's son and, urged on by his sister Elektra, he returned to kill his mother to avenge his father's death. He performed the deed unwillingly and afterwards suffered such remorse that the goddess Athena forgave him and lifted the curse from the House of Atreus. I hope I can be forgiven for dwelling on this story, (which I find fascinating and perhaps indicative of the bloody and back-stabbing era of Mycenae), but will not dwell on the site itself. The plan is self explanatory and there are detailed texts available to explain the successive layers of building and rebuilding. Like Tiryns it is the scale of the building, the walls up to 8 metres thick and the blocks of stone weighing up to 20 tons, that are impressive. There are the tombs where Schliemann found the remains and numerous gold objects including the mask of Agamemnon, the site of the palace, tunnels and storage rooms.

The city reached its zenith in the 13th century BC and declined abruptly with the Mycenean empire in the 11th century BC for no apparent good reason. Perhaps plague or some other disease, an unknown warrior race (perhaps the mysterious `sea people' who were ravaging the Aegean around this time), a natural disaster like a massive earthquake, or perhaps just a decline in the leadership and fortunes of the warrior race suddenly terminated an empire.

In the museum in Navplion (in the old Venetian arsenal in the square) there is a Mycenean suit of armour and this more than anything else has shaped my ideas of what a Mycenean looked like. The armour and the boar's tusk helmet look like something out of my boyhood books with illustrations of the Saracens, and seems strangely contemporary for the 2nd millennium BC. Add to the images the armour conjures up the thin cruel lips and hard features of Agamemnon's death mask, and add to that the horrors of the curse on the House of Atreus, and it can all send a chill down your spine that needs a brief spell sitting on the sun-warmed rock of Mycenae to dispel. It is evidently a common emotion once acquainted with the tragedy of the House of Atreus and Mycenae.

`Orestes, running out of the back door
Felt the wall's shadow lighten on his back,
Where blood and milk, mingled, seeped on the floor.
He looked one last time on that town the sack
Of Troy made famous, then forgot, and ran.
Free in the hills, no one could fetch him back.
`I am alone, free from the ties of men:
Odysseus drifts among the bladder wrack,
And swift Achilles lies as still as stone.
Behind the summit now my trodden track.'
That year the blood-red poppies did not bloom.
The land seemed dead, the rocks of Lethe cracked.
And I was glad to see the Furies come'.
At Mycenae Richard Stoneman

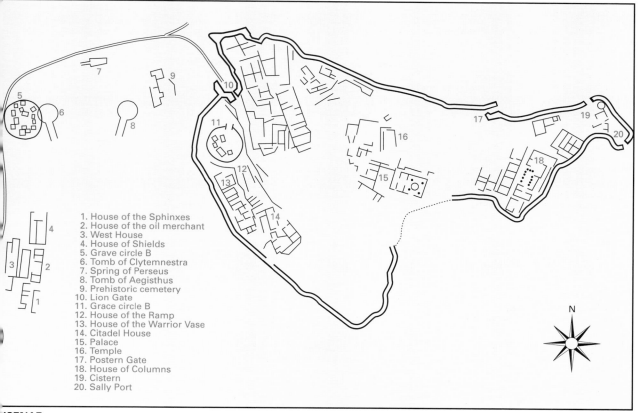

1. House of the Sphinxes
2. House of the oil merchant
3. West House
4. House of Shields
5. Grave circle B
6. Tomb of Clytemnestra
7. Spring of Perseus
8. Tomb of Aegisthus
9. Prehistoric cemetery
10. Lion Gate
11. Grace circle B
12. House of the Ramp
13. House of the Warrior Vase
14. Citadel House
15. Palace
16. Temple
17. Postern Gate
18. House of Columns
19. Cistern
20. Sally Port

YCENAE

Opposite The Lion Gate at Mycenae

thereafter, with successive occupations by the Franks, Venetians, Turks, and finally the Greeks in 1822.

The fortress on top of Palamidhi was built by the Venetians in three years from 1711 to 1714. Despite the thick walls, the successive defensive walls, and the impregnable-looking position on its sheer rocky site, the fort fell after only eight days' siege by the Turks just one year after it was completed. The fortress served the Turks little better. The Turkish garrison in the fort surrendered it without a shot being fired when the doughty Boubalina sailed up here and threatened the Turkish fleet with fireships – one can only imagine this woman put the fear of Allah into the Turks.

It can be reached by 857 steps from the town (take a bottle of water) or the indolent can be driven up to the summit via the new road to the

E. The views from the top, as you might expect, are stupendous. In places those who suffer from vertigo will be troubled when walking around the summit.

The other fortress at Navplion, somewhat overshadowed by the bulk of Palamidhi, is on the steep-sided headland sticking out to the W from Navplion town. Akronavplia was the site of the ancient Greek acropolis and of subsequent castles built by the Byzantines, added to by the Franks and again by the Venetians, who built the evocatively named Castel del Toro.

Navplion was the capital of Greece from 1828 to 1834 until Otto of Bavaria moved the capital to Athens. Ioannou Capodistriou, the first president of Greece, installed himself at Navplion and bestowed some of the fine neoclassical buildings on the city. He had to cope with much dissent and rebellion amongst the various guerrilla chiefs

Tiryns

Although not as well known as Mycenae, the ruins of Tiryns are impressive and worth a look at. The walled city sits on a low rocky outcrop with inner passages and storerooms. Originally it sat at the edge of the sea, but the geological tilting of the land and the silting up of the plain means it now sits on the large flat plain at the head of the Argolic Gulf.

Pausanias compared the site with the Egyptian pyramids and certainly the size of the building materials ensured much of it could not be carted away for other buildings. Some of the rocks used in the construction weigh as much as 30 tons and some of the walls are nearly 10 metres thick – it makes the construction at Mycenae look flimsy by comparison.

The city is said to have been founded by Proitos of Argos who enlisted the Cyclops of Lykia to help him build it. Amongst the descendants of Proitis was Eurystheseus who is credited with giving Heracles (Hercules) his twelve labours, and probably also for the popularity of the cult of Heracles which swept the Argolid and persisted for centuries. Heracles, to my mind, has always been the archetypal `kick-sand-in-your-face' sort of strongman, capable of astounding feats of strength but a little slow on the uptake and subject to all the duplicity going – so much so you have to sympathise with him in the end.

Tiryns was inhabited from around the third millennium BC right up to the Mycenean period when further walls were added and a palace built. It was still inhabited after the demise of the Myceneans and around the 8th century BC a Temple to Hera was built. The city was subjugated by the Argives in 486BC and the site was effectively abandoned.

who had fought the war and he was finally to fail in his diplomacy and pay with his life. In 1831 Capodistriou was assassinated in front of the Church of Áyios Spiridon by rebels from the Mani led by Kolkotronas. Kolkotronas was later imprisoned in Palamidhi. Otto of Bavaria was chosen as his successor and in 1834 moved the capital to Athens. Some idea of the anarchy which prevailed within the infant democracy is given in Julia Ward Howe's account from the mid 19th century.

'The evening of our sojourn in Argos saw an excitement much like that which blocked the street at Nauplia. The occasion was the same, the bringing home of a brigand's head; but this the very head and fount of all the brigands, Kitzos himself, upon whose very head had been set a price of several thousand drachmas. Our veteran with difficulty obtained a view of the same, and reported accordingly. The robber chief of Edmond About's 'Hadji Stauros', had been shot while sighting at his gun. He had fallen with one eye shut and one open, and in this form of feature his dissevered head remained. The soldier who was its fortunate captor carried it concealed in a bag, with its long elf-locks lying loose about it. He showed it with some unwillingness, fearing to have the prize wrested from him. It was, however, taken on board of our steamer, and carried to Athens, there to be identified and buried.'

Julia Ward Howe *From the Oak to the Olive* 1868

With the death of the brigand Julia Howe was able to proceed on to Mycenae, a journey which had been advised against while the brigand Kitzos was in the area. Today the only brigands around are confined to the bars in Navplion.

Navplion is the logical place to make excursions to Tiryns and Mycenae. Coach trips with a guide are organised in the summer, or you can take a taxi or hire a car or a motorbike. Do remember to take stout footwear, a hat, and a bottle of water – it gets warm at Mycenae in the height of summer.

Néa Kios

37°35'·0N 22°45'·0E

A small resort at the head of the gulf. In calm weather you can anchor off here, but the normal southeasterly sea breeze blows straight onto here and it is best not to stay. Local craft moor up in the shallow river above the bridge.

Míloi

37°33'·4N 22°43'·2E

A small resort in the NW corner of the gulf. In calm weather you can anchor off the S side of the stubby mole here, but when the southeasterly sea breeze gets up you will have to leave. Tavernas ashore with good fresh fish.

Míloi sits on the site of ancient Lerna where there was a cult celebrating the mysteries in honour of Demeter, and it is also where Heracles (Hercules) slew the many-headed Hydra. The site was occupied from as early as the 4th millennium BC and only declined with the Myceneans in 1100BC making it an important ancient site predating the Classical period.

Kiverion

A small village on the W side of Argolikós Kólpos approximately 3½M SW of Navplion. The cluster of houses of the village are easily identified. In the morning calm or in light southeasterlies you can anchor tucked into the bight off the village. There is a short mole here

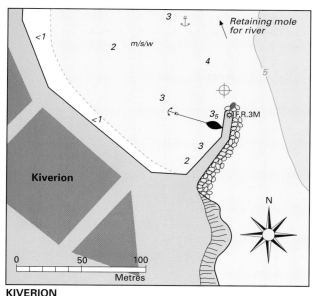

KIVERION
⊕37°31′·4N 22°044′·1E

and if you can find a berth under the outer end it affords reasonable shelter from the prevailing southeasterlies. Alternatively, if anchored, it's a good place for a lunch stop until the normal southeasterlies get up.

Tavernas and provisions ashore.

Ástrous

A fishing village and small resort tucked under Ák Ástrous, almost directly across the gulf from Toló.

Pilotage

Approach From the N and S the headland under which the harbour is tucked looks like an island. From the N and E the houses of the village will not be seen until around the headland. From the S the houses of the village and a few hotels around the beach are easily identified. The castle on the summit of the headland will be seen when closer in and the outer breakwater is easily identified. Entry is straightforward once up to the breakwater.

Mooring Go stern or bows-to the S mole where convenient. It is better to go bows-to as underwater ballasting extends out a short distance in most places, though it is generally deeper than it looks close to the quay. Care is also needed of the floating lines of permanent moorings. The bottom is mud and weed,

generally good holding, although there seem to be patches where the holding is indifferent. Good shelter from the prevailing wind and nearly all-round shelter. Occasionally at night a katabatic wind may blow off the mountains from the WNW, sometimes up to Force 7 or so, though generally less, so ensure your anchor is well in. No swell of any consequence is generated by this wind, but the force of the wind hits yachts beam-on on the S quay. A yacht should not go on the N quay which is used by a tripper boat and the hydrofoil.

Facilities

Services Water on the quay – the waterman will call round. Fuel can be delivered by mini-tanker.

Provisions Most provisions can be found in the village.

Eating out A good choice of tavernas. The *Elates*, the first taverna encountered when walking into the village, is a bit pompous, but has better than average food at reasonable prices. The *Bakxos* on the beach in the NW corner of the harbour serves honest Greek fare with a superb view. In the village several of the tavernas often have good fresh fish. Bars on the waterfront looking out over the harbour.

Other PO. OTE. Bank. Taxi. Hydrofoil to Piraeus.

Ástrous looking SW from the castle

127

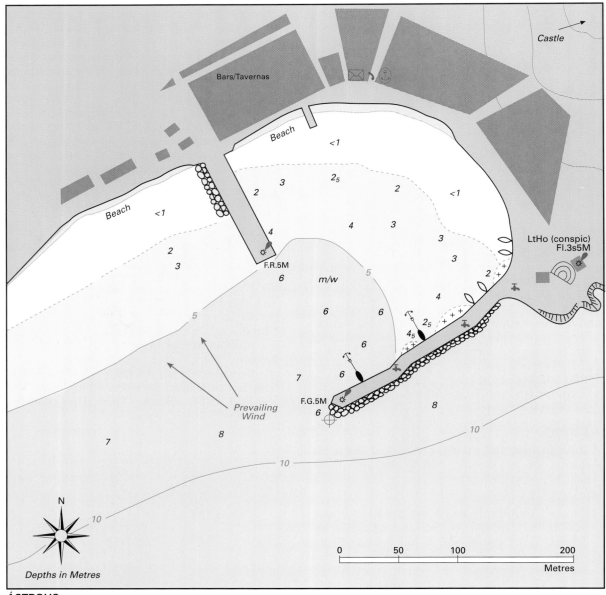

ÁSTROUS
⊕37°24´·9N 22°46´·1E

General

Ástrous is one of my favourite places in the gulf. Properly it is Paralion Ástrous, and Ástrous itself is the village 4 kilometres inland. It has enough tourism for a couple of good tavernas and bars, the harbour is clean enough to swim in (or you can pop over the breakwater to a small shingle beach) and the harbour offers more than adequate shelter in the summer. It is just a pleasant place to be, with a visit to the castle or right into Ástrous proper if you fancy a walk through agricultural land and orchards. There is nothing you 'should' see, but plenty of lazing around to be done.

The castle above the village does not entail a lot of energy to get to and is a pleasant ruin to wander around. Most of what remains was built by the Venetians, though originally an acropolis stood on the headland, possibly further to the NE of the castle. Ástrous was established around the 13th century BC and probably takes its name from the word *asti* (city) which was then corrupted to Astri and so Astros or Ástrous. In the ruins of Astri a caryatid was discovered, similar to those that adorned the Erechtheion in Athens but unique because it is the only caryatid discovered with its head intact. The Venetian castle is nothing exceptional, more homely than defensive, and local tales tell of a secret tunnel leading down to the cave by the sea, though I have never discovered any traces of it.

Órmos Ástrous

In calm weather and light southeasterlies you can anchor off the long sandy beach in the SW corner. Anchor in 5–8m on sand and weed. Here there is some protection from the prevailing southeasterlies although a swell tends to roll in. Good sandy beach.

Áy Andreas

37°22'·4N 22°47'·2E

A hamlet 3M S of Ástrous. There is a tiny fishing harbour here, really too small and shallow for even small yachts. The village of Áy Andreas inland has been identified as ancient Brasiae, though it was more likely to be at Leonídhion.

Órmos Áy Dhimitrios

37°20'·0N 22°48'·5E

A bay 3M S of Áy Andreas under Ák Áy Dhimitrios. In calm weather a yacht can anchor in here for a good lunch stop under steep slopes.

The slopes nearby have been subdivided into a development called the 'Arcadian Village', though it bears about as much resemblance to any Arcadian dream as do the suburbs of Athens.

Órmos Krionéri

37°18'·8N 22°49'·6E

Another bay about 1M S of Áy Dhimitrios suitable in calm weather. Anchor on the S side of the bay.

Órmos Zaritsi

37°16'·8N 22°50'·7E

Another large bay 2M S of Krionéri and suitable in calm weather. Anchor off the beach.

Tíros

Pilotage

Approach Three windmills on the ridge SE of the harbour are conspicuous. Closer in the mole shows up well against the beach. From the N care is needed of the rock off the N entrance point of the bay.

Mooring Go stern or bows-to the mole leaving the outer end free for the hydrofoil (see *Note*). Care is needed of a rocky patch about one third of the way up from the root of the mole. The resident fishing boats have laid moorings so care is needed not to foul them. Good shelter from the prevailing wind. With strong north to north-easterlies the harbour would be uncomfortable and may be untenable. In calm weather you can also go onto the short jetty on the beach or anchor off.

Note The locals say that the hydrofoil only runs in July and August so that the outer end of the mole can be used outside high season. However, schedules may change so seek local advice.

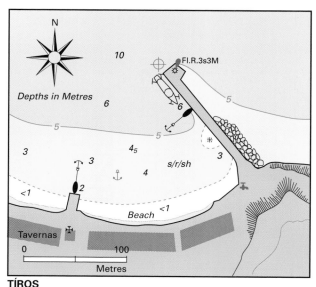

TÍROS
⊕37°14'·8N 22°52'·1E

Facilities

Services Water in the village. Fuel can be delivered to the harbour.

Provisions Most provisions can be found in the village. Ice available.

Eating out Lots of tavernas on the waterfront.

Other Bank. PO. Taxis. Hydrofoil to Piraeus and points along the way in July and August.

General

Tíros used to be a sleepy little village until in recent years it mushroomed into a sizeable resort. There are restaurants and bars all along the beach and the place fairly hums with the sound of cash registers ringing up the season's profits. There are 'zimmer frei' and 'rooms for rent' signs everywhere which is surprising as the beach is not all that great. At least at the harbour end you are in the

best part of Tíros. It is also a convenient place to get a taxi to visit the Monastery at Elona if you do not want to continue on down to Leonídhion.

Leonídhion

A small harbour at the end of the long sandy beach after Ák Sambateki.

Pilotage

Approach The harbour is difficult to identify from the distance as the beach continues along part of the breakwater and the breakwater itself blends into the rock behind. Head for the general vicinity, and closer in a windmill on the beach (converted to a house) and a white church will be seen. Closer still the buildings of the hamlet (all stone and brown tiles that blend

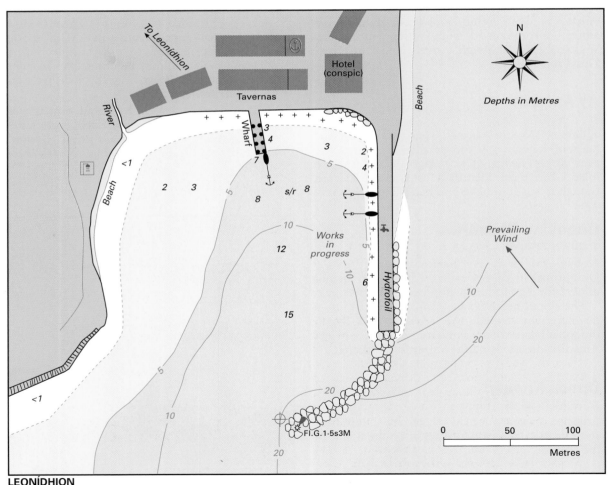

LEONÍDHION
⊕37°08′·7N 22°53′·6E

Facilities

Services Water on the quay.

Provisions Some provisions can be found. Good shopping in Leonídhion proper inland.

Eating out Several tavernas on the waterfront. *Mikhali's*, now run by his redoubtable daughter Margarita, serves good basic Greek food. Most of the tavernas have magical views out over the harbour.

Other Taxi. Hydrofoil to Piraeus.

General

The harbour and hamlet, correctly Skála Leonídhion (Skála means a ladder or staircase) or Pláka (which simply means 'beach'), sits under

Above Tíros looking E towards the mole from the beach
Right Leonídhion

into the landscape) and the end of the breakwater will be seen. There is usually a confused swell at the entrance with the prevailing winds so care is needed turning to enter the harbour.

Mooring Go stern or bows-to the mole leaving the hydrofoil berth clear. Care is needed of the underwater ledge that has been left sticking out from the quay with the harbour works which have been going on. It is probably best to go bows-to to rather than risking damage to the rudder when stern-to. The bottom is hard sand, rocks and weed, not the best holding so make sure your anchor is well in. Shelter in the harbour has been much improved by the breakwater extension, although the prevailing southeasterlies still cause some surge until they die down at night.

131

Monastery of Elona near Leonídhion

impressive precipitous slopes on the edge of the valley plain that extends back up to Leonídhion proper some 4 kilometres inland. It is a genial place, visited by a few backpackers and yachts, but with no established tourism yet. Leonídhion proper is built on either side of a river (usually dry in summer) on the floor of the valley. The town is the capital of the region and it is said that the local Tsakonian dialect preserves traces of the original Doric Greek. Some of the local rugs and tapestries are also said to preserve Doric designs and motifs.

Behind Pláka are the ruins of the ancient harbour and other buildings associated with Brasiae, about which little is known. It is thought ships used to moor at the mouth of the river and that the ruins, now a little way inland, would have been on the coast itself. When I first came to Leonídhion many years ago Mikhali would relate tales of the Second World War, when an Allied plane crashed into the sea nearby and the British pilot was hidden by the villagers until he could escape. He used to return here regularly for his summer holidays. You are less likely to hear of the gorge inland where a group of local communists were executed during the civil war that followed the Second World War. Their bodies are said still to be there in a mass grave.

From Leonídhion you can take a taxi to the Monastery of Elona tucked into a cliffside eyrie, though the drive up to the monastery with a local driver is more scary than standing on the edge of the monastery proper and looking down to the bottom of the cliff.

Poúlithra

A small fishing harbour 2M S of Leonídhion in the SE corner of the large bay. The cluster of buildings around the coast that make up Poúlithra can be identified, and closer in the short mole of the small harbour will be seen at the S end of the village. The harbour is very small with room only for a couple of small yachts amongst the local fishing boats. Go bows-to the end of the short mole, taking care of underwater rocks off the mole and the numerous laid moorings on the bottom. Good shelter from the prevailing southeasterlies but open N. In calm weather you can anchor off.

Water at the root of the mole. Ashore there are several tavernas, and some provisions can be found in the village.

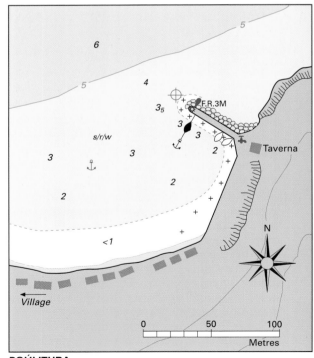

POÚLITHRA
⊕37°07'·1N 22°54'·2E

Poulithra mole looking northeast from the beach

Poúlithra is a quiet little spot off the beaten track. The coast road here turns inland so it is literally the end of the line for land-based tourists, who tend to turn round and hightail it to places like Pláka and Tiros.

Órmos Fokianos

A large bay lying 1M S of Ák Tourkovigla. Anchor at the head of the bay off the beach in 5–10m. At times nets are laid off the beach so

exercise some caution when entering. The surroundings here are magnificent and the bay is a wonderful spot, but the prevailing southeasterlies send a swell in. Try to tuck as far into the SW corner as possible.

Around Fokianos or a bit further S is the dividing line for the prevalence of the southeasterly sea breeze that blows up into Argolikós Kólpos. There may be either a southerly or a northerly here, or a flat patch where you catch only the swell but no wind.

Kiparíssi

The large bay lying 5M S of Fokianos.

Pilotage

Approach The entrance to the bay is difficult to make out from the N and S. On the N side of the entrance a conspicuous road scar runs around the coast and on the S side a pylon communications tower stands out well. Closer in, the light structure on the N side will be seen and from the S the rocky islet off the entrance can be identified, but the light structure on the S side will not be seen until you are into the bay. The houses of the village are obvious once you are up to the entrance.

Mooring There are three possibilities depending on the wind and ground swell.

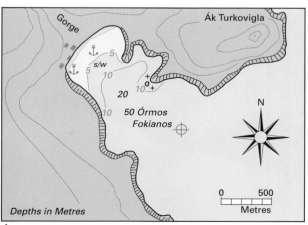

ÓRMOS FOKIANOS
⊕37°04′·1N 22°59′·3E

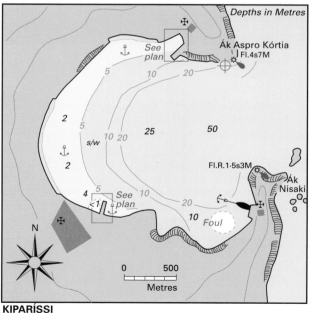

KIPARÍSSI
⊕36°59′·1N 23°00′·4E

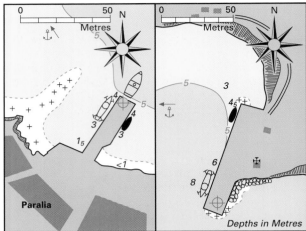

KIPARÍSSI: TOWN PIER
⊕36°58'·3N 22°59'·7E

KIPARÍSSI: NORTH PIER
⊕36°59'·0N 23°00'·0E

Kiparíssi. The anchorage off the village   *Nigel Patten*

ashore just SE of the quay, although care is needed of the permanent moorings on the bottom for local fishing boats. Good shelter from southerlies and northerlies send in a limited swell.

North pier Anchor in the N of the bay or tuck inside the new ferry quay. This is the best place to be in northerlies though unless you can get under the new quayed area it is not a good place in strong southerlies.

Note The hydrofoil uses either the town pier or the N quay, depending on whether southerlies or northerlies are blowing.

Kiparissi village Off the village in the SW of the bay. Anchor off in the bay or go alongside the E side of the pier. The bottom is sand and weed and not everywhere the best holding. With northerlies it is uncomfortable, though it only really becomes untenable in fresh or strong northerlies. Care needs to be taken of the rocky remains of an old pier to the W of the existing pier. You are close to all the facilities in the village here.

Chapel Cove Off the chapel in the cove on the SE side of the bay. Go stern or bows-to the quay off the chapel. There are 2–2·5m off the quay dropping off quickly to 15m a short distance off, so make sure you have plenty of scope for the anchor. Alternatively anchor and take a long line

The short quay off the chapel on the SE side of Kiparíssi

Facilities
Services Water in the village.

Provisions Most provisions can be found in the village.

Eating out There is a taverna and a café near the north quay and others in and around the village. Fresh fish is often available.

Other PO. OTE. Hydrofoil to Piraeus and S to Monemvasía.

General
The bay is quite simply majestic. Slopes rise precipitously to razor-sharp spines over which thunderstorms sometimes break in the summer. If you are off the chapel in the SE cove light the oil lamp for a little saintly intervention if the fishermen have not already done so. The mountainous setting gives a good idea of the backdrop to the coast further south – this is the sort of wild and savage country the Spartans lived and prospered in (although Sparta is a long way inland) and you can see where we get the word 'spartan' from.

Anchorages down to Ieraka

Between Kiparíssi and Ieraka there are some wild and wonderful anchorages that can be used in calm weather.

1. **Vathí Avláki** 36°51'·5N 23°02'·3E
   Under Ák Vathí Avláki there is a bay at the foot of a gorge which can be used. Just over 1M S there is another cove which can also be used, although it is quite deep for anchoring. Calm weather only.

2. **Chapel Cove** 36°49'·5N 23°04'·5E
   To the S of this anchorage just before you get to Ák Vathí (the next Ák Vathí after Vathí Avláki) a chapel (Evagelistrias) is conspicuous. In calm weather anchor in the cove underneath, although again it is quite deep for anchoring. With any wind at all this is not a good place to be.

Ieraka

A small village tucked into a rocky inlet 2M S of Ák Vathí.

Pilotage
Approach The crooked cleft in the cliffs that is the entrance is difficult to see even when you are quite close to it. From the N the chapel near Ák Vathí will be seen. From the S an islet,

Nisís Dhaskalio, can be identified in the large bay S of Ieraka. In the entrance the light structure on the N side will eventually be seen. With strong northerlies there can be a confused swell in the entrance as the waves rebound off the rocky cliffs.

Mooring Once into the inlet anchor or go stern or bows-to the quay off the village. Generally it is better to go bows-to as the quay is bordered by rocky shallows in places. Shallow draught craft can creep up quite a way to the W and anchor in the entrance to the lagoon. The bottom is mud, rocks and weed, reasonable holding. Good all-round shelter inside, although fresh to strong northerlies set up a surge which causes boats at anchor and on the quay to roll.

Facilities
Services Water in the village.

Provisions Basic provisions can be found.

Eating out Several tavernas on the waterfront which will often have fresh fish (and often little else, other than pork chops or chicken).

Other Taxi. Hydrofoil to Piraeus.

General
Ieraka (or Yeraka) is a gem of place that most people fall for on their first visit. The hamlet, a single line of houses, sits wedged along the quay-front hemmed in by rocky slopes on either side. At the eastern end you look out to the cliffs blocking off the entrance and the western end opens up into a shallow lagoon. The locals are a friendly lot who now ease their winter solitude

Ieraka looking W into the inlet from Ák Kástro

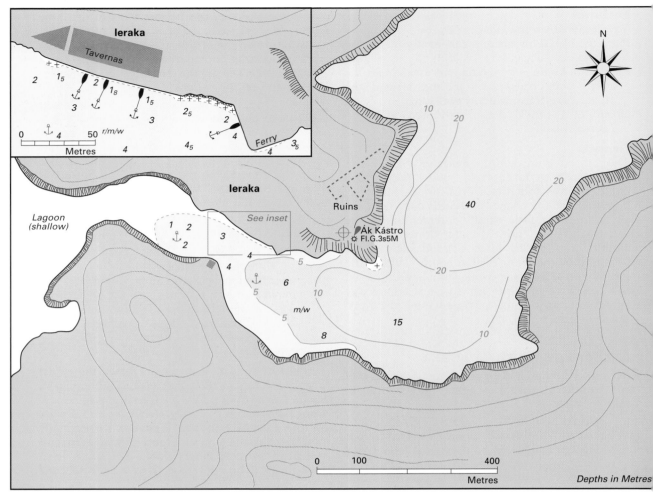

IERAKA
⊕36°47′·2N 23°05′·3E

with some summer income from the yachts that visit here.

On the northern entrance point are the ruins of ancient Ierakos or Ierax above the appropriately named Ák Kastro (Castle Cape). The ruins of the Mycenean acropolis are littered over the plateau above the cape. The inlet presumably served as the harbour for the ancient city.

Nisís Dhaskalio

36°45′·2N 23°05′·4E

The sheer-sided 'full-stop' of an islet in the large bay S of Ák Ierakas. In calm weather it is possible to anchor off in the bay although it is mostly fairly deep. There is also a cove to the S, just N of Ák Kremmidhi, where a yacht can anchor in calm weather. In either of these two bays there is a ground swell if any swell at all is running outside.

Órmos Kremmidhi

The large bay just over 1 M W of Ák Kremmidhi. In the approach care needs to be taken of a reef and shoal water off the coast just W of Ák Kremmidhi. The reef is deceptive and it is all too easy to cut the corner and shave it or worse. There are several anchorages around Órmos Kremmidhi:

1. On the W just inside the W entrance point. Subject to gusts off the land with the *meltemi*.
2. In the NE although care is needed of a reef off the shore. Subject to gusts with the *meltemi* but good holding.
3. In the NW corner. Also subject to gusts with the *meltemi*, but probably the best place to be with the *meltemi*.

Órmos Palaio (Monemvasía)

The cove in the NW corner of Kólpos Limaras. A tower on Ák Palaia Monemvasía is conspicuous and closer in the light structure on the E entrance point will be seen. Care needs to be taken of the reef running W from the E entrance point. Make your approach from the SW.

Anchor in 6–10m on sand and weed, good holding. Care needs to be taken of large permanent moorings on the bottom further in from the 6-metre line. There are gusts into here with the *meltemi*, but it affords good shelter from a strong *meltemi*. Ashore there is a small fishing hamlet but no facilities. Around the bay to the W is a camping ground and the ruins of ancient Epidhavros-Limera, established by colonists from Epidhavros in the Argolid.

Monemvasía

The huge hump-backed headland is easily identified from the distance and once seen is unmistakable.

Pilotage

Approach The high headland, looking like an

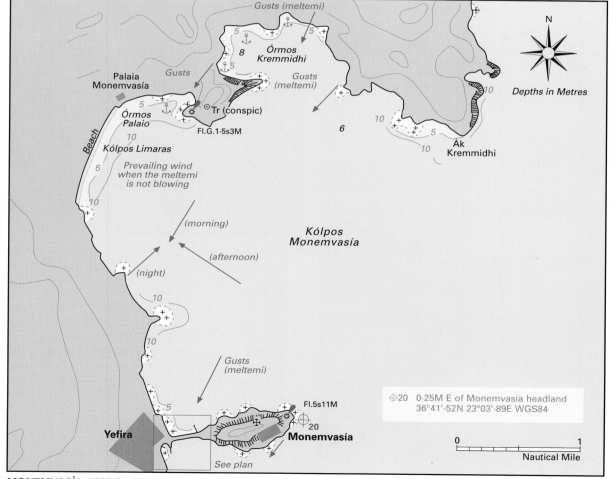

MONEMVASÍA APPROACHES

island from the distance, is conspicuous from some distance off. Closer in the houses of Yefira on the Peloponnese will be seen. From the N the mole on the N side is easily identified. From the S the old village on the headland will be seen, and the village of Yefira.

Mooring There are several places a yacht can go depending on the wind and sea.

North side mole Go stern or bows-to the inner half of the mole, leaving the ferry and hydrofoil berths clear. Near the root of the mole a yacht should take care as the rocky bottom is uneven and ballasting extends a short distance off the quay. The bottom is mud and rocks, reasonable holding. Good protection from southerlies, but with fresh to strong northeasterlies a surge builds up, causing yachts to roll and snatch on lines ashore. Strong westerlies sometimes blow

Áyia Sofia on the summit of Monemvasía   *Nigel Patten*

The fishing harbour at Yefira looking E towards Monemvasía

down off the hills onto the quay.

South side anchorage Anchor off the fishing harbour in 6–12m on sand, rock and weed, mostly good holding once you have got the anchor in. Good shelter from northerlies, and southerlies do not usually blow home in the summer. However, there is always some ground swell here causing yachts to roll at anchor.

Monemvasía marina A bit of a misnomer, as the present marina structure has deteriorated inside and many berths are taken up by local fishing boats. Go alongside the

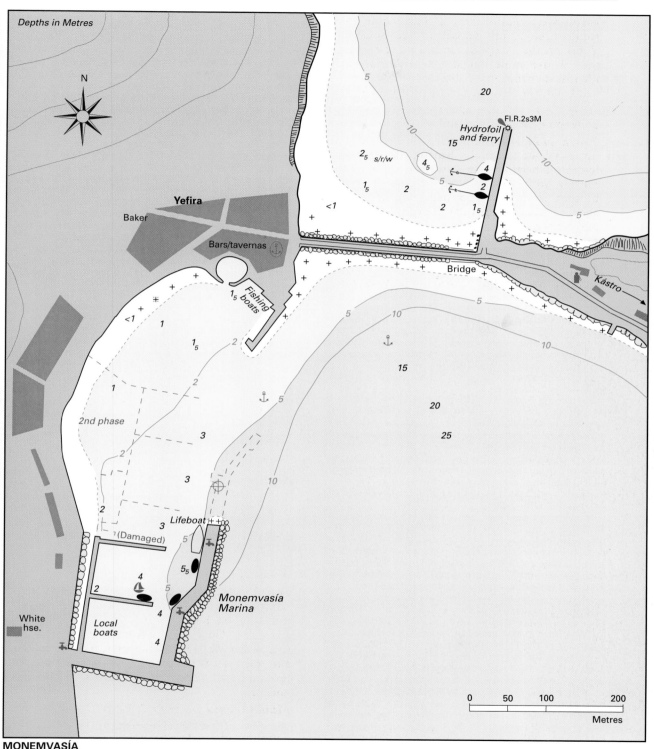

Depths in Metres

N

Yefira

Baker

Bars/tavernas

Fishing boats

Hydrofoil and ferry

Fl.R.2s3M

s/r/w

Bridge

Kástro

2nd phase

Lifeboat

(Damaged)

Monemvasía Marina

White hse.

Local boats

| 0 | 50 | 100 | 200 |

Metres

MONEMVASÍA

36°41´·03N 23°02´·38E WGS84

Monemvasía

The monolithic rock rising sheer out of the sea with the old village tucked onto the southern side is like an apparition, a chunk of the Middle Ages separated, as it is, by the causeway from the contemporary world. Monemvasía has been called the Gibraltar of the East for obvious reasons, but it is all the more impressive for being isolated from any rebuilding after the early 19th century and an historical preservation order should keep it that way. It is a `must' for anyone to see despite the inadequate shelter for yachts.

The name Monemvasía means `single entrance' (Moni Emvasis) from the only access across what is now a causeway. The headland was once joined to the Peloponnese and Pausanias refers to it as Ákra Minoa, Cape Minoa, suggesting there was a Minoan colony here. In AD375 a cataclysmic earthquake struck the region, sinking many coastal cities beneath the sea and severing the headland from the coast and turning it into an island. It was intermittently settled after this, but it was not until the 6th century that the Byzantines built a substantial town on the summit and fortified it with thick walls.

The lower town on the slopes was not built until some 400 years later when Monemvasía had become an important trading post for the Byzantines. From the fortified rock they could control the gateway to the Aegean around Cape Malea and their various settlements on the Peloponnese. It was briefly taken by the Franks under Villehardouin in 1249, but the Byzantines soon got it back in 1263 and were to hold it for another 130 years.

By now the Turkish threat was looming from the east and the city looked to the Venetians for security. Not surprisingly, the Venetians snapped up the offer and added Monemvasía to their already impressive list of fortresses around the Peloponnese protecting the trade route from Asia Minor. The Turks bided their time and in 1540 took the city, only to have the Venetians come back under Morosini and retake it in 1690, but in 1715 the Turks were back again to stay until the Greek War of Independence in 1821.

Monemvasía was well known around the world, as Malvoisie to the Franks and Malmsey to the English, for the sweet red wine which was shipped from here, but probably not produced here as is sometimes inferred. It is interesting that a heavy sweet wine will travel better than lighter more delicate wines, and Malmsey was much in demand for the long voyages of the time.

All these sieges and counter-sieges account for much of the continuous strengthening of the fortifications on the island. The Venetians beefed up the Byzantine walls and the Turks in turn added more walls and towers. The old town at the top was originally reached via a path from the causeway leading up to a huge gate, but in the 15th century the Turks closed it off with a thick wall, leaving the only access via the lower town. As you walk up the narrow winding path to what became the main gateway to the old town, it is not difficult to imagine what it was like for attackers told to get on up there and engage the enemy. To me the path up to the top, with thick walls and hedged in with banked corners, looks suspiciously like a giant pinball alley that a giant rock pinball released from the top would rattle down at

increasing speed, squashing any human flesh foolish enough to be in its way.

On the summit of the rock there is little left of the buildings of the old town save the defensive walls and the Byzantine church of Aghia Sofia. It sits precariously on the edge of the northern cliffs, as if perched on air, with a view out over the sea and coast that is giddying, and not for those who suffer from vertigo, especially if any wind is tugging at your clothes.

Down below, the lower town has been largely preserved and reconstructed. Many of the older houses are Byzantine with 16th and 17th century additions while there are also 18th and 19th century houses and adornments. The whole mixture of Byzantine, Venetian and Turkish with a bit of neo-classical thrown in is bordered by defensive walls with streets that were designed for donkeys and handcarts rather than motor vehicles – which mercifully are not allowed past the main gate into the town. Many of the houses have been converted into tavernas, bars, souvenir shops and boutiques which if sometimes a little precious, at least do not intrude on the character of the place. The stones of the main street are now worn smooth with the tramping of thousands of feet in the summer and `grippy' shoes rather than deck shoes should be worn.

The island was originally joined to the coast by a wooden bridge which the Venetians replaced with an elegant stone bridge. It had fourteen arches with a central wooden section which could be removed to prevent access in a siege. Bits of the bridge remain under the causeway now connecting the island to the mainland.

Monemvasia in a 17th century engraving by Coronelli

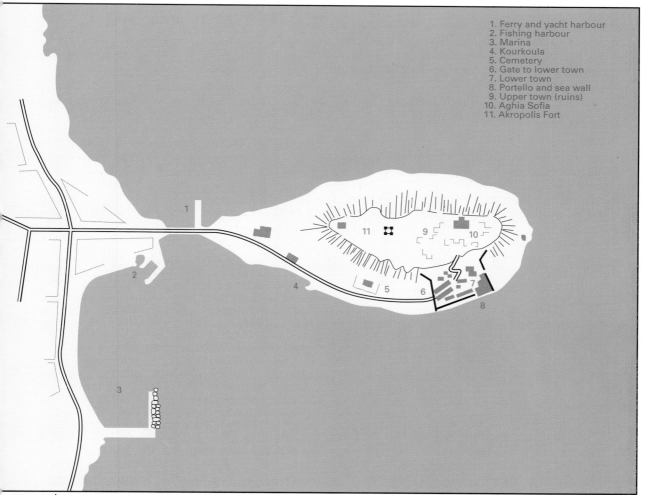

1. Ferry and yacht harbour
2. Fishing harbour
3. Marina
4. Kourkoula
5. Cemetery
6. Gate to lower town
7. Lower town
8. Portello and sea wall
9. Upper town (ruins)
10. Aghía Sofía
11. Akropolis Fort

ONEMVASÍA

breakwater quay behind the lifeboat or alongside on the second pontoon. Care is needed.

Facilities

Services Water on the quay in the 'marina' though it can be difficult to get at it. Water also delivered by mini-tanker. Fuel station on the causeway or it can be delivered by mini-tanker to the 'marina'

Provisions Good shopping for all provisions in Yefira. Ice available.

Eating out Numerous tavernas in the old town and in Yefira. The tavernas in the old town are inviting and the setting is romantic. Try the *Matoula* (the original here) or the *Castellano* at the *Lazaretto Hotel*, although really you should just make an inspired guess. In Yefira I favour one of the *ouzeries* on the edge of the fishing harbour which often have grilled octopus and good basic Greek fare. Alternatively try the *Monemvasía Hotel* restaurant or the *Nikolaos*.

Other PO. OTE. Bank. Hire motorbikes and cars. Malvasia Travel in Yefira can usually sort out anything you want. Ferry and hydrofoil to Piraeus and points along the way.

General

The settlement of Yefira (the name means 'bridge') on the Peloponnese coast is now the main settlement where most of the population lives. It is a likeable spot with the usual pour-and-fill somehow ameliorated by the bulk of

Monemvasía looming over it. To get across to Monemvasía either walk over the causeway, or from the 'marina' you can take the tender across to the old town itself, which in the summer saves dodging cars and people on the road leading to the gates of the old town.

Áy Fokas

36°35'·5N 23°03'·8E

A cove and small fishing harbour 5½M S of Monemvasía. I have never actually put in here as the wind and swell have always been a little too much for rock-hopping, but in calm weather it could be worth exploring. The bay and the mole are rock-bound so extreme care is needed and it would be wise to reconnoitre in the dinghy first.

Ák Maléas

The great rocky cape that a yacht must round before proceeding up into Lakonikós Kólpos. It is a stark, forbidding place, and worthy of what Strabo said was uttered by Greek sailors as they rounded it to head westwards: *Formidatum Malea caput* – roughly translated as 'Double Cape Malea and forget your native home'.

From the N the first thing you will see is the lighthouse perched on a splintered outcrop before the cape proper. Once round the cape, a hermitage with several sun-white dwellings and a church are like a saving signal from the confused swell always encountered here. When Alphonse de Lamartine rounded the cape in the middle of the 19th century he left this bleak account of the hermit on the cape.

'We doubled the cape so closely that we could distinguish his long white beard, his staff, his chaplet, his hood of brown felt, like that of sailors in winter. He went on his knees as we passed, with his face turned towards the sea, as if he were imploring the succour of Heaven for the unknown strangers on this perilous passage. The wind, which issues furiously from the mountain-gorges of Laconia, as soon as you double the rock of the cape, began to resound in our sails, and make the two vessels roll and stagger, covering the sea with foam as far as the eye could reach. A new sea was opening before us. The hermit, in order to follow us still farther with his eyes, ascended the crest of a rock, and we distinguished him there, on his knees, and motionless, as long as we were in sight of the cape.'

A. de Lamartine. *Travels in the East* 1850.

There is nearly always a S-going current from Ák Kamili to Malea, often as much as 1½-2 knots, which makes going S great but plugging up to the N from the cape a tedious affair. The current also causes a confused swell around the cape, with current lines and little overfalls which can become a problem with strong southerlies. The cape has a reputation for bad weather and it can be a dangerous place, but do not be put off by Lamartine's description, as in the summer, with luck and no depressions around, you can often get round in a near calm.

The lighthouse on Ák Maléas

Passage on to Kíthera and Lakonikós Kólpos

From Ák Maléas most yachts will head for either Áy Nikólaos or Kapsáli on Kíthera, or for Nísos Elafónisos or Porto Kayio. Care is needed in Stenó Elafónisos, the channel between Ák Maléas and Kíthera, of the large amount of commercial shipping passing through the strait. There will always be one or two ships around, at the very least.

Passage to Kíthera is straightforward, the island can be seen from Malea, though care is needed in the lee of the island where there can be strong gusts with the prevailing westerlies. Passage to Elafónisos is also straightforward, although there can be strong gusts into Órmos Vatíka and off Elafónisos with a strong meltemi.

For further pilotage information going westabout the Peloponnese see the author's Greek Waters Pilot (Imray).

⊕10 0·2M S of Ák Tainaron
36°22'·97N 22°28'·96E WGS84
⊕11 ½M E of Nisís Kranai light
36°45'·3N 22°35'·1E
⊕12 1½M S of Ák Elena (Elafonisos)
36°26'·4N 22°57'·8E WGS84
⊕13 0·4M S of Ák Zóvolo
36°25'·26N 23°07'·75E WGS84
⊕14 0·75M S of Ák Maléas
36°25'·48N 23°11'·62E WGS84
⊕15 1M N of Ák Spathí (Kíthera)
36°23'·9N 22°57'·0E

AKONIKÓS KÓLPOS (GULF OF LAKONIKA)

V. The Western Cyclades

Kéa, Kíthnos, Sérifos, Sífnos, Mílos, Kímolos and Políagos

The Cyclades are the islands that most correspond to the common perception of what Greece looks like. These are the brown sun-scorched islands with huddled cubist white houses dotted over the landscape: the waters around the islands are cobalt blue and mottled turquoise over a sand and rock bottom, and the sun blazes down out of a clear blue sky. It is the Greece on a thousand postcards and tourist brochures. Strangely enough, the islands don't experience as much tourism as some mainland resorts and you will be surprised that these islands, so close to Athens, feel a lot further away than the actual distance might suggest.

The Cyclades are the peaks of mountains that once stood on the vast Aegean plain. They poke up precipitously from the seabed and for the most part there are good depths right up to the coast. The northern islands are older than the southern islands, which are generally volcanic as at Mílos where the enclosed bay is one gigantic caldera.

The islands have probably been occupied from Neolithic times, although there have been few finds. Mílos was important from early on because of the abundance of obsidian (volcanic glass) on the island which was much valued for making cutting implements. With the rise of the Minoan empire on Crete the indigenous population was displaced and most Bronze Age artefacts are Minoan and later Mycenean. During the Minoan period the Cyclades produced distinctive sculpted figurines and pottery. Mílos in particular with its abundance of obsidian was a centre of trade, and the discovery of model boats suggests navigation between the islands was commonplace.

With the rise of the Myceneans, bronze became more widespread and the islands' importance declined. After the Myceneans mysteriously disappeared from the scene the Ionians moved in from Asia Minor, although it was not until the rise of Athens and the classical Greek period that the Cyclades started to hum again. The name Cyclades is derived from *kukloi*, which means 'rings', from the radiating circle they more or less form around the island of Delos. Delos was the sacred treasury of the Delian League, a place of worship and the centre of things until the Athenians decided it was better to control their loose empire of city-states from Athens itself.

It should be remembered that the received sanitised history of Athens and classical Greece, the notion that from here sprang all the fundamental ideas so essential to Western civilisation, was often nothing of the sort. The Athenians kept control by keeping the city-states under their thumb, and with a large navy were able to effectively stop any rebellion or defections from the League. The penalties for dissident city-states often included killing all the men and enslaving the women and children. Not surprisingly, some of the islands close to the Peloponnese were inclined to look fondly on the enemies of Athens over the water, even to the Spartans, who could not be described as the most tolerant or even-handed lot around.

With the rise of sea power in the Mediterranean the islands became more important. The Romans and later the Byzantines established ports on the islands for their trade routes, and when the Venetians, the trading nation above all others, arrived in the 13th century, the islands were given to various Venetian nobles to hold as part of the stepping stone route across the Aegean for Venetian ships. The prizes here were not anything the islands had to offer, but the safe passage to Venice of spices and cloth from the caravans arriving in Asia Minor.

In June 1645 the Turks invaded Crete and a period of war between the Venetians and the Turks continued for 24 years, until the Turks were victorious and the Cyclades came under

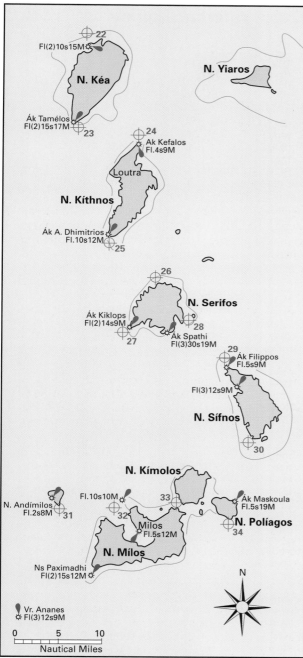

THE WESTERN CYCLADES

Useful waypoints

⊕22 1M N of Ák Perlevos (Kéa)
  37°42'·3N 24°21'·0E
⊕23 0·2M S of Ák Tamélos (Kéa)
  37°31'·14N 24°16'·50E WGS84
⊕24 0·25M N of Ák Kéfalos (Kíthnos)
  37°29'·21N 24°26'·01E WGS84
⊕25 1M S of Ák Áy Dhimítrios (Kíthnos)
  37°17'·1N 24°21'·9E
⊕26 1M N of Ák Volos (Sérifos)
  37°13'·8N 24°29'·5E
⊕27 1M W of Ák Kíklops (Sérifos)
  37°07'·4N 24°23'·7E
⊕28 0·2M W of Ák Amino (entrance to O.
  Livadhiou/Sérifos)
  37°07'·66N 24°31'·68E WGS84
⊕29 1M N of Vrak Tsoukala (Sífnos)
  37°03'·9N 24°38'·0E
⊕30 0·4M W of Ák Karavi (N. Kitriani/Sífnos)
  36°53'·50N 24°42'·91E WGS84
⊕31 1M S of Ák Vlikadhi (Andímilos)
  36°45'·1N 24°14'·6E
⊕32 0·5M W of Nds. Akrádhia light (Mílos)
  36°46'·9N 24°22'·7E
⊕33 0·25M N of Ák Pelekoúdha light
  (Stenó Mílou-Kimolou)
  36°46'·45N 24°31'·7E
⊕34 1M S of S end of N. Políagos
  36°43'·6N 24°38'·9E

Independence. After independence the islands declined in importance and were plagued by pirates. It is only in the 20th century that most of the populations have come down from the *chora*, the island capital, to settlements on the water's edge. The *chora* inland was usually atop a hill with a good view so that the inhabitants could flee any marauders before they got up the hill. Some had defences, but most were sited simply to be well away from the water's edge so the inhabitants had time to hide their valuables and flee with their daughters.

Piracy has always been a fact of life throughout the islands and from the time of the ancient Greeks through to the present day, pirates have shaped the trade, architecture and culture of these islands. The notion of the pirate should be qualified here. Odysseus on his voyages saw nothing amiss with a little plundering here and there. The loose confederation of city-states under the ancient Greeks and the Romans would often mount raids on one another to acquire booty and women. Under the Byzantines the Saracens held sway down through the islands; indeed, the common place-name 'Sarakiniko' means 'the place of the Saracens'. Under the Venetians the islands were prey to all sorts of adventurers who with quasi-legal approval carried

Turkish rule. Things were then comparatively calm for the islands, as the Turks required safe ports of call just as much as the Venetians had.

In 1821 the Greeks rebelled and the islands were thrown into the Greek War of

Prevailing winds

The prevailing wind in the Cyclades is the *meltemi*. Even those of us who have sailed in this area for a long time can curse it when the *meltemi* screams down through the Cyclades. As I was researching this book I sat in Vathí on Sífnos in August with two anchors out while the winds clocked up to 40 knots. It is important to remember that if you are on a charter boat out of one of the harbours around Athens, you may have problems getting back if the *meltemi*. gets up while you are in the southern Cyclades.

The *meltemi*. normally blows from June to the end of September. It starts off fitfully at first, is strongest in July and August, and starts to die down in September and October. It blows from the N to NE down through the western Cyclades and to some extent is modified by the high land mass of the islands.

It can blow anything from Force 4 to Force 8, though usually it blows at around Force 4–6. It may blow for one day, three days, or a week or more before dying down and there is no reliable way of knowing how long it will blow. While it does have a thermal component which causes it to blow strongest in the afternoon and lose strength in the night, it is not a pure thermal wind, and descriptions of it getting up around midday, blowing until sunset and then dying down, are patently wrong, as anyone who has sailed in the Cyclades will know. One thing you do need to be on the lookout for is gusts off the lee side of the islands. In places these gusts can be considerably stronger than the wind speed over open water – gusts of Force 7–8 can be experienced when the wind on the open sea is Force 5–6. At times small whirlwinds can accompany these gusts, which strike with great force and very quickly.

If you are in the western Cyclades and the *meltemi* is blowing, then to get N it can sometimes be worthwhile going across to the Peloponnese and working north to the Gulf of Ídhra and from there to Póros and Athens.

Outside the *meltemi* season winds are still predominantly from the N, though the average strength is considerably less. There are also a good number of days when southerlies will blow. Depressions do occasionally pass through the Cyclades in the spring and autumn, but are rare in the summer.

out raids on the islands. Some of this must have rubbed off on the islanders themselves, as shipowners trading between the islands thought nothing of a little piracy, and the British and French complained bitterly about raids by Greek vessels when they were ostensibly allies in the War of Independence.

The reversal in fortunes for the islands with the arrival of mass tourism is a comparatively recent affair. Only 20 years ago many of these islands saw few tourists and today it is still surprising just

Quick reference guide

	Shelter	Mooring	Fuel	Water	Provisions	Eating out	Plan
Kéa							
Limín Áy Nikólaou	A	AC	B	A	B	B	•
Órmos Pisa	C	C	O	O	O	C	•
Órmos Kavia	B	C	O	B	C	C	•
Órmos Orgias	O	C	O	O	O	C	•
Órmos Khalidhoniki	C	C	O	O	O	C	•
Órmos Polais	C	C	O	O	O	O	•
Kíthnos							
Órmos Kólona	B	C	O	O	O	O	•
Órmos Fikiadha	B	C	O	O	O	O	•
Órmos Apokriosis	B	C	O	O	O	C	•
Órmos Episkopis	C	C	O	O	O	C	
Mérikha	B	AC	B	A	B	B	•
Órmos Flamboriou	C	C	O	O	O	O	
Órmos Áy Dhimitriou	C	C	O	O	O	O	
Loutra	A	ABC	B	A	C	B	•
Órmos Áy Stefanos	B	C	O	O	O	C	•
Lefkes	O	C	O	O	O	C	
Órmos Kanala	C	C	O	O	O	O	•
Órmos Áy Nikólaos	C	C	O	O	O	O	•
Sérifos							
Livádhi	A	ABC	B	A	B	B	•
Órmos Ambeli	B	C	O	O	O	C	
Órmos Koutala	B	C	O	B	C	C	•
Órmos Mega Livádhi	C	C	O	O	O	O	
Órmos Avesalou	C	C	O	O	O	O	
Órmos Psili Ammos	O	C	O	O	O	O	
Sífnos							
Áy Yeóryios	B	C	O	O	O	C	•
Kamáres	B	AC	B	A	B	B	•
Órmos Vathí	B	AC	O	O	C	C	•
Órmos Fikiadha	C	C	O	O	O	O	•
Órmos Platí Yialos	B	C	B	B	C	B	•
Fáros	B	C	O	B	C	C	•
Órmos Kástro	O	C	O	O	C	C	•
Mílos							
Adhamas	B	AC	B	A	A	A	•
Órmos Mílou	C	C	O	O	O	C	•
Apollonia	C	C	O	B	C	B	•
Voudhia	C	C	O	O	O	O	•
Órmos Provatas	C	C	O	O	O	C	•
Kímolos							
Sikia	C	C	O	O	O	O	
Pirgonisi	B	C	O	O	O	O	
Psathi	C	AC	O	O	C	C	•
Sémina	C	C	O	O	O	O	
Prasonisi	O	C	O	O	O	O	•
Políagos							
Manolonisi	C	C	O	O	O	O	•

how many little places on the islands remain far from the madding crowd. With the easy rewards from tourism much of the agriculture on the islands has declined. Not so long ago many of these islands grew wheat on the terraces painstakingly constructed on the steep slopes. The wheat was milled by the numerous windmills which dot the island landscapes. The *meltemi* provided more energy than the windmills could use and they were equipped with sails that could be reefed when the wind got up. These days only yachtsmen are silly enough to use this antiquated method of propulsion.

Nísos Kéa

This is the first of the Cyclades you come to when heading east from Athens. The island lies approximately 12 miles from Sounion so it is a popular stepping stone for yachts bound to or from Athens. It is a mountainous craggy island with the main port at Áy Nikolaou on the northwest corner. There are a number of other anchorages around the island that can be used depending on the weather. In the summer, weather means the *meltemi* blowing from the northeast.

The island has been occupied from Neolithic times and has some of the few Neolithic remains (c.4000BC) found in the Cyclades at a site just near Ák Kéfalos N of Áy Nikolaou. In Áy Nikolaou itself a Minoan settlement has been excavated on the N side of the harbour. It was destroyed by an earthquake in 1500BC, around the same time that Thira erupted and, it is supposed, caused the rapid decline of the Minoan Empire on Crete.

In ancient times the island was of considerable importance. It was the first to send triremes to aid Athens against the Persians in the Battle of Salamís and was honoured by having its name mentioned first on the memorial tripod to Apollo at Delphi. The island had four cities: Korissia just W of the present-day port of Korissia, Ioulis where the present-day *chora* is sited, Karthaia in the SE at Órmos Polais, and Piessa at Órmos Pisa on the west coast. Little remains of most of them, although near the *chora* (about 20 minutes' walk) there is a half-finished sculpture of a large lion, though the rudimentary features of the face make it look more like a large pussycat than a ferocious beast.

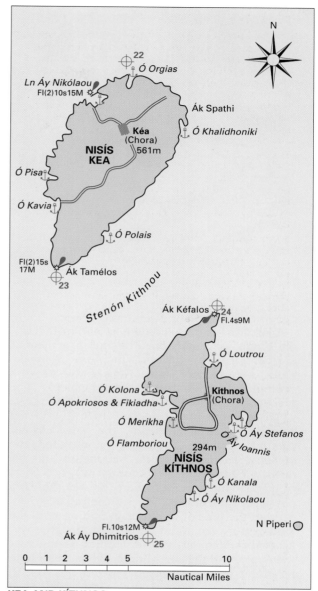

KEA AND KÍTHNOS

⊕22 1M N of Ák Perlevos (Kéa)
        37°42'·3N 24°21'·0E
⊕23 0·2M S of Ák Tamélos (Kéa)
        37°31'·14N 24°16'·50E WGS84
⊕24 0·25M N of Ák Kéfalos (Kíthnos)
        37°29'·21N 24°26'·01E WGS84
⊕25 1M S of Ák Áy Dhimítrios (Kíthnos)
        37°17'·1N 24°21'·9E

The pussycat lion near the *chora* on Kéa   *Nigel Patten*

The only really regular bus on the island is from Korissia to the chora. There is also an occasional service to Órmos Pisa and Órmos Orgias in the summer, but don't rely on it. There are a few taxis and probably the best thing to do is to get someone to call one up for you. Otherwise it is really down to hire motorbikes (Korissia is the place to get these), but you will need a bit of caution on some of the island's roads, which are not in the best of repair.

Apart from battles and temples and memorials, the Kéans were mentioned by ancient writers as having a bizarre custom, the *keion nomimon*. Kéans over seventy and no longer able to work committed suicide by drinking hemlock. The practice is supposed to have started during a siege when food was scarce and in order to save the younger, more able, Kéans, the older citizens committed suicide. The island was also the home of some ancient notables. Simonedes and his nephew Bacchylides (5th century BC), two poets of distinction, were born here, as was the early physician Erasistratus (4th–3rd century BC).

From the time of the Romans and up until the 19th century the island declined, although it was no doubt still important as a stepping stone across the Aegean. In the late Middle Ages it was a base for pirates and later Katsonis used it as a base to attack Tínos during the Greek War of Independence. During the age of steam there was a coal bunkering station at Áy Nikólaou, but with the introduction of fuel oil the ships bypassed the island and it declined in the 20th century until tourism touched its shores. Even today the southern end of the island remains largely uninhabited except for a few places on the coast where holiday villas have sprung up. Inland there are substantial groves of holm oak, the stunted oak native to the Mediterranean, and in times past the island used to export the acorns for use in the tanning industry. Acorns have now been supplanted by synthetic derivatives, but thankfully many of the oaks remain on Kéa and give us some idea of what these islands were like when they had more tree cover than the present day.

Limín Áy Nikólaou

The main port on the NW corner of the island.

Pilotage

Approach The white houses of the *chora* can be seen from the N, but the bay itself is difficult to spot from seawards. From the W the cluster of houses on the slopes around Vourkari will be seen and closer in the chapel-cum-lighthouse on Ák Áy Nikólaou will be seen. Entrance into the bay is straightforward although you need to keep an eye out for ferries and hydrofoils coming and going.

Mooring There are three possibilities:

Órmos Livádhi The S arm of the bay with the quay and breakwater at Korissía on the W side. Go stern or bows-to on the S end of the quay at Korissía or anchor off in the SE corner of the bay. Reasonable shelter from the *meltemi* on the quay and at anchor in the bay. There can be gusts with the *meltemi*, although not as strong as at Vourkari.

Órmos Vourkari The NE arm of Áy Nikólaou. You can go stern or bows-to the quay, although care is needed of the depths off the quay where it shallows up to 1·5–2m very quickly, with less depth in places. You can also anchor in the bay clear of the laid moorings. It is fairly deep here and you will usually be anchoring in 8–12m. The bottom is mud and weed, not everywhere the best holding, so make sure your anchor is well in. This is especially important on the quay as the *meltemi* gusts down straight onto it.

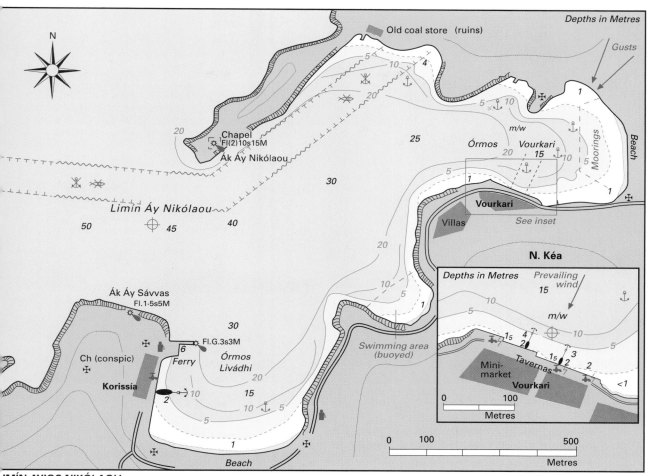

Depths in Metres

Gusts

Old coal store (ruins)

Chapel
Fl(2)10s15M
Ák Áy Nikólaou

Órmos   Vourkari

Vourkari

Villas   See inset

N. Kéa

Limín Áy Nikólaou

Ák Áy Sávvas
Fl.1·5s5M

Ch (conspic)
Ferry
Korissía

Órmos
Livádhi

Swimming area
(buoyed)

Depths in Metres   Prevailing wind

m/w

Tavernas

Mini-
market
Vourkari

0   100
Metres

0   100   500
Metres

Beach

IMÍN AYIOS NIKÓLAOU
37°39´·89N 24°18´·67E WGS84

The quay at Vourkari   *Lu Michell*

Coal Bunker Bay Anchor off the old coal bunkering depot in the N arm of the bay, keeping clear of the area where anchoring is prohibited because of a cable on the bottom. As elsewhere the bottom is mud and weed and not everywhere good holding.

Facilities

Services Water and electricity on the quay at Vourkari. Water on the quay at Korissía. Water is often in short supply on the island so it is not always possible to get it. Fuel can be delivered by mini-tanker.

Provisions Some provisions at Vourkari and Korissía. Ice available.

Eating out The tavernas at Vourkari looking out over the bay definitely have the edge over those at Korissía, although the cars passing along the road between the tavernas and the water don't

Korissia in the S arm of Áy Nikólaou

Lu Michell

do much for the atmosphere. Use your own judgment to pick a taverna as they are all fairly similar. The *ouzerie* near the head of the bay is worth a visit.

Other Bank. PO. OTE. Bus to the *chora*. Taxis. Hire motorbikes. Ferries to Lavrion, Piraeus and to the other Cyclades.

General

Áy Nikólaou is a popular place and in the season can get crowded with yachts on passage to or from the Attic coast. Both Korissia and Vourkari cope with the summer influx of tourists, but the place is definitely more amenable out of season, when it can be positively quiet. On the N side of Vourkari (near the church) are the excavations of the Bronze Age settlement, though there is little on the site to see.

From Áy Nikólaou a bus runs up to the *chora*, and it is well worth a brief excursion. It is situated in a fold in the hills which hid it from view from passing pirates. The sculpture of the lion ('the pussycat') is around 20 minutes' walk away, but you shouldn't feel any special compulsion to go and see it unless you fancy the walk.

Órmos Pisa (Pisses)

A small bay on the W coast under Ák Makropoundha. When the *meltemi* is blowing it affords some shelter, although a bit of swell curves around into the bay, more uncomfortable than dangerous. Anchor in 4–8m near the head of the bay on a sandy bottom.

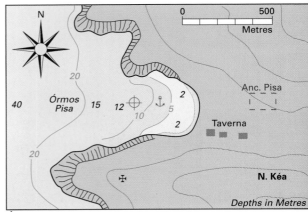

ÓRMOS PISA
⊕37°36'·1N 24°16'·6E

Ashore there are a couple of tavernas and a startling splash of green vegetation in the valley behind. This is one of the few places on the island that has some water, and the green swathe down the valley is emphasised by the brown rocky slopes around the bay. The existence of water here may have been the reason that the ancient city of Piessa (Poiessa) was built here. There are a few ruins lying about the valley but nothing too much to drag you away from one of the tavernas on the beach.

Órmos Kavia (Kondouros)

A ragged indented bay lying 1M E of Ák Makropoundha. In the approaches care is needed of the isolated reef lying approximately ¼M SSW of Makropoundha and ½M WNW of Órmos Kavia. Waves break on it with any swell and it is relatively easy to spot. Still, have someone up front keeping an eye out for it and describe a semicircle, as it were, when on passage between Órmos Kavia and Órmos Pisa. The bay of Órmos Kavia is relatively easy to identify as villas and hotels have been built around the slopes.

Anchor in 3–6m on a sandy bottom. A number of old mooring blocks and chains have been reported on the bottom so it would be wise to use

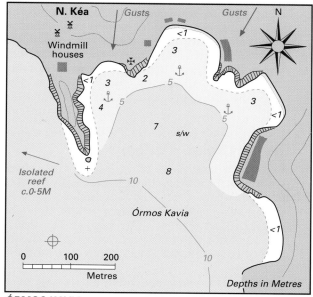

ÓRMOS KAVIA
⊕37°34´.44N 24°16´.13E WGS84

a trip-line on the anchor. The bay affords reasonable shelter from the *meltemi*, although if it blows hard some swell is pushed round into the bay. As at Pisa this is more uncomfortable than dangerous.

Órmos Kavia looking NNE from the entrance

Lu Michell

The bay has been developed for some tourism with numbers of villas and small hotels, although there is also a particularly ugly brown hotel on the slopes of the bay. The windmills here that look as if they have been converted into houses are actually new structures, built to look like windmills. There are several tavernas around the bay.

Órmos Orgias (Otzias)

A narrow bay on the N of the island. The *meltemi* blows straight into the bay so it can only be used in calm weather or with southerlies. Care is needed of a rock off the coast to the E of the approaches to the bay. The head of the bay is buoyed off for swimmers and you need to anchor clear of here in 5–6m. Take a long line ashore if necessary.

A number of villas and small hotels have been built around the slopes and there is some modest tourism in the summer when one or two tavernas aslo open.

Órmos Khalidhoniki (Spathí)

A small cove on the NE corner of the island under Ák Spathí. In a moderate *meltemi* there is reasonable shelter here, although some swell is still pushed into the cove. Anchor in 3–5m and take a line ashore to the N side of the cove if necessary.

A small hamlet ashore, and a taverna opens in the summer.

N of Khalidhoniki on the NE corner of the island is the monastery of Ayía Anna or Panayía Kastriani, sitting high on a bluff with vertigo-inducing views out over the sea. It was built relatively recently and you can reach it from Khalidhoniki, about an hour's walk.

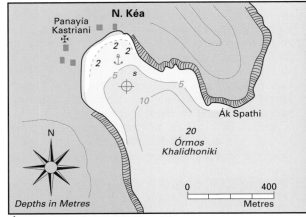

ÓRMOS KHALIDHONIKI (Spathí)
⊕37°38′·6N 24°24′·5E

Órmos Polais (Poles)

A small bay on the SE corner of Kéa. It offers poor shelter from the *meltemi*, but with light northerlies is a delightful spot to visit. A small islet joined to the shore by a reef bisects the bay. Anchor in the E side of the bay in 3–4m and take a long line ashore if necessary. The bottom is sand and weed with some rocks and not everywhere good holding.

Ashore are the ruins of ancient Karathia, one of the four cities of the tetrapolis. There are only scant remains of the city here, but the site above the bay is an evocative one and well worth a visit if the weather permits.

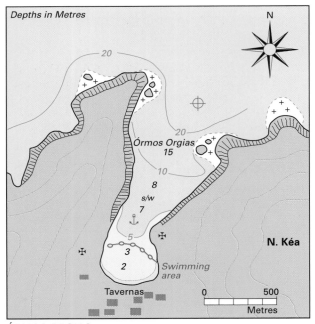

ÓRMOS ORGIAS
⊕37°40′·5N 24°21′·3E

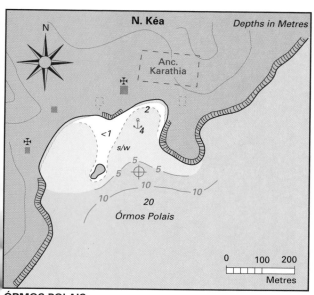

N. Kéa   *Depths in Metres*

Anc. Karathia

Órmos Polais

0   100   200

Metres

ÓRMOS POLAIS
⊕37°33′·4N 24°20·05′E

Nísos Kíthnos

Kíthnos lies a little over six miles south of Kéa. This rugged island, seemingly crumpled into steep ridges and rubbly slopes, gives the impression of being higher and bolder than Kéa although it is not. It is a savage landscape, inhospitable both from seawards and when you are in the interior, and like Kéa it has relatively little tourism despite its proximity to Athens. What tourism it does have is concentrated around Mérikha, and most of the other places are little touched by it. The island was a part of the Delian League and sent two ships to Salamís. Timanthes the painter (416–376BC) came from here and was described as a sort of ancient Impressionist: Pliny remarked that the less the artist depicted the more you were to able to imagine. In the Middle Ages the island was called Thermia after the hot springs at Loutra and elsewhere. Apart from this the island was largely ignored and only seemed to figure on the periphery of historical events in the Aegean. That is exactly the impression you get today and it is a blessing.

One of the things always mentioned about Kíthnos is that it produces good food, particularly cheese, honey, wine and figs. I can vouch for all of these with the exception of the local wine, which in my experience has been awful. Still, there is something gratifying about an island where the food takes precedence over lumps of

Getting around

There is a fairly regular bus service from Mérikha to the chora and a less frequent service from Loutra. There are also taxis, mostly based at Mérikha. Hire cars and motorbikes are available in Mérikha and hire motorbikes at Loutra. As on Kéa care is needed as the roads are primitive in places, with potholes that can swallow the front wheel of a scooter. There are lots of good, if rugged, walks: try the old paved road from the chora to the church of Áy Spiridhion and then follow the new gravel road to Driopis. The old paved road runs through a valley near the chora where ground water keeps things growing and green, something of a rare sight on Kíthnos.

ancient rock. A number of local dishes use Kíthnos cheese (*Kythneios tyros*) either fried or in baked dishes. A local drink (*Reklamata*) mixes the lethal *Tsoubouri* liqueur with cinnamon, cloves and honey and the whole lot is warmed up into a deceptive honey-flavoured but potent philtre. You may also be able to get a salad using hard-tack bread with tomatoes, herbs and oil over it, which, so I am told, was a staple on the caïques trading from the island – a sort of mariner's salad.

Kolóna, Apokriosis and Fikiadha

Three bays on the NW of the island which afford good shelter from the *meltemi*.

Pilotage

Approach These bays are situated about 1M N of Mérikha, where the huddle of buildings around the port are easily identified. Care is needed of strong gusts off the land with the *meltemi*.

Mooring You can anchor in any of the bays.

1. ***Órmos Kolóna*** (Sand Bar Bay) Anchor near the head of the bay in 3–6m on sand and take a long line ashore to the N side if necessary. Good shelter from the *meltemi*.
2. ***Órmos Fikiadha*** Care is needed of the rock off the eastern entrance point. Anchor in 3–5m on sand and weed, good holding once you get through the weed. Good shelter from the *meltemi*, although there are vicious gusts into the bay.
3. ***Órmos Apokriosis*** Anchor in 5–10m on sand and weed and take a long line ashore to the N side if necessary. Good shelter from the *meltemi*, although there are strong gusts.

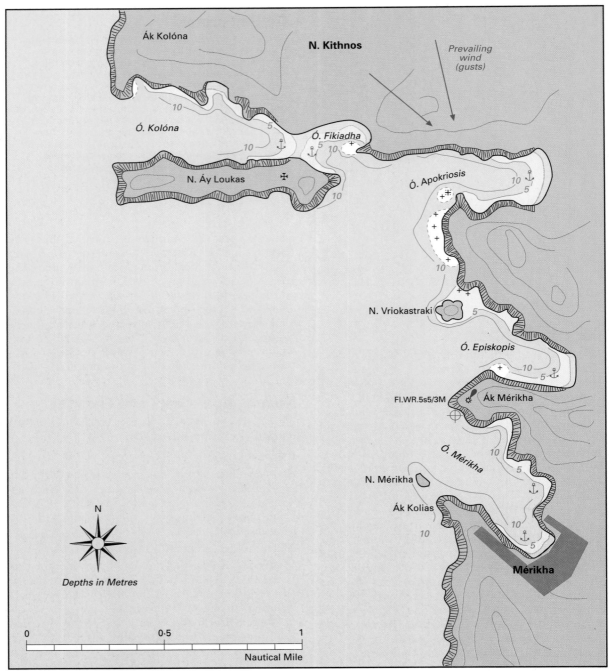

Ák Kolóna

N. Kithnos

Prevailing wind (gusts)

Ó. Kolóna

10

5

10

Ó. Fikiadha

5 *10*

N. Áy Loukas

10

Ó. Apokriosis

10
5

N. Vriokastraki

5

Ó. Episkopis

10
5

Fl.WR.5s5/3M

Ák Mérikha

Ó. Mérikha

10

N. Mérikha

5

Ák Kolias

10

10

5

Mérikha

N

Depths in Metres

0   0·5   1

Nautical Mile

ÓRMOS KOLÓNA TO MÉRIKHA
⊕37°23´·65N 24°23´·5E

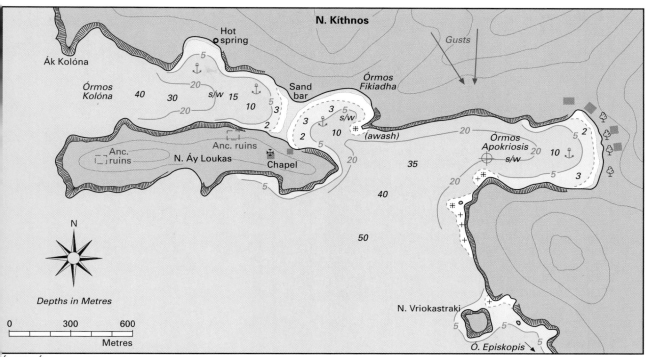

Ó. KOLÓNA, FIKIADHA AND APOKRIOSIS
⊕37°24'·9N 24°23'·5E

Órmos Episkopis looking NW towards Nisís Áy Loukas

Facilities

Taverna at Apokriosis opens in the summer.

General

The bays here are generally only frequented by yachts. A few tourists walk around, and locals sometimes bring speedboats round to here, but by and large it is a wonderfully peaceful place, except for the *meltemi* blasting off the hills in the height of summer.

On the S side of Apokriosis are the remains of the ancient capital of the island. Locally the site is known as Vriokastro and the islet off the cape is also called by that name. Associated with Vriokastro are the ruins on Nisís Áy Loukas where you can find the remains of the ancient *agora* (the ruins shown on the NE of the islet) and ruins of a temple and walls (on the W of the islet). On the slopes around the bays numerous tombs have been discovered which contained coins, clay vessels and jewellery. On the N side of Kólona there is a thermal spring.

Órmos Episkopis

The bay lying pretty much midway between Órmos Apokriosis and Órmos Mérikha. It affords reasonable shelter from the *meltemi* although a bit of swell may roll in here. Anchor in 3–10 metres near the head of the bay. A taverna opens in the summer.

On the slopes to the north are the scant remains of Vriokastro. The tower here is said to have been built by a local ruler to shelter the townswomen, and in particular one local beauty the ruler rather fancied, in the event of pirate attacks.

Mérikha

The principal port for the island.

Pilotage

Approach The buildings around Órmos Mérikha are easily identified and entrance is straightforward. When the *meltemi* is blowing there are strong gusts into the bay.

Mooring Go stern or bows-to the S end of the quay leaving the ferry berth clear. Shelter from the *meltemi* is good in here. The only problem you will have is the propeller wash from the ferries; often they will come in and tie up and then go slow ahead to keep themselves off the quay. Make sure your anchor is well in to withstand the turbulence from the ferry

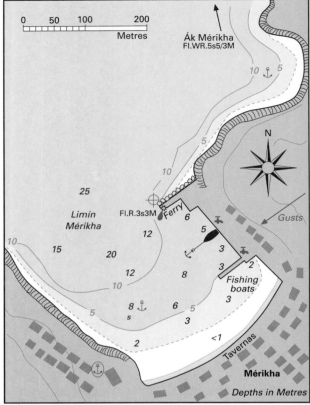

MÉRIKHA
⊕37°23′·45N 24°23′·75E WGS84

propellers. Alternatively you can anchor off although most of the bay is taken up with laid moorings. Make sure your anchor is holding as the gusts from the *meltemi* can be severe. You can also anchor off in the cove in the NE of the bay, though this is not the best place to be.

Facilities

Services Water on the quay when you can find the 'waterman'. Showers in a taverna nearby. Fuel can be delivered by mini-tanker.

Provisions Most provisions can be found in the village.

Eating out Try the tavernas along the waterfront which often have tables on the beach. There is something utterly magical about eating out while the sea gently breaks on the shore by your table. There is not a lot to choose between the different tavernas, so choose the one that appeals for its location.

Other PO. OTE. Bank. Bus to the *chora*. Taxis.

Órmos Mérikha, looking E to the harbour
Right Taverna on the beach at Mérikha

Hire motorbikes. Ferries to Lavrion and Piraeus and to the nearby Cyclades.

General

Mérikha has grown up to service the ferry port here and is to a large extent the hub of Kíthnos. Here you will find more hotels and tavernas than anywhere else, though for all that there are still not very many. It is a pleasant enough place and the tavernas on the water's edge are the best part.

It is worth visiting the *chora* from here; it is on a ridge in the interior and, although much larger than Mérikha, is a sleepy place with less in the way of services. It has nothing you should really see and most people end up sitting in the central square wondering why they are there. If you hire a motorbike to get to the *chora* it is worth continuing on to Driopis, the old capital of the island, which sits straddling a ravine. Its architecture is typically Cycladic and again, although there is nothing pressing for you to see or do here, it's worth a visit for a peep into the Cyclades of yesteryear. If you do hire a motorbike some care is needed on the island's roads, which are not in the best repair and have a lot of deep potholes.

Órmos Flamboriou

37°22'·2N 24°23'·7E

A large bay lying S of Mérikha. Shelter from the *meltemi* can be found here although some swell tends to curve around into the bay. Anchor in 5–10m off the beach on sand. With the *meltemi* there are gusts off the high land into the bay.

Órmos Áy Dhimitriou

37°19'·4N 24°22'·0E

A double-headed bay on the SW corner of Kíthnos. Some shelter from the *meltemi* can be obtained here. A taverna opens in the summer.

Loutra

A harbour on the NE coast that affords good all-round shelter.

Pilotage

Approach The bay in which Loutra snuggles is difficult to identify from the distance as the rubbly slopes all look much the same on this corner of the island. Once up to the entrance the houses on the S side of the bay will be seen and in the bay it becomes clear what is where.

Mooring Go stern or bows-to in the basin, except on the outside arm where yachts normally go alongside. This is simply to avoid anchors getting crossed over each other in the small basin. If the basin is full, yachts can go stern or bows-to the section of quay between the basin and the old loading gantry. Good shelter in the basin and adequate shelter from the *meltemi* on the quay outside.

Yachts can also anchor with a long line ashore in Órmos Áy Irini on the SE side of Órmos Loutrou. Anchor and take the line ashore to the NE side where there are a number of old iron rings set into the rock. Shelter here is adequate from the *meltemi* although some swell is pushed into the cove.

Facilities

Services Water and electricity on the quay in the basin at Loutra. Showers in the taverna nearby. It may be possible to get fuel delivered.

Provisions Some provisions in the village.

Eating out Several tavernas near the harbour and around the beach. Choose according to your fancy, but I'd recommend drinking something other than the local wine. *Vasilli*, right on the harbour-front, has good interesting food and good music. The *Trehandiri* taverna above Áy Irini is also good.

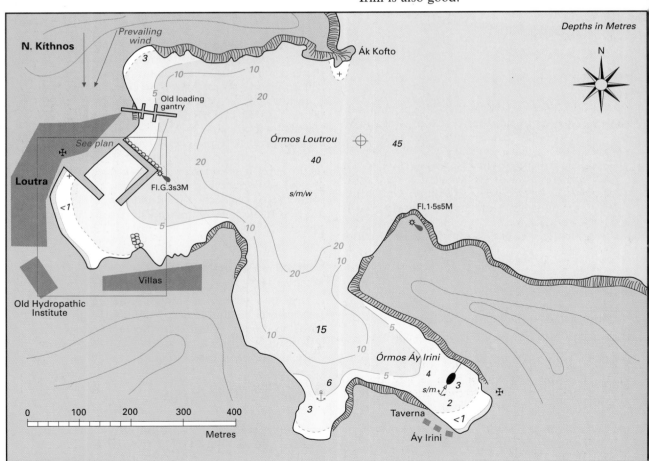

ÓRMOS LOUTROU
⊕37°26'·66N 24°25'·97E WGS84

Loutra harbour looking NW

Other PO. Taxi.

General

I've always liked Loutra, and the construction of the new basin giving all-round shelter means I like it even more. The place seems somehow more removed than its geographical position suggests – perhaps it is all those threatening rubble-strewn slopes and the *meltemi* screaming over the hills. Whatever it is, most people end up staying longer than anticipated here and most leave with warm memories of the place.

The old Hydropathic Institute, originally constructed by King Otto of Bavaria (Greece's first king) in 1858, still stands, though it has been largely rebuilt in a style reminiscent of correction institutions. It is all peeling paint and marble floors, with the individual baths behind solid doors with just a number on them. Non-residents at the institute can use the baths (0800–1400) and for around 3½ Euros you get a towel, a quick physical check-up to make sure you are up to it, and one of the cells with a bath. There are two springs here: one has a temperature of about 38·5°C (about body temperature) and the other of about 52°C. Apparently the springs are beneficial for rheumatism and arthritis. If you don't fancy the institute the hot springs flow down to the sea at the SE corner of the beach, so you can always wander down here for a dip.

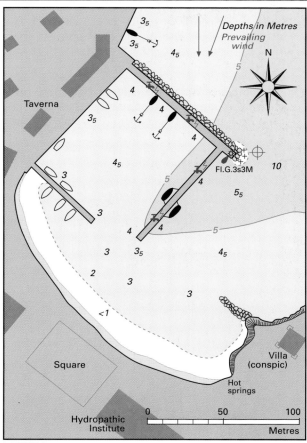

LOUTRA
⊕37°26'·6N 24°25'·7E

To the N around Ák Kéfalos are the ruins of Kástro, a medieval citadel and town. This was apparently sacked by Barbarossa (although poor old Barbarossa, a Greek himself, gets blamed for most things in this period) in 1537 and today little remains. Local folklore relates that the ruler of the Kástro escaped on horseback and the spot where his horse collapsed with exhaustion is where the present-day *chora* was built. Kástro is about two hours' tough walk – take a bottle of water.

Áy Stefanos and Áy Ioannis

The two much-indented bays on the E coast of Kíthnos. Both bays afford good shelter from the *meltemi* although there are severe gusts down into them. Care needs to be taken of the reef running out from the headland separating the two bays.

Anchor near the head of either bay and take a long line ashore if necessary. The latter is really only for the severe gusts from the *meltemi* as there is plenty of room to swing to an anchor. The bottom is sand and weed and not the best holding, so make sure your anchor is well in and if necessary set a second anchor.

A taverna opens in Áy Stefanos in the summer.

A number of villas, one palatial, have been built around the slopes, but by and large this remains a wonderful place. The chapel of Áyios Ioannis

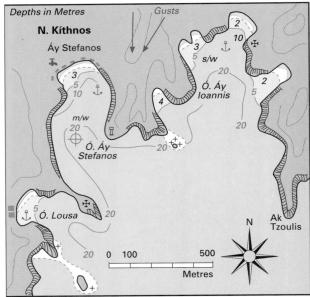

Ó. AYIOS STEFANOS AND Ó. AYIOS IOANNIS
⊕37°23′·6N 24°27′·6E

Theologos on the headland forming the western entrance to Áy Stefanos is wonderfully evocative and contains that essence of the Cyclades: the startling white of the chapel against the bare rocky headland caught between the glaring blue of the sea and sky. The chapel contains an icon to

Áy Stefanos and Áy Ioannis looking NE

KÍTHNOS SOUTHERN ANCHORAGES

⊕25 1M S of Ák Áy Dhimítrios (Kíthnos)
37°17'·1N 24°21'·9E

(Holy Virgin of the Canal), was founded when an icon of the virgin was found in a canal, though exactly where is uncertain. On the 15th August and the 8th September numbers of pilgrims come here for her feast days.

Órmos Áy Nikólaos (Skilou)

37°19'·8N 24°25'·3E

A bay nearly 2M further S of Kanala. It also affords indifferent shelter from the *meltemi* and is suitable in calm weather or light northerlies. Anchor near the head of the bay where convenient.

Nísos Sérifos

This dome-shaped island lies nearly 6M S of Kíthnos, separated by a strait with the slab-sided islets of Nisís Piperi and Nisís Serifopoula on the eastern edges. From the distance Sérifos looks like the other Cyclades, all brown sun-baked rock and little in the way of vegetation. So it comes as a bit of a surprise to those who venture inland to find that it has a number of valleys

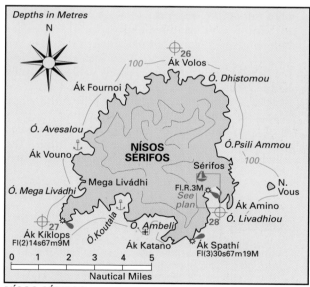

NÍSOS SÉRIFOS

⊕26 1M N of Ák Volos (Sérifos)
37°13'·8N 24°29'·5E
⊕27 1M W of Ák Kíklops (Sérifos)
37°07'·4N 24°23'·7E
⊕28 0·2M W of Ák Amino (entrance to O. Livadhiou/Sérifos) 37°07'·66N 24°31'·68E WGS84

Panayía Athenia (Holy Virgin of Athens) who is said to have swum to Kíthnos after the Turks captured Athens.

Lefkes

37°22'·4N 24°27'·0E

A tiny cove set at the foot of a ravine about 1M S of Órmos Lousa. It is exposed to the *meltemi* so is not really suitable in anything other than calm weather. There is a taverna on the shore and in calm weather this is a spectacular lunch stop.

Órmos Kanala

37°20'·7N 24°26'·2E

A bay 4½M SW of Ák Áy Ioannis. It affords indifferent shelter from the *meltemi* but can be used in calm weather. Care is needed of the isolated reef lying in the entrance to Kanala and the approach should be made from the S. Anchor in 5–8m at the head of the bay. Taverna ashore.

The monastery nearby, of the Panayía Kanala

where the almost corrosive green of the vegetation betrays the presence of water. The other surprise is that although the island looks amply rounded from the distance, when you venture inland, even just up to the *chora*, you find it is steeply folded, with the roads cut round deep gorges and ravines, and chapels built teetering on the edges of cliffs. It is a tough little nut of an island, with inhabitants who are also seen as tough, somewhat taciturn and withdrawn, but personable and friendly once you get to know them.

The island has bizarre mythopoeic origins. In Argos King Acrisius imprisoned his daughter Danae in a tower because an oracle had foretold that he would be murdered by a son born to his daughter. One day Zeus caught sight of her and, true to his satyriac nature, visited her as a shower of golden rain and slept with her. When her son, Perseus, was born, her father set them both adrift in a wooden chest which was washed up on the shores of Sérifos. The island was ruled by King Polydectes who fell in love with her, but Danae rejected his offers (no doubt when you sleep with a god, even as a shower of golden rain, a mere mortal is not enough). Polydectes pressed his offers over the years to no avail and eventually decided to win her by cunning. He sent Perseus on a mission to bring the Gorgon Medusa's head to Sérifos. The Medusa had writhing snakes for hair and her gaze turned men to stone, so Polydectes fondly imagined he had seen the last of Perseus. He didn't reckon with the gods. Athena and Hermes gave Perseus a helmet of darkness, a shield with which to reflect the stony gaze, and winged shoes. Perseus arrived back on Sérifos in the nick of time to stop Polydectes marrying Danae, and it is said that the fragmented rock cliffs at the *chora* are the bodies

The *chora* on Sérifos, looking up from the anchorage

of the king and his courtiers, turned to rock by the Medusa's gaze.

From this point on it was all downhill for Sérifos. It was a minor partner in the Delian League and during the Roman era it was a place of exile. From that time to the present it is hardly mentioned in the history of the Aegean, except for a bit of sacking by pirates or a stopover for the Venetians. Perhaps the islanders' reputation for being withdrawn is more a product of being isolated from the mainstream of Aegean history than some particular cultural trait, though I find a little reserve refreshing sometimes.

Livádhi

The main port on the southeast corner of the island.

Pilotage

Approach The exact location of Órmos Livádhiou is difficult to pin down from the distance. At times you will catch glimpses of the *chora*, but this does not necessarily help in locating the entrance to the bay. Once up to the entrance of Órmos Livádhiou all becomes clear and the approach is straightforward. When the *meltemi* is blowing there can be fierce gusts off the land in the approaches.

Getting around

A bus runs fairly regularly from Livádhi to the chora with times posted at the bus stop at the root of the yacht pier. There is an irregular summer service to Mega Livádhi and Kallistos in the N, but don't rely on it. There are several taxis all based at Livádhi or the chora. At Livádhi you can hire a car or motorbike. The island affords some good walks, in particular from the chora to Kallistos and the monastery of Taxiarhon in the N of the island. It is a good 2-hour walk to Kallistos and another 30 minutes to the monastery. It is probably best to get a bus or taxi to the monastery or Kallistos and walk back to Livádhi.

Mooring If there is room go stern or bows-to on the S side of the yacht pier. When the *meltemi* is blowing strongly only the bold will use the N side of the pier as the wind blows directly onto it. If you do intend going on the N side with a strong *meltemi* then go stern-to and ensure your anchor is laid a long way out and is holding properly.

The alternative to the pier is to anchor out in the bay. The holding here varies considerably and in places it can be difficult to get your anchor to hold. Just keep trying. At times

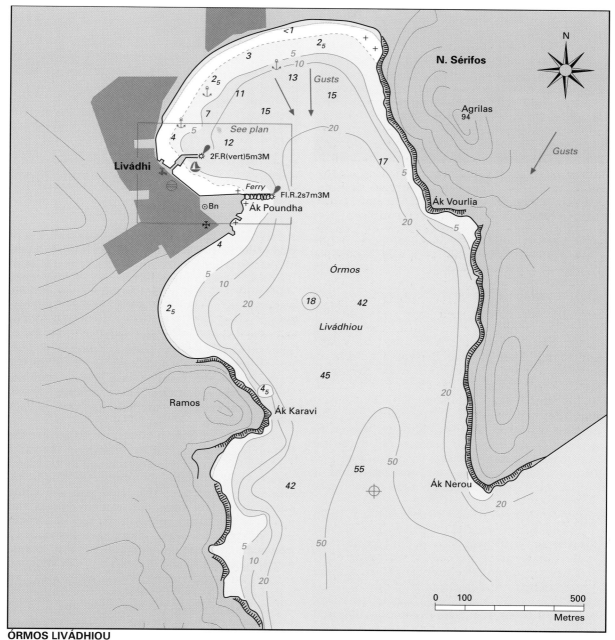

ÓRMOS LIVÁDHIOU
⊕37°07′·97N 24°31′·34E WGS84

Livádhi looking down from the *chora*   *Lu Michell*

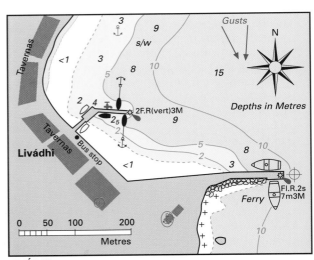

LIVÁDHI
⊕37°08′·49N 24°31′·19E WGS84

yachts will anchor and take a long line ashore to a tree behind the beach. The port police will occasionally object to this (it is a bit of a hazard to those using the beach) and will tell you to let go the lines.

Overall there is good shelter from the *meltemi* in the bay once you have got your anchor holding, either in the bay or on the pier, although there are strong gusts. The bay also affords good shelter from other winds except strong southerlies, when you must be tucked into the W side of the bay and even this will be uncomfortable.

Facilities
Services Water on the pier. Showers ashore in some of the bars and tavernas. Fuel can be delivered by mini-tanker.
Provisions Good shopping for most provisions at Livádhi. Two good bakeries right by the yacht pier.
Eating out A large choice of tavernas at Livádhi and all the way around the beach. The *Mokkas* taverna near the pier is good, but I suggest you just wander along and look at what is on offer. There are also a large number of bars playing everything from soft jazz to hard rap.
Other PO. OTE. Bank. Taxis. Bus to the *chora*. Hire motorbikes. Ferries to Sífnos, Mílos and Piraeus.

General
Livádhi is a busy spot in the summer with lots of yachts on the pier or at anchor, but it never seems all that crowded ashore and is a place that a lot of us look forward to returning to. I was once mightily relieved to get in here after struggling up from Sífnos against a Force 8 *meltemi*, with the engine overheating as I attempted to motor up to the entrance to the bay and doing all of 1½ knots against the force of the wind and the chop it set up in relatively sheltered water. Part of the attraction of the place is just getting into the sheltered bay, although as I have indicated above, getting the anchor to hold is not always straightforward.

While you are here it is well worth getting the bus up to the *chora*. It leaves from near the yacht pier and follows the winding road up to the island capital built around a rock buttress. Wandering around the streets of the *chora* you will come across wonderful views out over the gorges and valleys of the island and over the bay of Livádhi and adjacent coastline. There is really nothing exceptional to see here although most people wander around to the Kástro, the old Venetian fort set on a rocky defile with a giddy view out over Livádhi. There are a few tavernas around the village square where the bus stops, and a lot of locals sitting around sipping coffee and watching you.

Órmos Ambeli

37°07'·2N 24°29'·5E

The large bay on the west side of Ák Katano and Mikronisi. Care is needed of the isolated reef nearly in the middle of the entrance. In calm weather it will be seen, but with the *meltemi* gusting off the land it is lost in the white horses kicked up. Anchor in 5–10m in the NE corner. Reasonable shelter from the *meltemi*.

Órmos Koutala

The bay tucked up into the S side of Sérifos which affords good shelter from the *meltemi*. You can anchor in either of the two coves at the head of the bay, although care is needed in the W cove to avoid the area fouled by old mooring chains. There are strong gusts with the *meltemi* so make sure the anchor is well in. Taverna ashore.

Around the sides of the bay are the remains of the old iron ore mines and jetties. Most of the mines here have closed down and the population of Koutala has dwindled as a result. Although a number of new villas have been built recently, the place is still a little forlorn, though charming for all that, with the church still newly painted and a few tourists on the beaches.

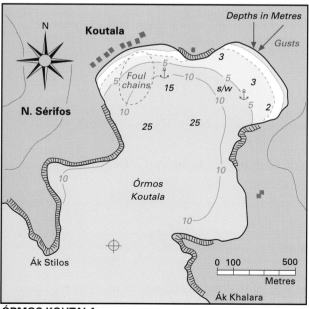

ÓRMOS KOUTALA
⊕37°07'·8N 24°27'·3E

Órmos Mega Livádhi

37°08'·5N 24°25'·8E

The bay N of Ák Kíklops. The bay is reported to offer good shelter from the *meltemi*. Taverna ashore.

Like Koutala this is an old mining area and until recently iron and copper ore were shipped out of here. Today the mines are all but abandoned and the machinery lies idle. Inland from here is Megalo Chorio, the ancient capital of Sérifos, though virtually nothing remains of it.

Órmos Avesalou

37°09'·8N 24°25'·8E

This bay on the E coast looks as though it should afford some shelter from the *meltemi*.

Órmos Psili Ammou

37°10'·0N 24°31'·7E

This is the best beach on Sérifos, but as it is situated on the E coast it is entirely open to the *meltemi*. In calm weather there are suitable depths for anchoring off the beach. Several tavernas open in the summer.

Nísos Sífnos

The sister island to Sérifos, lying across the often windy Sífnos Channel. Like the other islands it is all rough sun-baked rock cut by deep defiles and gorges, but go into the interior and there are cultivated fields and patches of green to relieve the bare rock. I always think of Sífnos as a tidy island run by tidy islanders. It has good asphalt roads and a reliable bus service. The houses and churches are newly painted and primped and ready for inspection. You almost feel that you have to do that very un-Greek thing of obeying signs which say 'no mooring' or 'no smoking' or 'no parking'.

In ancient times the Sífniots had a reputation for meanness and greed. The island was said to be rich in gold and silver mines and the Sífnians used to make an annual tithe of a gold egg to Delphi. The tithe was used to build the Treasury of the Sífniots in the sanctuary of Apollo at Delphi. Pausanias relates how one year the Síphniots offered a gilt egg in place of the gold one. Apollo, angered by this, caused the mines to collapse into the sea and thereafter the islanders were

NÍSOS SÍFNOS

⊕**29** 1M N of Vrak Tsoukala (Sífnos)
37°03'·9N 24°38'·0E

⊕**30** 0·4M W of Ák Karavi (N. Kitriani/Sífnos)
36°53'·50N 24°42'·91E WGS84

condemned to a life of poverty. On the northeast corner of the island at Áy Sostis there are ancient silver mines which were flooded when the land subsided, lending some truth to the old stories. The island was evidently wealthy, as around this time (6th–3rd century BC) it had three acropolises and a system of watchtowers (55 have been identified) for signalling between them.

After the 3rd century BC the island declined and passed variously to the Romans, Byzantines and finally, in 1464, to Venice via the Gozzadino family, who also controlled Kéa and Kíthnos as a

Getting around

Sífnos has the best roads and the best bus service in the western Cyclades. You can get to most places by bus, and get back again. At Kamáres and Apollonia you can hire cars and motorbikes for getting around the island, and given the good roads this is probably the best way to go.

little fiefdom owing allegiance to Venice. On Sífnos they chose Kástro as their capital for the island and the construction of the place was designed with defence in mind against the Turks and pirates that still roamed the Aegean. The houses are built on a rocky bluff with narrow streets, and rise up in a concentric ring that could be easily defended.

The Turks arrived in 1537 and, contrary to much popular folklore, were fairly benign rulers. The island practically ran itself, with an elected council which kept law and order and collected the taxes which were handed over to the Kaputan Pasha (the Admiral of the Turkish fleet) every year. Sífnos, like many of the other islands in the Cyclades, prospered during this time and had its own local trading fleet. Pottery was also big business and Sífnos is one of the last places where the huge handmade storage amphorae were made in the 20th century. The only thing to disturb this industrious little island at this time were the continuing pirate raids which even the large Turkish navy could not eliminate completely.

The Sífniots were not united in the Greek War of Independence. There were many on the island who were quite happy with the way business was prospering under Turkish rule and it took a little time before the islanders put their whole-hearted weight behind the war effort. After independence the island's fortunes waned and it declined, with mass emigration by many of the islanders to the USA and Australia. Only latterly has it recovered with some tourism and today it has ambitions to be an upmarket resort. The current Greek Prime Minister, (as I write this), Kostas Simitis, favours spending his holidays on Sífnos. Around the island camping is prohibited in most places, nudism is tolerated only on a few isolated beaches, and the locals tend to frown on anything or anyone that might reflect badly on their island.

Áy Yeoryios (Aghios Georgios, Khersonissos)

A narrow inlet right up on the northwest tip of the island under Ák Filippos. Care is needed of Vrak Tsoukala if you are coming from the E. The inlet provides good shelter from the *meltemi* and from most other winds except strong westerlies.

There is a quay on the SW side of the N bay where yachts can go stern or bows-to at the outer end taking care of underwater ballasting projecting out from it. There is also a quay on the NE side where there may be a space. A tripper boat also uses the quay in the summer so take care not to obstruct the space it uses. Alternatively anchor and take a long line ashore.

Ashore there are two tavernas and a ceramics workshop. Some of the last large amphorae used to be made here, vessels nearly as tall as a man that were used on the trading caïques to transport everything from wheat and other cereals to water and wine. The alternative name for the place, Khersonissos, means a peninsula or 'nearly an island'.

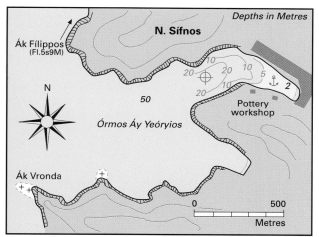

ÓRMOS ÁY YEÓRYIOS
⊕37°02'.2N 24°38'.8E

Vourlitha

37°01'.4N 24°39'.2E

The large bay lying just under Áy Yeóryios. It has been recommended as an anchorage, but I find that the swell from the *meltemi* is pushed around the corner into the bay making it uncomfortable. Moreover, it is a fairly bleak and desolate place and there are other good anchorages nearby.

North Bay

37°00'.5N 24°39'.7E

Just north of Kamáres there is an inlet which affords some shelter from the *meltemi*, though like Vourlitha, some swell enters with the *meltemi*. Cliffs surround the bay except where two gullies drop down into the bay. Anchor in 4–5m on sand and weed, not everywhere good holding.

Kamáres

The main ferry port for the island, situated in a deep cliff-lined bay on the W coast of Sífnos.

Pilotage

Approach The entrance is difficult to see from the distance and vessels seem to disappear or appear from nowhere. Closer in, the light structure on the N side will be seen and once up to the entrance the houses around the bay are easily identified. Care is needed of ferries leaving and entering the bay, which they do at speed. Care is also needed of strong gusts off the land from the *meltemi* and it is probably better to motor up into the bay rather than risk shredding sails in the gusts.

Mooring Go alongside or stern or bows-to on the inside of the mole. Ferries now berth on the outside end of the mole. Alternatively anchor in the bay in 2–5m. The bottom is hard sand and weed and not everywhere good holding. Good shelter from the *meltemi* on the mole and at anchor, although there are strong gusts off the high land. With westerlies the anchorage is not tenable.

Facilities

Services Water on the quay if you can find the 'waterman'. Showers ashore. Fuel can be delivered by mini-tanker.

Provisions Good shopping for provisions ashore – probably the best on Sífnos, so stock up if needs be. Ice available.

Eating out Numerous tavernas along the waterfront. Take a pre-prandial stroll to check them out. The *Mariena* at the far end of the beach is also worth looking at.

Other PO. Bank. Bus to Apollonia. Hire cars and motorbikes. Ferries to Mílos and Piraeus.

General

In the past I have been a bit negative about Kamáres, saying it lacked a certain something despite the spectacular location. While it is true that Kamáres does have a lot of awful pour-and-fill architecture straggling up the hillside, down below it has matured into a likeable little resort and now has more facilities, and certainly more tavernas, than Apollonia. It is busy, but in that island sense where everyone gets excited because the ferry is coming in and that means mail, long-awaited packages arriving, relatives visiting, and hopefully some tourists to keep the local cash registers ticking over. If you want to explore

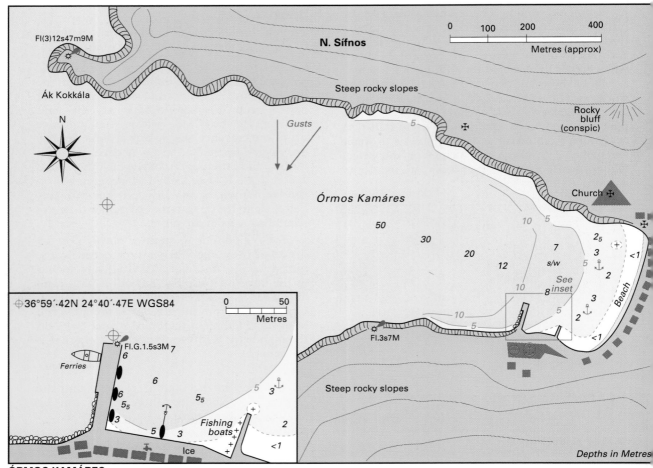

ÓRMOS KAMÁRES
⊕36°59´.50N 24°39´.21E WGS84

inland and visit Apollonia and Kástro, then Kamáres is the logical place to head for. After that you can visit the other anchorages around the coast.

On the other side of the bay sit Áyios Marina and Ayía Anna with their own churches. It's worth a wander round at dusk, and you can always stop on the way back for a drink at the *ouzerie* on the beach to watch the sun go down.

Órmos Vathí

Pilotage

Approach Like Kamáres, it is difficult to see just where the entrance to the bay is. The light structure on the S side will be seen, as will the villa on the N side. Once in the entrance the villas around the slopes will be seen. Care is

needed of the above and below-water rocks just off the N entrance.

Mooring Most yachts anchor in the bay. The depths shelve gently to the shore on the N side of the bay and you can drop anchor in 3–5m. The bottom is sand and weed and it can be difficult to get the anchor to hold at times. It may also be worth laying a second anchor if the *meltemi* is blowing strongly. A few yachts can also go stern or bows-to the stubby quay where there are 2–2·5m depths at the end.

Shelter from the *meltemi* is good in the bay and in fact there is shelter from all directions except W to SW, when a considerable swell is pushed in. Shelter on the quay is good although a strong *meltemi* causes a bit of a surge and boats on the quay will often jerk and roll uncomfortably.

Kamáres looking WNW from the slopes behind the bay

Nigel Patten

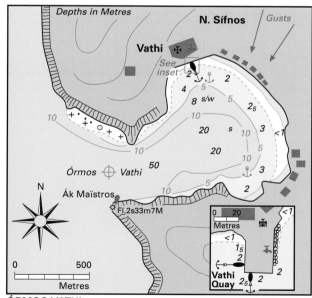

ÓRMOS VATHI
⊕36°55'·62N 24°41'·01E WGS84

Facilities
Services Water near the church, although the tap itself is often removed.

Provisions A small shop in the hamlet.

Eating out Tavernas in the hamlet and around the beach. The two tavernas on the beach near the road leading to the bus stop are worth a visit.

Other Bus to Apollonia.

General
There are some villas around the slopes and a pretty awful development on the road leading to Apollonia, but despite this the hamlet in the corner is a hymn to Cycladic architecture, with a pile of houses and buildings huddled around the water and the church on the stubby pier. There are tavernas here with locations to die for, and there are few who do not retain affection for the place. You can easily lose a few days just swimming and sitting by the water with a drink and some *mezes*, content that there is nothing else important to see or do.

The church on the pier is part of the small monastery of the Archangel (Taxiarchis) with cells in the courtyard formerly inhabited by the monks. On the northern slopes above Vathí is the

The short yacht quay at Vathi   *Lu Michell*

Vathi   *Lu Michell*

church of Áyios Andreas and the remains of one of the acropolises of ancient Sífnos. If you make the climb don't expect to see much of the acropolis apart from the foundations of the walls and some buildings.

Fikiadha

A narrow rocky inlet 1½M S of Vathí. It affords reasonable shelter from the *meltemi*, although a bit of swell is pushed into here – more uncomfortable than dangerous. Anchor in the inlet with a long line ashore or go bows-to the short pier below the chapel which has 1·5m depth on the end. The bottom is sand and mud with some rock, not everywhere good holding.

The inlet is hemmed in by the steep slopes and can feel a little scary at times, but in settled weather it is a wonderful place to spend the night.

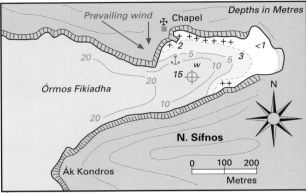

ÓRMOS FIKIADHA
⊕36°54'·4N 24°41'·6E

Órmos Platí Yialos

The U-shaped bay just round the corner from Ák Kontos and partially sheltered by Nisís Kitriani on the SW side. There are good depths (25m) in the fairway between Nisís Kitriani and Sífnos and passage through the channel is straightforward. You can anchor anywhere off the beach at Plati Yialos, but the best place to be with the *meltemi* is in the NE corner where the gusts from the *meltemi* are not as strong as elsewhere. Anchor in 5–7m clear of the boats on permanent moorings here. The bottom is sand and weed with some rock and not everywhere the best holding, so make sure your anchor is well in.

Ashore there are lots of tavernas and bars and some provisions can be found. This is the most popular resort on Sífnos, a fact attested to by the ugly strip of concrete buildings along the beach which do nothing but detract from the place. It is indistinguishable from any other resort and is arguably the most ugly part of the island. On the other hand, if you like late-night clubs and a loud

Platí Yialos looking NE   *Lu Michell*

bass beat, then you may like the place more than I do.

Fáros

A bay on the SE corner of Sífnos providing good shelter from the *meltemi*.

Pilotage

Approach The monastery on Ák Petalos (Panayía Chrysopigi) is conspicuous and once into the entrance of the bay the buildings of Fáros at the head will be seen.

Mooring There are a number of possibilities:

1. **Fáros head** At the head of the bay anchor and take a long line ashore to the rocky bluff between the beaches (with the *On the Rocks* taverna above). This is the best place to be as the *meltemi* blasts directly out of the bay here and the long line takes the strain.

2. **Fáros quay** On the E side of the bay there is a short quay with a stubby mole. There may be space here, although a strong *meltemi* blows straight down onto the quay.

3. Anchor in the bay or in either of the two coves

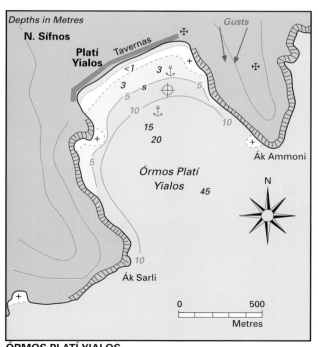

ÓRMOS PLATÍ YIALOS
⊕36°55'·6N 24°44'·0E

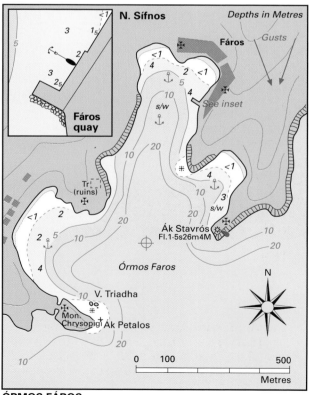

ÓRMOS FÁROS
⊕36°56'·3N 24°45·2E

Fáros, looking NW from the stubby mole on the E side of the bay

Below Fáros, looking NE towards the head of the bay

Nigel Patten

near the entrance. Of these the cove on the W side is usually best with a strong *meltemi*.

Facilities

Services Water ashore. Showers at some of the tavernas.

Provisions Limited provisions, although you can always get the bus into Apollonia.

Eating out Several good tavernas along the waterfront. The *On the Rocks* and the *Kyma* are both worth a try.

Other Bus to Apollonia. Taxi.

General

Fáros has a more earthy and intimate charm than neighbouring Platí Yialos. It attracts quite a lot of people to the small beach in the summer, though many of them are locals who disappear by early evening. There are a few good tavernas and bars ashore and, despite the *meltemi* gusting into the bay, you feel comfortable here.

The monastery of Panayía Chrysopigi (Virgin of the Golden Fountain) on the headland at the entrance to the bay is worth a visit, though if you

have only a small outboard on the tender and several people to transport, then leave the expedition until after the *meltemi* dies down. There is a small landing stage on the N side of the rock. The Panayía Chrysopigi is the patron saint of Sífnos and has been credited with a number of miracles. Legend has it that the icon of the Virgin was found floating out at sea by fishermen and brought to this rock. Another tale relates how several young girls fled to the rock to escape pirates intent on deflowering them. Just before the pirates got to the rock, the deep cleft that separates the church from Sífnos opened up, and the pirates could not get across.

Kástro

On the N side of Ák Miti and under the old medieval capital there is a cove suitable in calm weather only. The *meltemi* pushes a considerable swell straight into here so during the *meltemi* season it is better to visit Kástro by land from another safe anchorage.

In calm weather anchor in 3–5m off the tiny beach. The bottom is sand and weed with some rocks and not everywhere good holding. Taverna on the tiny beach at the head of the bay.

The Kástro above is well worth a visit. It is a steep walk up to the houses built in a defensive concentric pattern on the rocky bluff. The outer houses make up a defensive wall with just five gates leading into the interior. The larger houses have a crest on the front denoting which noble family lived there, and many of the houses have

Kástro on Sifnos   *Lu Michell*

incorporated bits of ancient masonry into the construction so that you find a column here, a sarcophagus there, and bits of old veined marble cemented into the walls or used as doorsteps. It is worth going up here for lunch as there is nearly always a pleasant breeze cooling things down and several of the tavernas within Kástro have good food in aristocratic surroundings.

Nísos Mílos

Mílos is a huge volcano that erupted in prehistory to scoop out the huge caldera that is Órmos Mílou. It takes a while to realise that this huge bay is the volcano and bubbling away under the surface is the hot magma that heats the numerous hot springs around the island. Like Thira, its neighbour to the E, the island is surrounded by ash and pumice cliffs and basalt pillars that, despite millennia of weathering, are the result of

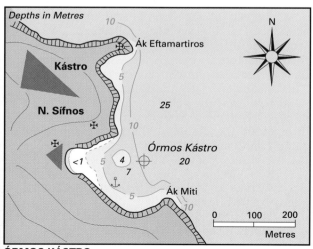

ÓRMOS KÁSTRO
⊕36°58'·3N 24°45'·1E

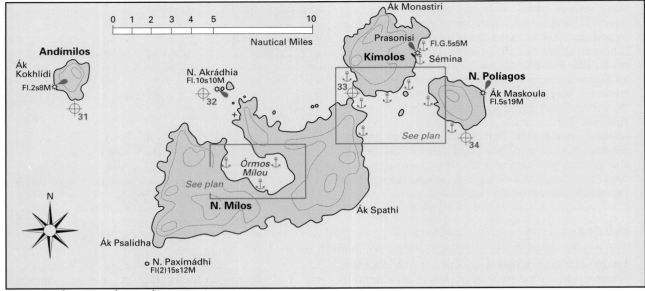

NISOI ANDÍMILOS, MÍLOS, KÍMOLOS AND POLIAGOS

the cataclysmic eruption that shaped the island. You should spend a little time contemplating the caldera, while thinking about the magnitude of the volcanic explosion needed to excavate a hole two miles in diameter and 60 metres deep.

The island is still important for its mineral reserves and there are huge opencast mines around the eastern side of Órmos Mílou. Alum, sulphur (there are hot sulphur springs), barium and kaolin are mined. Alum and sulphur were important in antiquity as well as nowadays. Alum was used to fix dyes in cloth and sulphur was used for medicinal purposes and in smelting metal.

The volcanic island was important in prehistory because of its rich reserves of obsidian or volcanic glass. Obsidian can be split to make sharp cutting edges for knives and spears and was used even after the introduction of copper and bronze. At Filokapi on the NE corner of Mílos there is a settlement which was continuously inhabited from 3000BC through the entire Bronze Age to the end of the 2nd millennium BC. A model of a boat from this period suggests that navigation between the islands was commonplace. During the second phase of building at Filokapi there is evidence in the pottery styles and frescoes that this was a Minoan outpost along with Thira. After the decline of the Minoans the same site was rebuilt and occupied by the Myceneans. Mílos occupies a sort of 'halfway house' position

⊕31 1M S of Ák Vlikadhi (Andímilos)
36°45'·1N 24°14'·6E
⊕32 0·5M W of Nds. Akrádhia light (Mílos)
36°46'·9N 24°22'·7E
⊕33 0·25M N of Ák Pelekoúdha light (Stenó Mílou-Kimolou) 36°46'·45N 24°31'·7E
⊕34 1M S of S end of N. Políagos
36°43'·6N 24°38'·9E

between the centre of the Minoan empire at Knossos on Crete and the centre of the Mycenean empire at Mycenae in the Argolic Gulf and quite possibly Mílos was pivotal in the Mycenaean advance down through the Aegean to Crete.

At the end of the Bronze Age Filokapi was abandoned and never again inhabited. Dorian settlers came down from the N and chose to build their capital on the eastern side of the entrance to the bay between present day Pláka and the sea. The Ionians and later the Romans also chose to build here, and the ruins of ancient Mílos are a jumble of ancient rubble from the Dorians through to the Romans. There are the usual columns and building blocks and part of a Roman theatre with one of those fantastic views over the sea. The site is interesting for a brief look and you can also take in Pláka and the fishing village of Klima nestled by the sea.

It was near here that the statue called the Venus di Milo was recovered. This statue of Aphrodite from around the 1st century BC, reproduced endlessly in history and art history books, was found in the 19th century by a farmer collecting stones for a dry wall. He removed the top half and negotiated to sell it to the French consul who took it to his house for safe keeping. The French ship sent to collect the statue arrived to find that the governor had seized it and put it aboard a Turkish ship bound for Istanbul. Captain de Marcellus decided to take it back and boarded the Turkish ship with an armed party and, after a brief skirmish, got the statue back on board the French ship. It is said that the Venus di Milo lost her arms during the skirmish and these were spirited away by a local. The statue was safely transported to the Louvre where it now sits, still without any arms, waiting for somebody in Mílos to turn up with the missing limbs.

Like all volcanic islands, Mílos possesses soil which is fertile in the extreme. Everything grows well and the name Mílos itself is derived from the Greek *melo*, apple, which presumably grew here in antiquity. Classical Greek coins minted on Mílos had an apple on the reverse side and descriptions by ancient commentators talk of the figs, honey, olives and apparently its fighting cocks which were described as the best in the (known) world. On the pottery from Mílos there are pictures of flowers and fish and the impression is one of a fecund island overflowing with fruit and vegetables, an impression hard to reconcile with the fairly arid landscape of today.

Mílos also figures in one of the darker deeds of classical Greece, the Melian deeds described by Thucydides. During the Peloponnesian Wars Mílos wanted to remain neutral. Eventually they opted for the Spartans across the water on the Peloponnese and Athens, enraged by what they saw as an act of betrayal, mounted an expedition against the island. Eventually Mílos had to surrender to the might of Athens and did so unconditionally. From Athens the order came to massacre the entire male population and enslave the women and children.

After the Romans the island passed in succession to the Byzantines, the Franks and then to the Turks, until it finally became Greek in 1830. Under the Turks and after the Greek War of Independence it was infamous as a pirate base. The pirates based themselves at Mílos and Kímolos and sold their booty onward at an open market, all of it pretty much sanctioned by the local inhabitants. In 1677 the Greek pirate Yiannis Kapsis decided to declare himself King of Mílos and the locals readily acquiesced. Kapsis was crowned king in the island's cathedral by the Catholic Bishop to the acclaim of the population. He lived here in a fine house with his piratical band and everyone seemed happy except the Turks who no longer received taxes. In 1670 he was lured onto a Turkish galley and taken to Istanbul where he was hanged.

Like many of the other islands, Mílos declined in the 20th century. The large natural harbour was used by the British as a naval base in the First World War. Today it has some tourism, though much of it is concentrated in the July-August period and outside high season many places are all but deserted. One thing the island, along with its neighbour Kímolos, does have, is the only venomous snake in Greece. All snakes in Greece are harmless with the exception of the vipers. The horned viper, *vipera ammodites*, found in Greece, is mildly poisonous and only really dangerous to the very young and very old. The viper found on Mílos and Kímolos (and Cyprus and North Africa), *vipera lebetina*, has a more dangerous venom, though it is usually not fatal to a healthy adult. The Lebetina viper is protected, though its numbers are declining as species are smuggled to collectors in northern Europe.

Nisídhes Akrádhia and lighthouse in the approaches to Órmos Mílou looking N

Getting around

Buses run regularly from Adhamas into the chora in the summer and there is also a reasonable service to Apollonia and Voudhia. In Adhamas you can hire a car or motorbike to get around the S and SW of the island and this is really the only way to go.

Adhamas

The main harbour for Mílos on the N side of Órmos Mílou.

Pilotage

Approach The entrance to Órmos Mílou is straightforward, if nearly always windy and bumpy in the summer. The *meltemi* blows straight down into the entrance, and there is always a heavy confused swell in the entrance with the *meltemi*. The lighthouse on Nisidhes Akrádhia and the village of Mílos (Pláka) on the peak on the E side of the entrance are easily identified. The passage between Nisidhes Akrádhia and Mílos is deep and poses no problems apart from the confused swell usually found here. The port of Adhamas will not be seen until you round Ák Bombardha.

When the *meltemi* is blowing care is needed of strong gusts down off the high land into Órmos Mílou, especially around Ák Bombardha, and it is prudent to take down

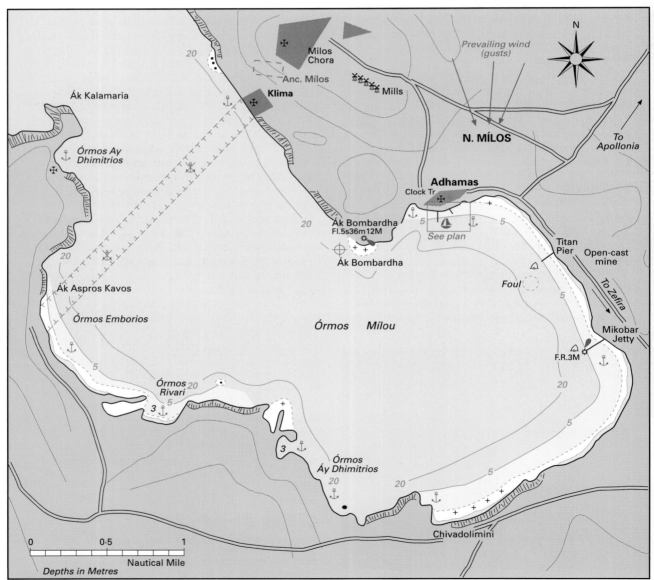

ÓRMOS MÍLOU
⊕36°43´·3N 24°26´·0E

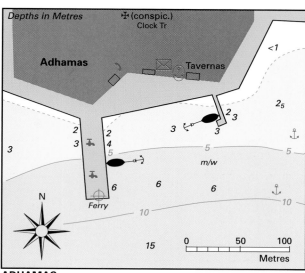

ADHAMAS
⊕36°43'·5N 24°26'·7E

Yacht pier at Adhamas

your sails and motor down into Órmos Mílou before you get to Ák Bombardha.

Mooring Go stern or bows-to the E side of the ferry quay or bows-to the short pier to the E of it. Alternatively anchor off the port to the W or E of the ferry quay, leaving plenty of room for the ferries to manoeuvre. Care is also needed of the numerous permanent moorings here. Shelter is good on the piers, where there is a bit

of a lee from the gusts, and is also good in the anchorage as long as your anchor is properly in. The bottom is mud, rocks and weed, poor holding in places, so if the *meltemi* is blowing strongly it is advisable to lay a second anchor.

The port of Adhamas is open to the S for the fetch across the large bay and with strong southerlies is untenable. With southerlies you should move to an anchorage on the S side of Órmos Mílou.

Facilities

Services Water on the ferry quay. Fuel can be delivered by mini-tanker.

Provisions Good shopping for provisions at Adhamas. Ice available.

Eating out Tavernas on the waterfront at Adhamas, though some of them serve some pretty awful fare for passengers waiting for the ferries. Try the *Navagio* and the *Flisvos* towards the beach.

Other PO. OTE. Bank. Hire cars, motorbikes and bicycles. Ferries to Piraeus, Thíra and Crete. Internal flights to Athens.

General

Adhamas is a comparatively new place, settled by Cretan refugees fleeing a failed uprising against the Turks in 1841. It has that sort of feel, although if the *meltemi* is blowing strongly outside you get to quite like the place. There are a number of interesting churches in typical

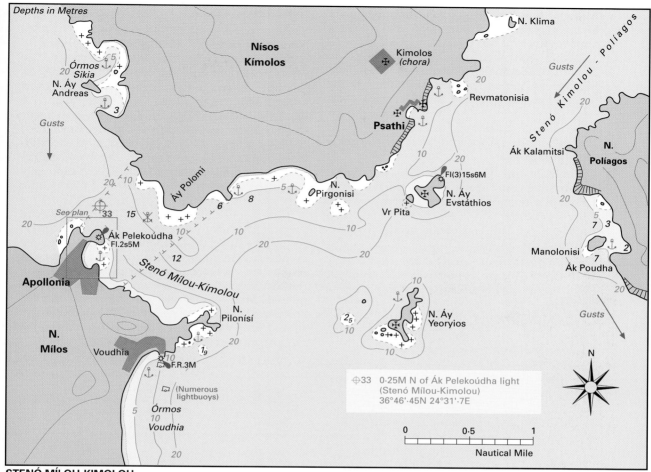

Depths in Metres

N. Klima

Nísos Kímolos

Kimolos (chora)

Órmos Sikia

N. Áy Andreas

20

Gusts

Revmatonisia

Stenó Kímolou - Políagos

Gusts

Psathi

Ák Kalamitsi

N. Políagos

Áy Polomi

N. Pirgonisi

Fl(3)15s6M

N. Áy Evstáthios

Vr Pita

See plan 33

Ák Pelekoúdha Fl.2s5M

Manolonisi

Ák Poudha

Apollonia

Stenó Mílou-Kímolou

N. Pilonísí

N. Áy Yeoryios

Gusts

N. Mílos

Voudhia

F.R.3M

(Numerous lightbuoys)

Órmos Voudhia

⊕33 0·25M N of Ák Pelekoúdha light
(Stenó Mílou-Kimolou)
36°46'·45N 24°31'·7E

N

0   0·5   1

Nautical Mile

STENÓ MÍLOU-KIMOLOU

Cycladic style and a few fair tavernas towards the beach.

From Adhamas you can get the bus up to the *chora* (Mílos or Pláka, an odd name for a place on top of a hill since it means 'beach') which is well worth a wander, as is ancient Mílos which straggles down the slopes to the sea near Klima. Also nearby are the early Christian catacombs although only the beginning of the tunnel is illuminated.

If you want a look around the interior then Adhamas is the logical place to leave the boat and hire a car or a bike. The island is scored and pitted by deep gullies and conical peaks where wind and water have eroded the limestone away to create a spectacular landscape and it's well worth exploring inland.

Opposite Looking up towards Plaka from Órmos Mílou

Anchorages around Órmos Mílou

There are a number of anchorages around Órmos Mílou that can be used in calm weather or with southerlies.

1. ***Titan and Mikobar piers*** On the E side of the bay are two long piers used by ships loading ore from the opencast mine on the slopes above. You wouldn't usually want to come to this dusty mining wasteland, but if you want to visit the Mining Museum here then it is possible to anchor off the beach in 4–6m just S of Titan. Strangely enough it is quite pleasant here, and in calm weather the anchorage off the beach to the N of Titan pier is really quite a good place to be. To the S of

Mikobar pier hot springs well up into the sea and you can move around to find just the temperature you want.

Inland from here was the old medieval capital of Zephyria, presumably so named because you got a gentle breeze rather than the *meltemi* bowling you over. Until recently it was largely deserted, having been abandoned in 1770 after an epidemic. Recently some of the houses have been rebuilt and it is not the ghost town it once was.

2. *Chivadolimini* On the S side of Órmos Mílou. The long beach here is very popular although it really doesn't compare to those on Kímolos nearby. In calm weather you can anchor at the SW end of the beach. Taverna ashore in the summer.

3. *Órmos Áy Dhimitrios* The bay immediately W of Chivadolimini. Suitable in calm weather. Small yachts may be able to creep in under the headland to get a bit more shelter.

4. *Órmos Rivari* The small bay in the SW corner of Órmos Mílou. Open to the *meltemi* but sheltered from southerlies.

5. *Órmos Emborios* The large bay on the W side of Órmos Mílou. Here there is a hamlet with some of the typical fishermen's houses, built on top of the boat-sheds, where boats would be hauled out of the water for lack of good shelter – something to bear in mind here. There is a good taverna, recommended by a Greek friend of mine, serving fresh fish and in calm weather it is well worth the effort to visit this picturesque little place.

6. *Klima* The small fishing village on the NE side of Órmos Mílou. In light northerlies you can anchor off here at the foot of the steep slopes. There is usually a bit of ground swell even in calm conditions so it is not the most comfortable place to stay. Klima is a picturesque little place with the same boatsheds under the houses as at Emborios. Taverna ashore.

Northeast coast

The northeast coast of Mílos between Nisidhes Akrádhia and Ák Pelekoúdha is a hostile impossible coast when the *meltemi* is blowing. The sea crashes right onto the coast and there are no safe anchorages. In calm weather you can potter around here and there are a few places to anchor on the W side of Ák Pelekoúdha. With even a hint of a northerly you should leave straight away.

This north coast is a picturesque place, with steep gullies and jagged basalt. The basalt pillars of the Glaronisia (Seagull islets) are especially impressive, rearing up out of the sea like some seascape out of *Lord of the Rings*.

Further offshore to the NW is Andímilos, a precipitous rock of an islet. It is apparently home to a rare breed of chamois, those goat-like creatures who supply all the soft leather for car enthusiasts to while away their Sundays polishing the car. With the *meltemi* there are fierce gusts off it, with little whirlwinds swirling across the sea and if you are on passage to the Peloponnese you should keep well clear of the islet before shaping the proper course to your destination.

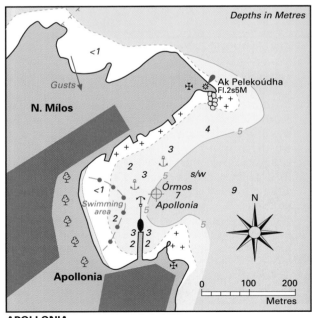

APOLLONIA
⊕36°45'·9N 24°31'·6E

Apollonia (Pollonia)

The bay tucked under the E side of Ák Pelekoúdha.

Pilotage

Approach The buildings around the bay are conspicuous and the location just S of the channel between Mílos and Kímolos is obvious. With the *meltemi* there are savage gusts through the channel and until you get to the entrance of the bay there is a surprising amount of short choppy sea. Care is needed of the reef running out E of Ák Pelekoúdha and also the reef running N from the southern entrance to the bay.

Mooring Anchor in the bay in 2–4m clear of the area buoyed off for swimmers. The bottom is mostly sand and good holding. In calm weather you can go stern or bows-to the end of the pier on the S side of the bay if there is room. This latter berth is not the best place to be with the *meltemi* as there are strong gusts into the bay directly onto the pier. Overall shelter in the bay is better than it looks.

Facilities

A mini-market and tavernas and bars along the beach.

General

Apollonia is the most popular beach on Mílos and it is busy in the summer. Really it's not one of my favourite places, much too noisy and crowded when there are a number of other good anchorages around. The *meltemi* gusting over the low-lying Ák Pelekoúdha makes it popular with the sailboard brigade and one of the bars, *Okto Bofor* (Eight Beaufort), gives you a pretty good clue to how windy it gets here.

Órmos Voudhia

The large bay lying about 1M SE of Apollonia. The loading gantries for the opencast mine on the slopes behind make it reasonably easy to identify. Care is needed of a 1·9m patch approximately 0·2M S of Pilonisi, the islet connected to Mílos by a causeway. Anchor in 5–8m in the N corner of the bay off the hamlet. Good shelter from the *meltemi* although a bit of swell is pushed around into the bay – more uncomfortable than dangerous.

Ashore there are a number of tavernas (the *Captain Nikolaos* has been recommended) and despite the despoiled slopes and the trucks rumbling around to load ore, you can sort of get to like the place. Along the shores there are a number of hot springs.

Palaiakhora

36°40'·4N 24°31'·0E

A rocky bay on the SE corner of Mílos. In calm weather you can anchor off here to enjoy the hot springs that well up into the sea. Care is needed of rocks running out from the shore and you should anchor well off. In the event of northerlies or southerlies it is best to leave.

Several tavernas ashore open in the summer and one of the beaches on the W side is an unofficial naturist beach.

Órmos Provatas

A large bay on the S side of Mílos between Ák Akrotiri and Ák Zefiros. In calm weather or with light northerlies this is a wonderful place which in settled weather can be used for an overnight stay. With a strong *meltemi* some swell is pushed around into the bay and it is probably best not to stay the night here in these conditions.

Anchor in either side of the bay on the W or the E. The bay on the W is generally favoured although there are suitable depths for anchoring

Apollonia *Nigel Patten*

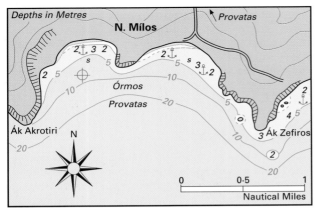

ORMOS PROVATAS
⊕36°40'·0N 24°26'·7E

in either bay. The bottom is sand with some rock, generally adequate holding.

There is some development here but the setting under the cliffs is wonderful. Several tavernas open at Provatas.

Nísos Kímolos

The island of Kímolos almost touches Mílos at the NE corner and is separated by the narrow Mílos-Kímolos strait. Kímolos is the poor cousin of Mílos. It has a few tourists in the summer, a bit of mining for chalk and fuller's earth, though most of that has gone, and no water to speak of. What it does have for yachts are a number of good indentations to shelter in where the paucity of tourists is a blessing for some of us.

Like Mílos, Kímolos is a volcanic island, although topographically it appears to be less so than its neighbour. It is a low treeless island without any of the soaring layered cliffs of Mílos, almost as if it has been worn down by the *meltemi* which screams over it in the summer. In ancient times it was called Echinoussa, probably after the sea urchin, but also possibly after the poisonous viper (*ehidna*) that the island shares with Mílos. The island was known for its deposits of chalk, and mines have existed here since ancient times. There is a strange story about cooling shafts on the island, where jars of water would be lowered down shafts at the mines and cooled in the underground caverns before being hauled to the surface.

The ancient capital was at Órmos Sikia on the SW corner of the island. The present day capital is the *chora*, which is about fifteen minutes' walk

from Psathi. Also near Psathi is a defensive huddle of houses like that at Kástro on Sífnos and built around the same time.

Órmos Sikia (Ellinika)

The anchorage on the SW side of Kímolos with the islet of Áy Andreas in the middle of the bay. The anchorage is suitable with a light *meltemi* blowing, but if it blows with any force this is not a good place to be as a considerable swell is pushed into the bay. You can always go round the corner to Apollonia or Pirgonisi anchorage. Anchor in 3–5m on the N or S side of the islet. The bottom is mostly coarse sand, patchy holding in places.

This is the site of Ellinika, the ancient capital of Kímolos. It is supposed that the islet of Áy Andreas was joined to Kímolos by a causeway in ancient times and there are the remains of walls and buildings on the islet, some now just under the water. On Kímolos itself there are further ruins and numerous graves. Ellinika was inhabited from around 1000BC right up until the Christian era and must have been of some importance, as an inscription found here tells of a quarrel between Mílos and Kímolos over the ownership of the nearby island of Políagos.

Pirgonisi anchorage

A long sandy beach stretches right around the S side of Kímolos and although it looks quite open, this anchorage affords good shelter from the *meltemi*. Care is needed when closing the beach of a rocky shelf around 1m underwater which fringes the beach for some way out. Nose into suitable depths and anchor. The *meltemi* blows more or less straight off the beach and the water here is relatively flat. At the eastern end of the beach there is the low rocky islet of Pirgonisi connected to the shore by a reef. With care you can tuck under the islet and reef off the beach in attractive and usually deserted surroundings. The bottom is sand and weed, good holding.

Ashore there is the hamlet of Aliki and in the summer one or two tavernas open, depending on inclination and whether anyone is prepared to gamble on a good season.

Psathi

The ferry port for the island on the SE corner of the island.

Pilotage

Approach The approach is straightforward, although if the *meltemi* is blowing it screams down the strait between Kímolos and Políagos. The cathedral in the *chora* and four windmills on a ridge behind are conspicuous.

Mooring Go stern or bows-to the stubby pier on the N side or bows-to behind the mole on the S side. It is best to go bows-to the mole as there is some underwater rubble off it. Otherwise anchor and take a long line ashore to the N side between the ferry pier and the stubby pier. If the *meltemi* blows strongly it can get very bumpy in here and you may have to leave. The Pirgonisi anchorage is just round the corner.

Facilities

You can get some provisions in the *chora* around fifteen minutes' walk away. At Psathi there are several tavernas and cafés including the recommended *Kyma* taverna on the beach. Ferry to Voudhia on Mílos.

General

Psathi is a wonderful sleepy little place that, weather permitting, you should visit. From here you can visit the medieval Kástro, much like the one on Sífnos except that here there has been no

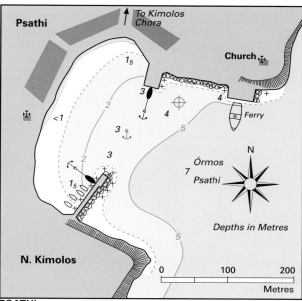

PSATHI
⊕37°47'·1N 24°35'·0E

real reconstruction of the place. Inside there is the large Catholic church of Khryssostomos. The *chora* too is worth a visit, simply because it is there and it makes few concessions to tourism. Just wander around, have a drink or two in the square, and then wander back to the little port.

Sémina Creek

36°48'·4N 24°35'·4E

A narrow fjord-like cove lying approximately 1¼M N of Psathi. It affords poor shelter from the *meltemi* and any good spots in here are used by local boats. Visit it in calm weather. Anchor in 4–6m and if necessary take a long line ashore.

Prasonisi anchorage

Under the NE end of Kímolos there is a bay with an islet in the middle. The *meltemi* blows straight into here so it should only be used in calm weather or light westerlies and northerlies. Anchor in 4–6m on the N or S side of the islet. The islet is connected by a reef to the shore.

Tavernas open in Prassa in the summer. There are radioactive hot springs here which are said to be beneficial for a wide range of complaints including skin diseases and 'women's problems'.

Psathi on Kímolos looking SW   *Nigel Patten*

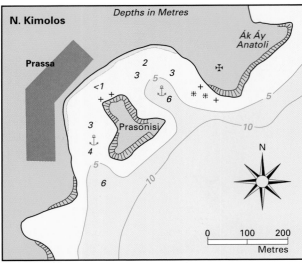

PRASONISI

Nisís Áy Evstathios and Áy Yeóryios

N. Áy Evstathios light (N end)
36°46'·7N 24°35'·0E

These two islets lying S of Psathi have anchorages which can be used in calm weather, but with any hint of the *meltemi* you should head for a safer anchorage. On Áy Evstathios anchor on the W or E sides. On Áy Yeóryios anchor off the W side. Care is needed of the reefs fringing Áy Yeóryios.

Nísos Políagos

The uninhabited island lying off the SE side of Kímolos. Apart from a large herd of goats, there is nothing here.

Manolonisi

On the W side of Políagos there is a bay with the islet of Manolonisi in the entrance. Anchor on the S side of the islet in 2–4m. Manolonisi is connected to Políagos by a reef and sand-bar. There is reasonable shelter from the *meltemi* in here and the surroundings are wonderful.

Políagos south side

⊕**34** 1M S of S end of N. Poliagos
36°43'·6N 24°38'·9E

On the S side of Políagos there are several anchorages which can be used in calm weather. When the *meltemi* is blowing there are strong gusts off the land and a swell is pushed around the island, making the anchorages uncomfortable.

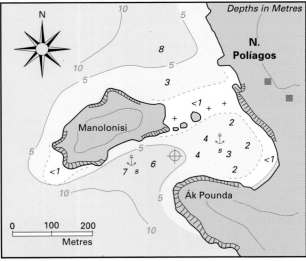

MANOLONISI
⊕36°46'N 24°36·5E

Appendix

GLOSSARY

Common Greek terms and abbreviations used in the text and plans

Ákra (Ák)	Cape
Andí (Anti)	Opposite
Áyios (Áy)	Saint
Dhíavlos	Strait or channel
Dhiórix	Channel or canal
Dhrómos	Roadstead
Fáros	Lighthouse
Ífalos (If or I)	Reef
Isthmós	Isthmus
Kávos	Cape
Khersónisos	Headland
Kólpos	Gulf
Limín (L)	Harbour
Mólos	Breakwater or mole
Moní	Monastery
Nisáki	Islet
Nísos/Nisí/	
Nisía (N)	Island(s)
Nótios	Southern
Órmos (O)	Bay
Ormiskos	Cove
Óros	Mountain
Pélagos	Sea
Pírgos	Tower
Porto	Small harbour
Potamós (Pot)	River
Pounda	Cape or point
Stenó	Strait
Thálassa	Sea
Vórios	Northern
Vrakhonisis	Rocky islet
Vrákhos	Rock

A few useful words in Greek

General

yes	né
no	ókhi
please	parakaló
thank you	efharistó
OK	endaksi
hot	zeste
cold	krió
here	ethó
there	ekí
hello	herete
goodbye	adío
good morning	kalaméra
good evening	kalíspera
good night	kalíníkhta
good	kaló
bad	kakó
today	símera
tomorrow	ávrio
later	metá
now	tóra
I want	egó thélo
where is	poú inai
big	megálo
small	mikró
one	éna
two	dhío
three	tría
four	téssera
five	pénde
six	éxi
seven	eptá
eight	octó
nine	eniá, enéa
ten	dheca

Shopping

apples	míla
apricots	veríkoka
aubergines	melitzána
baker	foúrnos
beans	fassólia
biscuits	biscóttes
bread	psomí
butcher	hassápiko
butter	voútiro
carrots	caróta
cheese	tirí
chicken	kotópoulo
chocolate	socoláta
coffee	kafés
cucumber	angouri
eggs	avgá
fish shop	psaróplion
flour	alévri
garlic	scórdo
green pepper	piperiá
grocer	bakáliko
ham	zambón
honey	méli
jam	marmeláda
lamb	arnáki
lemon	lemóni
margarine	margaríni
meat	kréas
milk	gála
mutton	arní
oil	ládhi
onions	kremmídia
oranges	portokália
parsley	maïdanós
peach	rodhákino
pepper	pipéri
pork	khirinó
potatoes	patátes
rice	rízi
salt	aláti
sugar	zákhari
tea	tsái
tomatoes	domátes
veal	moskhári
water	neró
watermelon	karpoúzi
wine	krassí
yoghurt	yaoúrti

USEFUL BOOKS

Admiralty Publications

Mediterranean Pilot Vol IV Covers the Aegean Sea.

List of Lights Vol E Covers the Mediterranean, Black and Red Seas.

Yachtsman's Pilots

Greek Waters Pilot Rod Heikell (Imray). Covers all Greek waters in a single volume.

The Ionian Islands to Rhodes H M Denham (John Murray). Covers the Ionian islands through Crete to Rhodes. Classic guides though no longer revised and kept up to date.

Imray Mediterranean Almanac Ed. Rod Heikell (Imray). Biennial publication covering all major Mediterranean harbours and marinas, although not in detail.

Other Guides

Blue Guide to Greece Ed. Stuart Rossiter (A & C Black).

Yacht Charter Handbook Rod Heikell (Imray). Covers charter destinations worldwide.

Berlitz Guide to Athens (Berlitz). Compact guide.

A Travellers History of Greece Timothy Boatswain & Colin Nicolson (Windrush Press). With a name like that how could a sailor resist it?

The Greek Islands Lawrence Durrell (Faber). Good photos and eloquent prose.

The Greek Islands Ernle Bradford (Collins Companion Guide).

The Rough Guide to Greece Ellingham, Jansz and Fisher (RKP). Down to earth guide.

Fortresses and Castles of Greek Islands and Fortresses and Castles of Greece Vol II

Alexander Paradissis (Efstathiados Group). Detailed guides available in Greece.

The Venetian Empire Jan Morris (Penguin). Readable account of the Venetian maritime empire.

General

A Literary Companion to Travel in Greece Ed. Richard Stoneman (Penguin).

The Ulysses Voyage Tim Severin (Hutchinson).

Eleni Nicholas Gage (Fontana/Collins).

Hellas Nicholas Gage (Collins Harvill).

The Colossus of Maroussi Henry Miller (Penguin). Arguably his best piece of writing, fiction included.

The Hill of Kronos Peter Levi (Zenith).

Flora and Fauna

Flowers of Greece and the Aegean Anthony Huxley and William Taylor

Flowers of the Mediterranean Anthony Huxley and Oleg Polunin. Both the above have excellent colour photos and line drawings for identification.

Trees and Bushes of Britain and Europe Oleg Polunin (Paladin).

The Hamlyn Guide to Birds of Britain and Europe Bruun, Delin and Svensson (Hamlyn).

The Hamlyn Guide to the Flora and Fauna of the Mediterranean A C Campbell (Hamlyn). Good guide to marine life.

Food

Greek Cooking Robin Howe

Food of Greece Vilma Chantiles

The Best of Greek Cooking Chrissa Paradissis

BEAUFORT WIND SCALE

B'fort No.	Wind Descrip	Effect on sea	Effect on land	Wind speed knots	mph	Wave ht (metres)
0	Calm	Like a mirror	Smoke rises vertically	less than 1		
1	Light	Ripples, no foam	Direction shown by smoke	1–3	1–3	–
2	Light breeze	Small wavelets, crests do not break	Wind felt on face, leaves rustle	4–6	4–7	0·2–0·3
3	Gentle breeze	Large wavelets, some white horses	Wind extends light flag	7–10	8–12	0·6–1·0
4	Moderate breeze	Small waves, frequent white horses	Small branches move	1–16	13–18	1·0–1·5
5	Fresh breeze	Moderate waves, some spray	Small trees sway	17–21	19–24	1·8–2·5
6	Strong breeze	Large waves form, white crests, some spray	Large branches move	22–27	25–31	3·0–4·0
7	Near gale	Sea heaps up, white foam, waves begin to streak	Difficult to walk in wind	28–33	32–38	4·0–6·0
8	Gale	Moderately high waves	Twigs break off trees, walking impeded	34–40	39–46	5·5–7·5
9	Strong gale	High waves, dense foam, wave crests break, heavy spray	Slates blow off roofs	41–47	47–54	7·0–9·75
10	Storm	Very high waves, sea appears white, visibility affected	Trees uprooted, structural damage	48–56	55–63	9·0–12·5
11	Violent storm	Exceptionally high waves, wave crests blown off, badly impaired	Widespread damage	57–65	64–75	11·3–16
12	Hurricane	Winds of this force seldom encountered for any duration in the Mediterranean.				

USEFUL CONVERSIONS

1 inch = 2.54 centimetres (roughly 4in = 10cm)
1 centimetre = 0.394 inches

1 foot = 0.305 metres (roughly 10ft = 3 metres)
1 metre = 3.281 feet

1 pound = 0.454 kilograms (roughly 10lbs = 4.5kg)
1 kilogram = 2.205 pounds

1 mile = 1.609 kilometres (roughly 10 miles = 16 km)
1 kilometre = 0.621 miles

1 nautical mile = 1.1515 miles
1 mile = 0.8684 nautical miles

1 acre = 0.405 hectares (roughly 10 acres = 4 hectares)
1 hectare = 2.471 acres

1 gallon = 4.546 litres (roughly 1 gallon = 4.5 litres)
1 litre = 0.220 gallons

Temperature scale

$t°F$ to $t°C$ is $5/9(t°F-32) = t°C$
$t°C$ to $t°F$ is $9/5(t°C+32) = t°F$

So 70°F = 21.1°C   20°C = 68°F
   80°F = 26.7°C   30°C = 86°F
   90°F = 32.2°C   40°C = 104°F

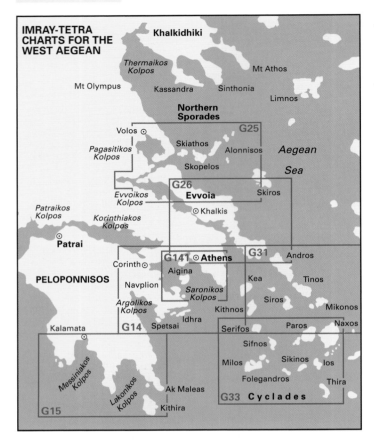

IMRAY-TETRA CHARTS FOR THE WEST AEGEAN

Khalkidhiki
Thermaikos Kolpos
Mt Athos
Mt Olympus
Kassandra Sinthonia
Limnos
Northern Sporades
Volos ☉
Skiathos G25
Pagasitikos Kolpos
Alonnisos *Aegean*
Skopelos
Sea
G26
Evvoikos Kolpos **Evvoia**
Skiros
Patraikos Kolpos
Korinthiakos Kolpos
☉ Khalkis
Patrai
G141 ☉ **Athens** G31 Andros
Corinth ☉
Aigina
Kea Tinos
PELOPONNISOS Navplion
Saronikos Kolpos
Argolikos Kolpos
Siros Mikonos
Idhra
Kithnos
Kalamata G14 Spetsai
Serifos Paros Naxos
Sifnos
Milos Sikinos Ios
Folegandros Thira
Ak Maleas
G15 G33 **Cyclades**
Kithira

Imray Tetra
Charts for the Ionian and Aegean
Designed by Rod Heikell

Imray Tetra Charts for the Ionian and Aegean provide coverage of popular areas on sheets especially designed for the needs of yachtsmen.

The charts contain large scale port insets in addition to all the small craft information so well known to users of Imray charts. Modifications include graduated meridians and parallels, satellite derived position offset data and the addition of land contours. Imray charts are printed on waterproof material and are updated by correction notices on leaving our offices and may also be corrected from our web site.

The charts are 640 x 900mm and they are available as flat sheets or folded (A4 format).

G1   **Mainland Greece and the Peloponnísos**
1:729,000 WGS 84
Plans Approaches to Piraeus and O. Falírou

G13 **Gulfs of Patras and Corinth** 1:218,800
Plans Mesolongi, O. Loutrákiou, Kiato, Patrai, O. Andíkiron, O. Aiyiou, Krissaíos Kólpos, Dhiórix Korínthou (Corinth Canal)

G14 **Saronic and Argolic Gulf** 1:189,000
Plans Marina Alimos, O. Falírou, Limín Porou (N. Póros), Steno Spétson (N. Spétsai), Limín Aiyinis (N. Aiyina)

G141 **Saronikós Kólpos**
Corinth Canal to Akra Sounio and Póros
1:109,000 WGS 84

G15 **Southern Peloponnísos**
O. Navarínou to Nísos Kithíra and Akra Tourkovigla 1:189,700
Plans Kalamata, O. Navarínou, Yíthion, Monemvasía (Yefira), Methóni, Koróni

G16 **Western Peloponnisos – Killini to Kalamata**
1:189,000
Plans Killini, Kiparissia, Kalamata, Katakolon, Pilos, Steno Methonis

G2   **Aegean Sea (North Part) Passage Chart** 1:720,500
WGS 84
Plans Canakkale Boğazi (The Dardanelles)
Plan Limín Ródhou (N. Rodhos)

G3   **Aegean Sea (South Part) Passage Chart** 1:758,800
WGS 84

G31 **Northern Cyclades** 1:189,700
Plans Mikonos Marina (N. Mikonos) O. Gávriou (N. Andros), Limín A. Nikolaou (Nísos Kea), Limín Sirou (N. Siros), O. Naoisis (Paros)

G32 **Southern Sporades and Coast of Turkey**
1:189,700
Plans Kuşadasi Liman, Limín Karlóvasi – N. Sámos, Limín A. Kirikou – N. Ikaria, Steno Samou – N. Sámos, Limín Pithagóriou – N. Sámos, O. Patmou – N. Pátmos

G33 **Southern Cyclades (Sheet 1 – West)** 1:190,000
Plans Steno Kimolou (N. Kímolos), O. Livadhiou (N. Sérifos), Steno Andíparou (N. Paros), O. Náxou (N. Naxos)

G34 **Southern Cyclades (Sheet 2 – East)** 1:190,000
Plans O. Kalímnou (N. Kalimnos), O. Analipsis (N. Astipálaia)

Index